Caribbean Currents

Caribbean Music from Rumba to Reggae

PETER MANUEL

with
KENNETH BILBY
and
MICHAEL LARGEY

TEMPLE UNIVERSITY PRESS
Philadelphia

In a neighborhood house with a patio on the Caribbean,
Here I am with my gruff-toned guitar,
trying to bring out a song.
A song of frenzied dreaming,
a simple song of death and life
with which to greet the future that's drenched in blood,
red as the sheets, as the thighs, as the bed
of a woman who's just given birth.

Nicolás Guillén

Temple University Press, Philadelphia 19122

Copyright © 1995 by Temple University

All rights reserved

Published 1995

Printed in the United States of America

Library of Congress Cataloging-in-Publication Data

Manuel, Peter Lamarche.
    Caribbean currents : Caribbean music from rumba to reggae / Peter
Manuel, with Kenneth Bilby and Michael Largey.
      p.   cm.
    Includes bibliographical references (p.   ) and index.
    ISBN 1-56639-338-8 (cloth) : — ISBN 1–56639–339–6 (pbk.)
    1. Music—West Indies—History and criticism. 2. Music—Caribbean
Area—History and criticism. I. Bilby, Kenneth M., 1953–
II. Largey, Michael D., 1959–   III. Title.
ML3565.M36 1995
780′.9729—dc20   95–3152
                                                             CIP
                                                             MN

Caribbean Currents

Caribbean Music from Rumba to Reggae

Contents

Preface

This book arose originally out of a simple necessity, which the authors encountered in trying to assemble readings for their overflowing Caribbean music classes. The amount of English-language academic literature on Caribbean music is growing, but most of this is, in one way or another, unsuitable for the general reader or for college students. Journalistic articles on the region's pop music also abound, but these are scattered in a thousand sources and represent nearly as many perspectives and topics. Clearly, there has existed a need for a readable guide to Caribbean music, oriented toward a broad audience.

A more fundamental need, of course, is for greater knowledge of Caribbean music and culture in general, both in the United States and in the Caribbean itself. Caribbean immigrant communities now constitute significant and dynamic parts of North American society. City neighborhoods throb to the pulse of Caribbean music, and Caribbean stores and products have become familiar and colorful parts of urban America's cosmopolitan landscape. And as the United States government and economy continue to dominate the Caribbean, the two regions have become more closely intertwined than ever.

This book is oriented toward a few distinct yet overlapping sets of readers. One group contains the music lover who has taken a fancy to some kind of Caribbean music and would like to know more about the background of that style and about the region's music as a whole. Another set includes the student of Caribbean society or of pan-American society in general, who seeks an introduction to this most dynamic aspect of our hemisphere's culture. Last, but not least, are readers of Caribbean descent, increasing numbers of whom now populate college classes. Many such students love their own culture's music and are proud of their ethnic identity but know woefully little of their musical heritage beyond the current hit parade. Ignorance of other local Caribbean cultures is even greater, inhibiting the formation of pan-regional alliances and contributing to the perseverance of petty rivalries and stereotypes. So far, North American universities have done little to rectify this situation. Even in a Caribbean cauldron like New York City, very few colleges have made any effort to recognize the musical cultures of their immigrant populations, whether out of a Euro-American ethnocentric disdain or because of a lack of qualified teachers and suitable course materials.

Caribbean Currents attempts to address this need, providing a readable and informative overview of Caribbean music for the student and general reader. This book does not pretend to be an original scholarly monograph, although it does contain much new information, especially on aspects of Afro-Jamaican, Indo-Caribbean, and Surinamese music that have yet to be described elsewhere. Similarly, it does not attempt to be a comprehensive reference book for Caribbean music, for such a volume would have to be several times the size of this one. Instead, we have chosen to circumscribe the book's scope. For one thing, we have adopted the relatively narrow rather than the broad conception of the "Caribbean Basin," excluding, for example, the musics of coastal Venezuela, Central America, and Mexico, however interesting these may be. We have included Suriname and, to some extent, Guyana because of their overwhelmingly Caribbean orientation, and indeed, these countries are best regarded not as South American nations but as mainland appendages of the West Indies. Further, even within such limits, we have tried to highlight the most important and representative aspects of each musical culture, rather than attempting to include all possible genres and subcategories. As a result, the range of subjects not covered is considerable, from Cuban *criolla* to Jamaican *jonkonoo*. But, as our title promises, rumba and reggae are definitely present, as are many other genres, and they are given more thorough treatment than could be provided in a sketchy survey that tried to mention everything. To the Cubanophile interested in *abakuá* chants or the Tortola immigrant wishing to learn more about the island's *funji* music, we offer our apologies—and a set of recommended readings.

There are also a few musical cultures that are too marginal to merit full chapters of their own and that do not fit nicely into any other chapters, but that are nevertheless too substantial—and interesting—to be omitted altogether. In Chapter 9, we take a look at two such sets of musical traditions: the music of East Indians and the music of Suriname, a nation that, although in South America, is, as mentioned, best seen as a Caribbean country. As for the authorship of this book, Ken Bilby wrote Chapter 7 and the Suriname sections in Chapter 9, and Michael Largey wrote Chapter 6. Peter Manuel wrote and takes sole responsibility for the rest.

Readers of this book are encouraged to get hold of the double CD titled *Caribbean Currents: A Panorama of Caribbean Music* (Rounder Records), which is intended as a companion recording to this book. The CD is the first, and at this point the only recording of its kind, providing a panoramic survey of all the major and several minor genres of Caribbean music, traditional and modern. It includes several pieces that are discussed or analyzed in this book and, aside from being an ideal pedagogical tool, contains a lot of wonderful music—"Greatest Hits of the Caribbean," as it were.

In writing this book I have drawn heavily from the earlier work of such writers as Alejo Carpentier, Fernando Ortiz, Gordon Lewis, Argeliers León, John Storm Roberts, Leonardo Acosta, Donald Hill, Gordon Rohlehr, Juan Flores, and, among my own generation of scholars, Deborah Pacini, Paul Austerlitz, Steven Cornelius, Frank Korom, Hal Barton, Roberta Singer, and Lise Waxer, to name but a few. Journalistic articles by Enrique Fernandez, Daisane McClaine, Gene Scaramuzzo, and others have also been useful, and I am indebted to them not only for their information content but for more than one felicitous turn of phrase that I have borrowed.

More specific thanks are due to the many individuals and institutions that have assisted me in completing this volume. Delfín Pérez and Chris Washburne have been invaluable Latin music gurus in this project, as in previous ones. Edgardo Díaz Díaz provided particularly helpful comments on Chapter 3. With regard to the researching of Indo-Caribbean music, I mention Jeevan Chowtie, who guided me through Guyana, and such informants as Mangal Patasar, H. Mohabir, Moean Mohammad, and Kries Ramkhelawan. I have also been fortunate to have another set of excellent informants in my many Caribbean students at John Jay College; Michael Blugh, Aggrey Dechinea, Gilda Benjamin, Kirk Louison, Judith Williams, and others too numerous to mention have been of great help in putting me in touch with current developments and in providing their own perspectives on music. In collecting photographs for the volume, thanks are due to the Ethnic Folk Arts Center, Roberta Singer of City Lore, and Sandra Levinson of the Center for Cuban Studies. Don Hill was of particular assistance in guiding me through the treacherous world of copyright permissions. Thanks are also extended on behalf of Michael Largey to Lolo Beaubrun, Gage Averill, and Allison Berg, and on behalf of Ken Bilby to Jake Hom- ink, Dermott Hussey, and George Eaton Simpson. Finally, I must thank Publishers' WorkGroup for their fine copy editing and above all, Doris Braendel, for the care, attention, and enthusiasm with which she has guided this book through the publication process.

Peter Manuel

Map by the Center for Cartographic Research and Spacial Analysis, Michigan State University

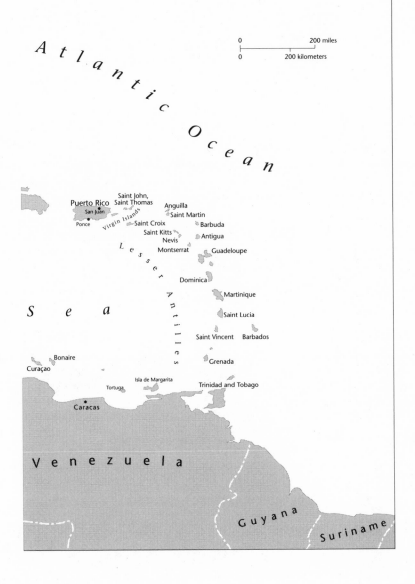

Atlantic Ocean

200 miles

0   200 kilometers

Saint John,
Saint Thomas

Puerto Rico

Anguilla

San Juan

Saint Martin

Ponce

Virgin Islands

Saint Croix

Barbuda

Saint Kitts

Antigua

Nevis

Montserrat

Guadeloupe

Lesser Antilles

Dominica

S e   a

Martinique

Saint Lucia

Saint Vincent   Barbados

Bonaire

Curaçao

Grenada

Isla de Margarita

Tortuga

Trinidad and Tobago

Caracas

V e n e z u e l a

G u y a n a

S u r i n a m e

The Caribbean at a Glance

(Country, Capital, 1990 Country Population)

THE DUTCH CARIBBEAN

Netherlands Antilles (Aruba, Bonaire, Curaçao, Saba, St. Eustatius, St. Maarten) (Neth.): Willemstad; pop. 187,000.

Suriname: Paramaribo; pop. 408,000 (31 percent African, 37 percent East Indian, 15 percent Javanese)

THE ENGLISH-SPEAKING CARIBBEAN

Anguilla (U.K.): The Valley; pop. 7,000.

Antigua and Barbuda: St. John; pop. 64,000.

Bahamas: Nassau; pop. 251,000.

Barbados: Bridgetown; pop. 260,000.

British Virgin Islands (U.K.): Road Town; pop. 13,000.

Cayman Islands: George Town; pop. 23,000.

Dominica: Roseau; pop. 74,000. English and French creole spoken.

Grenada: St. George; pop. 84,000.

Guyana: Georgetown; pop. 765,000 (30 percent African, 51 percent East Indian, 14 percent mixed).

Jamaica: Kingston; pop. 2,513,000.

St. Kitts-Nevis: Basseterre; pop. 40,000.

St. Lucia: Castries; pop. 153,000. English and French creole spoken.

St. Vincent and the Grenadines: Kingstown; pop. 106,000.

Trinidad and Tobago: Port of Spain; pop. 1,270,000 (43 percent African, 40 percent East Indian, 14 percent mixed).

Turks and Caicos Islands (U.K.): Grand Turk; pop. 9,000.

U.S. Virgin Islands (St. Croix, St. John, St. Thomas) (U.S.A.): Charlotte Amalie; pop. 106,000.

THE FRENCH CARIBBEAN

French Guiana (Fr.): Cayenne; pop. 94,000.
Guadeloupe (Fr.): Basse-Terre; pop. 340,000.
Haiti: Port-au-Prince; pop. 6,409,000.
Martinique (Fr.): Fort-de-France; pop. 336,000.

THE SPANISH CARIBBEAN

Cuba: Havana; pop. 10,582,000.
The Dominican Republic: Santo Domingo; pop. 7,253,000.
Puerto Rico (U.S.A.): San Juan; pop. 3,700,000

1

Introduction:
The Caribbean Crucible

In his 1962 book *The Middle Passage,* a caustic and dourly Eurocentric V. S. Naipaul wrote, "History is built around achievement and creation, and nothing was created in the West Indies." Naipaul's disparagement of his homeland—and by unspoken extension, of the region as a whole—has often been quoted and debated. His cut evidently touched a nerve, perhaps because of the persistence of its implicit colonial concepts of "history," involving great European kings, wars, artworks, and inventions. Yet, leaving aside the Cuban Revolution, which constitutes "history" by any standard, by 1962 the Caribbean people had already made cultural history in creating a set of original and dynamic musical genres. An archipelago populated mostly by descendants of slaves might seem an unlikely site for cultural vitality, but by Naipaul's time, the Caribbean had become a crucible for some of the most unique musical developments of the century. Indeed, when elitist neoconservatives derisively issue the challenge to find a Zulu Tolstoy or a Haitian Mozart, they, like the early Naipaul, may be blinded by their narrow conception of art, for popular and folk music styles, as much as fetishized individual classical pieces, can constitute "Great Works" of art, and the Caribbean has been a remarkably fertile source for music genres.

As styles like reggae and Cuban dance music achieve international popularity, they become part of world cultural history as well as that of the Caribbean. Ultimately, Caribbean music can scarcely be compartmentalized as a local, regional entity, when over four million people of Caribbean descent populate the cities of North America and Great Britain, and when the world is united as never before by the mass media and international capital. In a global village where Sri Lankan schoolboys sing Bob Marley tunes, Hawaiian cowboys sing Puerto Rican *aguinaldos,* Congolese bands play mambos, and Vietnamese urbanites dance the bolero, Caribbean music has truly become world music and, in its own way, world history as well.

1

Some of the vitality of Caribbean music seems to derive from its importance within Caribbean society and the sheer amount of attention and creative energy it commands. Caribbeans are well aware of the international prominence of their music, and they accord it a preeminent symbolic status at home. Cubans readily cite music, health, and education as the three arenas in which their Revolution has excelled. Similarly, though we may smile at the way Jamaicans made pop singer Millie Small a national hero for her 1964 ditty "My Boy Lollipop," we can nevertheless appreciate how Bob Marley's fame has far outstripped that of any of his fellow citizens. Likewise, in Trinidad, calypso not only spreads news, it *is* the news, with politicians, journalists, and other public figures endlessly debating and denouncing the latest songs. Indeed, when Muslim militant Abu Bakr attempted to seize power in a 1990 coup, one of his first acts was to set up an all-calypso radio station. Music, in a word, is the most visible, popular, and dynamic aspect of Caribbean expressive culture.

With music so beloved by Caribbeans of all stripes and persuasions, it is not surprising that the region's ethnic and class variety has generated an extraordinary degree of musical diversity. Caribbean music has long offered something to practically everyone, from the nineteenth-century Parisian aristocrat dancing a genteel habanera to the Jamaican peasant finding release in an ecstatic *Kumina* dance. Accordingly, Caribbean people have always been divided by linguistic, political, ethnic, and geographical barriers and by the legacy of colonialism in general. Nevertheless, Caribbean musical cultures have been shaped by many similar sociohistorical factors, which enables us to make certain generalizations about the region as a whole. The entire Caribbean shares a history of European colonialism, slavery, ethnic and class conflict, nationalism, and, in the twentieth century, North American imperialist influence. Within this framework, Caribbean musics have evolved in a complex process of creolization, in which Caribbean peoples have fashioned new, distinctly local genres out of elements taken from disparate traditions—primarily African and European. Caribbean musics are thus the products of the dialectic interaction of distinct ethnic groups and social classes, and they often combine elements of cultural resistance as well as dominant ideology and of local traditions as well as those borrowed from international styles.

THE INDIAN HERITAGE

The prehistory of Caribbean music begins with the culture of the region's first inhabitants, the Amerindians, whose fifteenth-century population historians have estimated, not very helpfully, at somewhere between 250,000 and 6,000,000. The currently favored guess at their population numbers is around half a million, with the largest concentration on the island of Hispaniola. The Ciboneys of Cuba had been in the region the longest but became outnumbered by other groups, especially the more advanced Taino Arawaks and, in the Lesser Antilles, the warlike Caribs. Because of the presence of these Indians, it may be better to speak not of a "discovery" of the region by Europeans but of the "encounter of two cultures," although the actual period of cultural interaction lasted less than a century, by which time most Indians had perished. Nevertheless, any historical account of Caribbean music and culture must commence with the practices of the Amerindians, as described by the Spanish.

Indigenous Caribbean music centered around a socioreligious ceremony called *areito,* in which as many as a thousand participants would dance in concentric circles around a group of musicians. The musicians sang mythological chants in call-and-response style, playing rattles (later called "maracas"), gourd scrapers (*güiros*), and slit drums called *mayohuacan.* These last were hollowed logs with H-shaped tongues cut into them. Although most scholars think the Indians of the Caribbean originally came from what is now Venezuela, the use of slit drums suggests some affinity with Aztecs and other Mexican Indian groups, who played similar instruments called *teponaztli.*

The Spaniards, far from bringing progress and civilization to their Caribbean subjects, enslaved and effectively exterminated them. The Indians were forced to work in mines, while Spanish pigs overran their crops. Those who did not perish from starvation, disease, or forced labor were killed outright or committed mass suicide. Christopher Columbus himself set the tenor, presiding over the death of a third of the population of Hispaniola during his sixteen-month governorship (1496–1497). By 1570, the Caribbean Indians were effectively extinct, except for a few villages in Dominica and the African-intermixed "Black Caribs" of St. Vincent, later exiled to Honduras. To fill the need for labor, the colonists had to turn to slaves from Africa; as Trinidad's prime minister Eric Williams put it, the Europeans "used negroes they stole from Africa to work the land they stole from the Indians."

To a certain extent, early colonial-era culture emerged as a mixture of European, African, and Amerindian traditions; the still-popular Cuban cult of the Virgen de la Caridad del Cobre, for instance, mixes elements of the worship of the Taino god Atabey, the Yoruba deity Oshun, and the European Virgin of Illescas. On the whole, however, little remains of Indian culture except for place-names, foods, and words like "hammock," "manatee," "yucca," "hurricane," and "tobacco"—the last surviving as the In-

Taino dancers in Hispaniola, as portrayed by seventeenth-century artist R. P. Labat

dians' parting gift (or retributive curse) to the world. But if Indian culture and music are largely lost, the Indian past has continued to be invoked as a symbol for various purposes. Still celebrated in Cuba are the names of the Arawak princess Anacaona and the chieftain Hatuey, for their valiant struggle against the Spaniards. Puerto Ricans still use the Taino name for their island, Borikén, as a symbol of independence, which lives on as a memory and a goal. In other contexts, a mythical Indian heritage has often been asserted as a way of denying the reality of the region's African heritage. Thus, obscurantist folklorists such as Cuba's Eduardo Sánchez de Fuentes have tried to argue that their country's non-Hispanic folk music derived mostly from Tainos rather than from Yorubas and Bantus. Even some blacks and mulattoes have tried to deny their own ancestry, for instance, in the Dominican Republic, where a negrophobic ideology has led many to refer to themselves euphemistically as *indios* or *indios oscuros* (dark-skinned Indians).

If the Amerindian heritage has played little role in post-Columbian music, then we must look elsewhere for the roots of Caribbean music—specifically, in the musical cultures of Europe and Africa.

Taino dancers as imagined, perhaps more accurately, by a modern artist (adapted from O. J. Cardoso and M. García, *Los Indocubanos,* Havana, 1982)

THE AFRICAN HERITAGE

The Caribbean is host to a variety of ethnic groups, including East Indians, Chinese, Syrians, and Caucasian Europeans. However, throughout the region, descendants of the four or five million enslaved Africans brought by the colonists are a common denominator. In islands such as Haiti, they constitute nearly the entire population, while even in the more Caucasian Puerto Rico, black communities have exerted a musical influence quite incommensurate with their size. Moreover, just as Afro-American musics and their derivatives like rock have come to pervade world culture in the twen-

tieth century, so have the African-derived elements in Caribbean music provided much of what has distinguished it and made it internationally famous.

For the last two centuries, scholars (and pseudoscholars) have argued
about the degree to which black communities in the Caribbean and the
United States have been able to retain elements of their traditional African
cultural roots. A persistent white view had been that Africa had little particular culture to begin with, and that the slaves had lost touch with that as
well. Anthropologist Melville Herskovits challenged this conception in his
The Myth of the Negro Past (1941), and in his wake, scholars have devoted
many volumes to documenting or claiming the existence of African-derived
elements in modern Afro-American and Afro-Caribbean cultures. Such
writing has also criticized the tendency to regard slaves as passive victims of
circumstance, instead stressing the ways in which slaves and free blacks fashioned their own culture—"the world the slaves made," as the subtitle reads
in historian Eugene Genovese's influential *Roll, Jordan, Roll* (1974). In recent decades, the scholarly pendulum may have swung a bit too far in the
direction of emphasizing the ability of slaves to retain and construct their
own cultures. Within the Caribbean itself, the degree to which diverse black
communities were able to retain African traditions has varied considerably
from place to place.

Regional variation notwithstanding, there are many specific features of
Caribbean music that can be traced directly to Africa. Such correlations are
particularly evident in religious musics, which tend throughout the world to
be more conservative than secular musics, preserving archaic features. Thus,
in music associated with Afro-Caribbean religions like Cuban *santería,* Haitian *vodou,* and Jamaican *Kromanti,* one finds song texts in West African
languages and the use of drums that closely resemble African drums with
the same names. While few, if any, specific songs or melodies can be linked
to modern African ones, many other features of these religious traditions,
including the associated belief systems and social practices, can be matched
closely with their current African counterparts. Some such music traditions
can be regarded as "neo-African" in the sense that they reflect little Euro-
American influence.

On the whole, the sorts of Africanisms evident in most Caribbean music
consist more of general principles than specific elements. Slave communities
usually combined people from different African regions and ethnic groups,
whose musical traditions tended to blend accordingly. Acculturation with
European musics further diluted the original African practices, as did the
relative cessation of contact with Africa after the slave trade stopped. Moreover, Afro-Caribbean musicians have always applied their own creativity to

their art, so that the music has tended to take on its own life, departing from its original transplanted forms. Given these conditions and the diversity of sub-Saharan music itself, it is best to speak of general rather than particular elements of African music that survived the infamous Middle Passage and the cultural repression of the slave period.

During the colonial era, as now, sub-Saharan Africa was home to hundreds of ethnic groups[1] with different languages and social structures, ranging from simple hunter-gatherer clans to more elaborate societies with substantial towns, trade networks, and specialized occupation groups. Although African music is similarly diverse, it is possible to speak of a set of general features that are common throughout most of the continent (excluding the culturally Arab north), and which continue to pervade Afro-Caribbean and Afro-American musics as well.

One sociomusical characteristic of much African music is *collective participation,* a feature typical of many classless societies lacking occupational distinctions between performers and consumers. Soloists and specialists do play roles in Africa, but it is extremely common for all or most members of a rural community to participate actively in musical events, whether by singing, clapping, dancing, or playing instruments. This convention accompanies a conception of musical talent as something innate, albeit in different degrees, to everyone, rather than being the property only of specialists. Likewise, collective participation, starting as early as the baby bound to the dancing mother's back, tends to promote the cultivation and development of musical talent to a greater degree than in more stratified societies. The persistence of communal music-making in the New World has naturally been dependent on social structure as a whole, but it has been perpetuated by the fact that most Afro-Caribbeans have tended to occupy the same social classes—that is, the lower ones.

In the realm of more distinctly musical features, the most often noted feature of African music is its *emphasis on rhythm.* African music is rich in melody, timbral variety, and even two- and three-part harmony, but rhythm is often the most important aesthetic parameter, distinguishing songs and genres and commanding the focus of the performers' and listeners' attention. Accordingly, the rhythms of African and Afro-Caribbean traditional music are often formidably complex, in ways that lack any counterparts in Western folk or common-practice classical music. Much of the rhythmic interest and complexity derives from the interaction of regular pulses (whether silent or audible) and offbeat accents. This feature is often described as "syncopation," but that term is vague and problematic, as is indeed the notion of a single, regular pulse in the multiple, distinct layers of much African ensemble music. When two or more regular pulse patterns are combined, the result is what musicologists call *polyrhythm*, or polymeter, which is a common kind of African rhythmic organization. Polyrhythm is most typically performed by an ensemble, in which a "cell" consisting of twelve beats is divided by different instrumental patterns into groups of twos and threes (a division not so possible with the four- or eight-beat meters that pervade most contemporary North American and Caribbean pop music). Often a "time-line" played on an iron bell provides a referential pattern.

Playing a Polyrhythm

The schematic example below (Musical Example 1) shows a simplified polyrhythm, using the so-called standard time-line, which is common throughout West and Central Africa as well as in neo-African religious musics in Cuba, Haiti, and Brazil. For those who do not read Western notation, the equivalents are given both in staff and in what is called TUBS (time-unit boxes) notation, in which each box represents a regular pulse unit (of which there are twelve, in this case).

MUSICAL EXAMPLE 1

Staff Notation

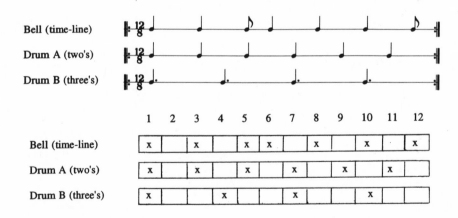

You can try tapping twelve regular beats with your left hand and tapping the time-line with your right, repeating the pattern without pause. The next step is to add the subsidiary parts, one of which divides the twelve beats into groups of twos and the other into groups of threes. Once you get the feel of the time-line, try tapping that with one hand, and tapping the twos with the other. (This can be challenging for musicians as well as non-musicians.) Then try combining the time-line with the threes (which is even harder for most people). So far we do not yet have a polyrhythm. But if you get a friend to help out, you can put together the time-line, the twos, and the threes, and the result is a polyrhythm, in which duple and triple pulses, or meters, are combined with the time-line.

In a typical West African or similar Afro-Caribbean ensemble, the accompanying drum parts would be more interesting than simple reiterations of two- or three-beat pulses. For example, in the Ghanaian *agbadza* rhythm, which uses the standard time-line, the *kidi* drum establishes the duple pulse with the following rhythm, alternating muted ("m") with open ("o") strokes:

m o o o m m m o o o m m

A few more distinct, interlocking accompanying parts—played on drums and shakers—complete the composite *agbadza* rhythm, which would then be supplemented by singing and dancing. The dancing itself might stress either the duple or the triple pulse, or in some cases, one's feet are moving to one pulse and one's shoulders to the other. The result is uniquely expressive and rewarding for listeners and performers. From the aesthetic point of view, the individual polyrhythmic cell is interesting enough that one does not mind hearing it repeated again and again, especially when combined with a varying vocal part or with improvisation by a master drummer.

Another widespread feature of African music is vocal *call and response,* which is well suited to communal performance in general. It is also found in many types of Afro-Caribbean music. A related characteristic is what I call *cellular structure,* meaning that pieces tend to be constructed by repetition and variation of a short musical cell or ostinato. Variety is provided by altering the pattern or by combining it with another feature, such as a narrative text. This way of structuring pieces pervades Afro-American as well as Afro-Caribbean music, including countless rock, R & B, and rap songs based on a repeated riff ("Super Freak," "Satisfaction," "I'm a Man," and thousands of others). Pieces using this format are open-ended, additive entities, loosely expandable or compressible in accordance with the desires of the performers, the audience, or the occasion. This sort of structure contrasts with that of most European-derived music—from sonatas to Frank Sinatra ballads—in which a song or piece has a finite, symmetrical structure, such as the thirty-two-bar *AABA* form typical of American popular song.

PATTERNS OF MUSICAL RETENTION

The sort of classic polyrhythm shown in example 1 above, although common in Afro-Cuban and Haitian religious music, is unusual in most Caribbean creole and popular music forms. These generally use simpler rhythms, although they are often animated by syncopations and cross-rhythms influenced, however indirectly, by older polyrhythmic forms. The degree to which neo-African traits like polyrhythms are retained in contemporary musics is dependent on various factors and raises broad questions having to do with the relative ability of Afro-Caribbean communities in different regions to maintain cultural autonomy over the generations. Why, for example, are polyrhythms and neo-African musics common in Haiti, with its population of only six million, when such features have long since disappeared from the music of the much larger Afro-American population, which now numbers some thirty million? Why are such musics so strong in Cuba, with its large white population, and far less common in overwhelmingly black Jamaica? Why do we find certain African-derived features in one part of the Caribbean and other features elsewhere?

There are many factors involved in answering such questions, which have engaged the interest of scholars for decades. We can start with the last question, which is in some respects the simplest. Although most slave communities combined people of diverse ethnic origins, in certain regions slaves from one distinct area of Africa predominated. For example, in the early 1800s, the collapse of the great Yoruba kingdom led to that people's subjugation by the Dahomey and other rival groups, who sold many Yoruba as slaves to the Europeans. The British, however, had withdrawn from the slave trade by this time; as a result, the tens of thousands of captured Yoruba went primarily to Iberian-ruled Cuba and Brazil, whose imports continued through the 1860s. Accordingly, Yoruba-derived music and religion are much more prominent in these countries than in the former British colonies, or in Haiti, whose own slave imports ended with the Haitian Revolution in the 1790s. In this way also, the cultural heritages of Akan and Congolese slaves, from the Gold Coast and Central Africa, respectively, are more influential in Jamaica.

A more problematic issue is whether the different policies and attitudes of individual colonial powers allowed for different degrees of African cultural retention. This question overlaps with a hypothesis, first argued in the 1940s by historian Frank Tannenbaum, that slavery in the Roman Catholic colonies—especially those of Spain and Portugal—was milder than in the British and Dutch colonies. This "Tannenbaum thesis" has been much rehashed and rebashed by subsequent scholars. Critics have pointed out that there are several criteria by which the severity of slavery should be measured. In terms of diet, longevity, and reproduction rates, for example, the North American slaves seem to have fared considerably better than Caribbean and Brazilian ones. In other respects, however, practices and attitudes in the Iberian and, to some extent, in the French colonies may have favored greater degrees of cultural autonomy for blacks. For one thing, it was much easier for slaves in Spanish and French colonies to buy their own freedom (manumission) than it was in North America. The large communities of free blacks in Cuba and elsewhere were able to form socioreligious clubs (*cabildos*) and maintain considerable cultural independence, including traditional musical practices.

Of greater relevance to the study of music than matters of diet and the like is the argument that the Iberian and French colonists may have been culturally more tolerant of neo-African practices than were the northern European slave owners. French and Iberian Catholicism, with its elements of saint worship and ritual, blended more easily with African religions than did Protestantism. The early Spanish and Portuguese colonists, unlike the bourgeois, more economically advanced English, were premodern, precapitalist peoples who, however racist in their own way, recognized Africans as human beings with their own culture. Unlike the inbred, blue-eyed, ethnically isolated English, the olive-complected southern Europeans had a certain Mediterranean cosmopolitan nature bred from centuries of contact with diverse Arabs, Jews, Gypsies, and Africans—according to this hypothesis.[2]

Such arguments might partially explain, for instance, why in the United States neo-African drumming was effectively outlawed everywhere except in New Orleans, where, because of the city's distinctively French Caribbean cultural orientation, it was tolerated until 1845. This thesis might also help explain why neo-African music and religion are so widespread in Cuba and so marginal in the British Caribbean, and why some Protestant missionaries in Haiti today, unlike local Catholic priests, demand that their congregations abandon all their traditional, African-influenced musical practices.

However, there are other factors that may better explain the different degrees of African retentions in the New World. One of these concerns the time that has elapsed in the various areas of the Caribbean since the end of slave imports. In the British colonies, importation of slaves ended in 1804, and by 1860, there were no African-born slaves in the United States. Hence it was natural for neo-African practices in British colonial areas to weaken during the subsequent long period of isolation from Africa. Cuba, by contrast, continued to receive slaves—and fresh infusions of African culture—through the 1870s. Similarly, the only neo-African religion in Trinidad,

Shango, survives as the legacy not of the slave period but of Yoruba indentured servants who arrived in the mid-1800s. (Haitian slave imports also ended early, in the 1790s, but at the time of the Haitian Revolution, most slaves were African-born, and the subsequent absence of Europeans allowed neo-African culture to flourish unimpeded.)

Perhaps the most important factor involved in the different degrees of African retentions is the difference between plantation colonies like Jamaica, whose populations consisted primarily of slaves, and settler colonies like Cuba, which had a more diverse balance of whites, free blacks and mulattoes, and slaves. In Jamaica, slaves, who constituted 88 percent of the population in 1800, were subject to rigid cultural repression and could exert little cultural influence on local whites. In contrast, sugar plantations came relatively late to Cuba and had to adapt themselves to the already well formed and more lenient creole culture with its substantial freed black population (20 percent in 1774). The communities of freed Afro-Cubans played important roles in preserving neo-African culture, including musical practices based in the *cabildos.* Thus the cultural attitudes of the colonists, although not insignificant, were only one among many factors influencing the nature and degree of African retentions in the New World.

THE EUROPEAN HERITAGE

The other primary ingredient in the formation of Caribbean music consists of the diverse forms of music introduced by the European colonists—primarily the Spanish, British, and French. These forms included not only the well-documented classical music of the era but, more importantly, the various folk and popular songs and dances of contemporary Europe. Thus, more influential than the rarefied music of Bach and Beethoven were the innumerable sailors' chanteys, church hymns, military marches, and social dances like the quadrille, mazurka, waltz, and contradance. These "set" (i.e., suite) dances were popular throughout the Caribbean and were played on ad hoc ensembles of fiddles, guitars, fifes, and whatever else was around. As in Europe, most were round or line dances led by a caller, although ballroom-style couple dancing gradually became popular. As performed over the generations by Afro-Caribbeans, the dances eventually became creolized and came to incorporate typical syncopations and other distinctly local features.

Several of these European musical genres shared some of the aforementioned features associated with African music, and indeed, scholars have commented on the considerable degree of compatibility between African and European musics. Spanish fandangos and zapateos, for example, have lively cross-rhythms, while Protestant hymns used call-and-response "lining out." The French and Spanish, like many African communities, had traditions of seasonal carnivals with festive music. Further, most European folk musics were, like African music, orally transmitted traditions rather than written ones. Perhaps as a result of such precedents, oral poetry—especially as sung—has long played a much more prominent role in Caribbean culture than in more "developed" countries like the United States, where poetry is cultivated only by a few literati. Caribbean people still take great interest in amateur versification, whether in the form of calypso, Jamaican dancehall, or Spanish *décimas*. Indeed, Caribbean popular culture in general is primarily oral rather than written; and for that matter, the same could be said of Caribbean politics with its prominence of brilliant orators, from Eric Williams to Fidel Castro.

The nature and extent of European influence have varied in accordance with several factors, some of which have already been discussed—for example, the distinction between plantation colonies, where large slave populations were managed by a handful of white entrepreneurs, and settler colonies, which attracted substantial numbers of European immigrants. In the settler category, with some qualifications, would fall Cuba and Puerto Rico, which received hundreds of thousands of European immigrants. These settlers (primarily but not exclusively Spanish) brought a rich spectrum of European musics with them and, over the generations, played crucial roles in developing distinctive creole cultures in their new homelands. The British colonies, in contrast, attracted relatively few settlers. Most of those who came were what historian Gordon Lewis pithily described as "scum"—that is, social derelicts and mountebanks out to make a quick killing in the tropics. For their part, the British upper-class owners and managers generally came for limited periods, remaining attached to England, where they invested their earnings and sent their children to be educated. The contrast between the two sorts of colonies could be seen in their cities: colonial Havana was an opulent and beautiful metropolis with fine cathedrals, mansions, and promenades, whereas the British Caribbean ports consisted of dreary warehouses surrounded by shantytowns, with a few bleak barns passing as the "great houses" of the rich. Similarly, because the British colonial elites made little attempt to develop their own art forms, it may be said that the musical heritages transmitted by the Spanish to Cuba and Puerto Rico were considerably richer than whatever the British bequeathed to their colonies.

In general, the European heritage brought to the Caribbean included instruments, chordal harmony, sectional formal structures (rather than the reliance on cellular ostinatos), concepts of ensemble orchestration and arrangement, the practice of notating music, and a vast repertoire of written and orally transmitted musics. The Spanish musical heritage was particularly distinctive and influential. Documentary films on Latin music seem invariably to represent this musical culture with footage of flamenco, the most famous kind of Spanish music; but flamenco, a product of settled urban Andalusian gypsies, did not emerge until the later 1800s, and there is no evidence that it was transmitted to the Caribbean in the colonial period. However, other Andalusian folk musics sharing certain features with flamenco were definitely brought to the New World. The Spanish predilection for triple meter survives only in the most purely Iberian genres, but Hispanic influence remains widespread in the use of guitars and guitar-like instruments and in the so-called Phrygian or Andalusian tonality (epitomized by the progression Am–G–F–E, where E is the tonic).

CREOLIZATION

A key concept in the formation of Caribbean culture and music is identified by the rather inelegant term *creolization,* which connotes the development of a distinctive new culture out of the prolonged encounter of two or more other cultures. The process is also described as "syncretism," although "creolization" is particularly appropriate in the Caribbean, due to the long usage of the term *creole* there and its ability to suggest some of the complex sociocultural issues also involved in the process.[3] In linguistic terms, a creole language is one evolved through the blending of two or more prior languages; the creole language subsequently becomes a native tongue to later generations, who may forget or lose contact with the original languages. This process is more than, say, the mixing of blue and yellow to make green, since people are active, creative agents, not inert chemicals, and the new human product, whether a language or a musical style, takes on a life of its own.

Caribbean creolization has primarily involved the encounter between Africans (mostly from West and Central Africa) and Europeans (mostly Spanish, British, and French). Other groups like the East Indians, the Chinese, and the Dutch have also played roles, some of which we consider later. There have been various stages and subsidiary developments in the creolization process. One can speak of an initial stage in which new forms of both neo-African and European-derived musics began to develop in the Caribbean. Cuban rumba can be regarded as such a genre, evolving partly through the interaction of slaves from different African regions. European influence is obvious in the use of the Spanish language, but stylistically, the rumba is essentially neo-African. However, whereas *santería* music is largely a transplanted Yoruba entity, the rumba is not a transplant but a distinctly Cuban creation. Likewise, the nineteenth-century Puerto Rican *danza* reflects little Afro-Caribbean influence, and in terms of style it can be regarded as essentially European-derived. It is not, however, a European genre but a Puerto Rican one and has been celebrated as a symbol of Puerto Rican nationalism. Both the *danza* and the rumba are, in a preliminary sort of way, creole entities.

The more definitive sort of creolization occurs when African- and European-derived musical styles and elements mix together. In most cases, this creative mixing started among the Afro-Caribbean lower classes, whose products, such as the early calypso, were generally denounced by Eurocentric elites (whether black, white, or mulatto). In the typical pattern, these lower-class, syncretic forms gradually percolate upward, acquiring more musical sophistication and eventually coming to be enjoyed by the upper classes. When all classes and races of a given population come to embrace local syncretic genres—whether merengue, reggae, calypso, the Cuban *son,* or the Puerto Rican *plena*—as nationalistic symbols, then one can truly speak of a creole national musical culture.

The evolution and acceptance of creole musics in the Caribbean have thus been closely bound up with nationalism and elite recognition of the Afro-Caribbean heritage. Cuban nationalists, for example, prized the habanera partly because it was a local creole invention rather than an archaic product of despised Spain; part of what distinguished the habanera was the use, however diluted, of Afro-Caribbean syncopations. With the emergence of the Cuban *danzón* in the late 1800s, the Afro-Caribbean element became more overt and, accordingly, more controversial. The *danzón,* with its felicitous combination of genteel melodies, sophisticated ensemble writing, and jaunty rhythms, quickly gained popularity in elite and petit bourgeois circles. To the modern ear, the genre may sound quite tame and quaint, but many negrophobic purists, because of the music's bouncy Afro-Caribbean rhythm, denounced it as barbaric, grotesque, and somehow foreign. Other obscurantists tried to legitimize it by falsely attributing its distinctive rhythm to Taino influence.

In the Spanish and French Caribbean, the *negritud* movement of the 1930s and 1940s did much to discredit such foolishness and to force Eurocentric elites to acknowledge and accept the African heritage in their national cultures. The later scholarship of Cuban ethnologist Fernando Ortiz, the writings of Puerto Rican essayist Tomás Blanco, and the poetry of Aimé Cesaire, Nicolás Guillén, Luis Pales Matos, and Luis Llorens Torres played important roles in this movement and in many cases explicitly celebrated the role of Afro-Caribbean music in national culture. In subsequent years, the attainment of political power by black and mulatto leaders further legitimized Afro-Caribbean culture. For that matter, the Cuban Revolution, although dominated by whites, has led the region in integrating its nation's black underclass into the economic and cultural mainstream of society.

In the twentieth century, urbanization, emigration, the mass media, and the internationalization of capital have brought new dimensions to musical syncretism to the Caribbean. Gone are the days of isolated peasant communities cultivating their traditional creole songs in ignorance of the wider musical world. Flipping the radio dial anywhere in the Lesser Antilles, one can pick up everything from salsa, soca, *zouk,* and reggae to East Indian film songs—not to mention rock and rap. As such radio signals crisscross the sea and satellites transmit MTV International, musical trends spread and proliferate in days, not decades, and geographic, linguistic, and international boundaries seem to melt into the airwaves. In metropolitan hubs like New York, Toronto, and Birmingham, immigrants mingle with one another and with longtime locals, developing intricate multiple senses of identity reflected in the most eclectic musical tastes. Meanwhile, musical styles and influences cross-pollinate and multiply, spawning every conceivable sort of fusion, from Spanish-language reggae to merengues in Hindi. As creolization reaches a new level and the internal and external musical borders of the region dissolve, any book attempting to take stock of the contemporary music scene is doomed to rapid obsolescence. But snapshots have their own utility, and the authors of this book have done their best to cover the present as well as the past, starting with the largest and most influential island of all.

BIBLIOGRAPHY

For general reading on the Caribbean, an excellent social, cultural, and political overview is Catherine Sunshine's *The Caribbean: Survival, Struggle and Sovereignty* (Washington, D.C.: EPICA, 1988); also see Gordon Lewis *The Growth of the Modern West Indies* (New York: Monthly Review, 1968); and Franklin Knight, *The Caribbean* (New York and Oxford: Oxford University Press, 1990).

2

Cuba

A DAY IN HAVANA, 1986

It is a sultry Saturday in Cuba's capital, a few years before the collapse of the Soviet bloc and the economic problems it caused. At this point, the economy is running smoothly, in its idiosyncratic way, and most Cubans are more concerned with how to enjoy their weekend than with the size of the sugar harvest. My friends and I—Latin music fans visiting from the United States—are also trying to decide how to spend the day. The problem is that there is too much to choose from. The options are dizzying: for the afternoon, they include the *Sábado de la rumba* (Rumba Saturday), performed weekly by the national folkloric group; a set of free concerts in the old city; some touristy facsimile of a campesino (white peasant) festival out of town; and, for the less energetic hotel guests, the poolside band. As for the evening, there are salsa-style dance clubs, joyously kitsch cabarets at the Tropicana and the Havana Libre Hotel, a bunch of Soviet-bloc pop bands at the Karl Marx Theater, and more hotel folkloric shows featuring Afro-Cuban music and dance. Or we could rent a car and find our way to a real campesino music festival, which I see advertised in the newspaper. All this is either cheap or free. Eventually, I opt for the old-city concerts, not knowing what to expect, and we decide to regroup in the early evening.

I head off by bus for old Havana, the waterfront area dominated by colonial-era buildings, including the cathedral and the national museum, where free concerts often take place. It's Saturday, and no one is in a particular hurry—certainly not the bus driver, who at one point stops the bus, full of people, calmly steps out, and walks into a drugstore to make a purchase. This gives me some time to savor the atmosphere of this part of the old city. Havana, like other Cuban cities, has a timeless charm hard to find in more modernized Caribbean countries. Most of the buildings are either colonial or early-twentieth-century edifices, many with the most majestic

17

and ornate facades. They are rather run down, to be sure, but they retain their faded elegance. There are few billboards, few neon lights, and no Burger Kings. The cars enhance the sensation that one is in some sort of time warp, for most of them date from the 1950s, before the U.S. government cut off trade with Cuba; so one sees DeSotos, Thunderbirds, and even the occasional Edsel chugging along, miraculously kept running by Cuban ingenuity and a local cottage industry producing spare parts for otherwise extinct vehicles. I notice that in an open-air tavern at the corner, among the patrons seated in front of the long mahogany bar and an immense rusted mirror, a man is strumming a guitar and crooning to the woman next to him.

Soon enough, our driver is again at the wheel, honking at passing girls and hailing friends as we proceed. As we near the museum, I hop out, noting that I have forgotten my umbrella; the morning has been clear and sunny, but in the Caribbean, one never knows. I arrive in time to hear the last pieces by a large wind orchestra playing in front of the museum to a relatively elderly audience. The ensemble is performing a mixture of European light classics and Cuban nineteenth-century salon-dance pieces—habaneras and *danzones*. The latter have a marked Afro-Caribbean rhythmic flavor to them, provided especially by the prominent timpani. The tubas are as battered as the T-Birds, but the playing is sweet and professional.

As soon as they stop, I hear another band starting up in the courtyard, playing a 1950s-style mambo. As I enter the courtyard, I am amazed to see that the performers consist of eight or nine rather ancient, matronly women. Several of them are wizened, stooped, and bespectacled, but the music is hot, and a few couples are already dancing. "What the Fidel is going on here?" I wonder. I ask someone who the performers are, and it turns out that they are Orquesta Anacaona, an all-woman dance band formed in 1939, which is still going strong, with the addition of a few new members. Eventually, they are followed by another cultural institution, the Septeto Habanero, which has been performing, with similarly replenished membership, since 1925. They play old-style *son* with the traditional format of guitar, *tres* (like a guitar), bass, and percussion. Their style and repertoire date mostly from the 1920s and 1930s, and they preface each piece with a sort of "name that *son*" contest, whose winners get little prizes. The audience, as could be expected, is mostly middle-aged and older, but they are dancing in the most suave and supple style. I am just starting to wish that I were a sixty-year-old Cuban skilled in Latin dancing when a torrential downpour puts an abrupt end to the concert, sending musicians and listeners scurrying for cover under balustrades.

Donning a newspaper in place of my forgotten umbrella, I make my way back to the hotel, to learn that my friends and I have been invited to attend a *bembé*—a sort of dance party connected to the Afro-Cuban religion *santería* (or *Regla de Ocha*). These are semiprivate affairs, so this invitation is not to be passed up. Our Cuban friend soon arrives to take us in his car to Matanzas, a nearby town famous for its Afro-Cuban traditions. It is dark when we reach our destination, a nondescript, one-story private home in a black neighborhood. We enter the house, in which one room is dominated by a *santería* altar; blood and feathers scattered in front of the altar suggest that either a chicken sacrifice or a violent pillow fight has recently taken place. We pass through to the backyard where the *bembé* is already in progress. About a hundred people are crowded into the yard, and the atmosphere is festive. About half of those present, mostly women, are either singing a refrain in call and response with a lead vocalist or dancing in a roughly circular fashion. Drowning out their voices are the instruments— three drums looking like oversized congas, two cowbells, and a tamborine.

I soon deduce that the person to watch is the lead drummer, who is improvising, beating the drum with a stick in his right hand and the palm of his left. Being so accustomed to music relying heavily on melody and harmony, I have never imagined how drumming could be so expressive. I am mesmerized by his playing, in which he repeatedly starts a basic pattern, twists it around in different syncopations, and then abandons it for another, while different duple and triple pulses in the polyrhythmic accompaniment come in and out of focus. Finally, his playing reaches a crescendo as he works up to a frenetic acrobatic passage. It seems as if electricity sweeps through the yard as people whoop and cheer, and two women dancing in front of me stiffen and collapse into the arms of their neighbors, their eyes glazing over. They are acting as if possessed—and indeed, they have been possessed by Elegba, the *santería* god of crossroads. Their friends, laughing, carry them into the house, where they pass the next few hours in a trance, awakening later to remember nothing.

THE CUBAN CRUCIBLE

The array of musical events happening on any given weekend in Havana is representative of the extraordinary richness and diversity of Cuban musical culture. In the nineteenth century, the Cuban habanera charmed European audiences and worked its way into operas like *Carmen*. In the mid-twentieth century, Cuban dance music dominated urban Africa, and it has continued to flourish in all the Spanish-speaking countries of the Caribbean Basin, providing the backbone for salsa. Within the Caribbean itself Cuba's influence is perhaps not surprising, as it is by far the largest and most populous island. But its remarkable musical richness seems to derive from other factors as well, including the way that both African and European musics have been able to mix and enrich each other.

Since the mid-nineteenth century, Cuba's population has consisted of relatively even proportions of whites, blacks, and mulattoes (with smaller groups of Chinese, Lebanese, and others). By 1570, the native Taino and Ciboney Indians had died out along with their language, culture, and music, including the massive *areito* dances. Over the subsequent centuries of Spanish rule, Cuba, unlike most of the British West Indies, received large numbers of European settlers (mostly from Spain and the Canary Islands). These colonists brought with them a wealth of European music, from opera and sacred choral music to vibrant Spanish folk musics.

At the same time, conditions favored the dynamic flourishing of neo-African music in Cuba. For one thing, since it was much easier for Cuban slaves to buy their freedom than it was in the United States or British West Indies, by the early eighteenth century, Cuban towns hosted large communities of free blacks. These, together with urban slaves, were allowed to celebrate various sorts of musical and religious festivities, especially in the aforementioned *cabildos* (mutual-aid societies). The Spanish authorities tolerated the *cabildos,* partially because they tended to divide the blacks along ethnic and religious lines, thereby lessening the chance of unified slave revolts. Most rural slaves, despite brutal work schedules, were also allowed to sing, drum, and dance as they wished on their days off, and many were even permitted to leave their plantations to attend fiestas. Moreover, while the import of slaves to the United States and the British colonies had dwindled by 1800, most Cuban slaves (especially the Yoruba) were brought in the subsequent sixty years, so that neo-African musical traditions continued to be invigorated by fresh infusions of hapless captives.

Under such conditions, both traditional African and European musics were able to flourish in Cuba, at the same time blending and giving birth to a variety of syncretic styles in a process dubbed "transculturation" by ethnologist Fernando Ortiz.

AFRICAN-DERIVED MUSICS

The enslaved Africans brought to Cuba came from a variety of regions and ethnic groups. The larger of these were able to maintain many of their musical and religious traditions, especially in the realm of musics associated with religious ceremonies. One of the two largest ethnic groups among the slaves was the Yoruba, most of whom came from what is now Nigeria. The Yoruba in Africa had a highly developed culture, with large towns, social classes, trade networks, and sophisticated musical and religious heritages. While much of Yoruba culture—including language, kinship systems, and social structure in general—was lost in slavery, the Cuban Yoruba (called *lucumí*) were able to maintain a considerable amount of their traditional music and religion.

The Yoruba-derived religion in Cuba is called *santería*. *Santería* is a syncretic religion in the sense that traditional Yoruba elements have fused with Roman Catholic ones to form a new, coherent set of beliefs and practices. The West African pantheon of deities is retained, but they are identified with Catholic saints—for example, Changó, the thunder god, with Saint Barbara and Ogún, the god of iron, with Saint Peter. Each god, or *orisha*, is associated with particular colors, myths, herbs, dances, and songs. *Santería* devotees, most of whom are black or mulatto, believe that the *orishas* are powerful presences who should be regularly honored. Worship centers in ceremonies in which participants sing, dance, and in some cases undergo possession, as in the *bembé* described above.

The *bembé* is one kind of *santería* event, with its own kind of musical ensemble, repertoire, and rather festive character; Cubans describe it as a sort of "party for the *orishas*." The more typical *santería* function is a *toque de santo*, which uses different music and has a somewhat more serious character. A *toque* usually takes place at a devotee's home, which doubles as a temple. The occasion may be the anniversary of someone's initiation, an *orisha*'s sacred day, or an honoring of the spirits in thanks for or anticipation of a boon. The first part of the ceremony (called *oru del igbodú*—"ceremony in the *orisha*'s room") starts in the afternoon, when the musicians, with a few guests watching, play a sequence of drum invocations before the altar. The musical ensemble consists of three hourglass-shaped *batá* drums, resembling traditional Yoruba drums of the same name. In *batá* music, there is no improvised jamming as in *bembé* drumming; instead, the drummers play a set of largely precomposed rhythmic patterns, consisting of a complex series of salutes and transition passages. Each drum pattern is associated with a particular *orisha*, and parts of the patterns, in African "talking-drum" tradition, imitate the speech inflections of old Yoruba praise poems, which themselves are now largely forgotten.

After the *oru del igbodú*, guests start to arrive, and the musicians honor each initiate by briefly playing rhythms associated with his or her patron *orisha*. From then on, the main singer (who, like the drummers, is a paid professional) leads the ensemble and participants in performing various songs invoking the *orishas*. The songs are mostly in Yoruba, praising or even insulting the deities in order to encourage them to "descend" and possess the appropriate participants. The lead vocalist's job is to get people to sing and dance and, ultimately, to help induce spirit possession. When possession does occur, the possessed individual—now regarded as the *orisha*—is led into another room, dressed in appropriate garments, and often asked for advice or blessings.

While most North Americans have never heard of *santería*, they have heard something of Haitian *vodou* (voodoo), which is in many respects quite similar. Due in part to racist stereotypes of Haiti, *vodou* has a negative image abroad, and one can find references even in academic literature to "wild and drunken voodoo orgies." But there is nothing wild about either *santería* or *vodou* ceremonies. Actually, *batá* music and the dancing it accompanies have a rather stately and restrained character. Drunkenness and lewd behavior are forbidden at such functions, and there is no erotic couple dancing; instead, the dancers execute their traditional steps in a loosely collective fashion. *Santería*, of course, is not everyone's cup of tea, and most educated Cubans (especially whites) tend to regard it as backward and part of the lumpen underworld. Nevertheless, *santería* remains extremely widespread among lower-class Cubans, and the Revolutionary government has made no attempts to curtail it. Furthermore, the important role of Afro-Cuban culture in national identity in general has long been widely acknowledged, especially in the wake of the intellectual *negritud* movement of the 1930s, led in Cuba by ethnologist Fernando Ortiz, poet Nicolás Guillén, and others.

Meanwhile, since the mid-twentieth century, *santería* has flourished in Latino communities in the United States, especially in New York City and the Miami area, each of which hosts tens of thousands of adherents. Many of the practitioners are from Puerto Rican or other Latino backgrounds; some are Afro-Americans trying to get in touch with their African heritage. In New York and other North American cities, there are dozens of stores called *botánicas* that sell herbal medicines, statuettes, booklets, talismans, and other articles related to *santería*. In 1993, the U.S. Supreme Court legalized animal sacrifices practiced by a *santería* temple in Florida, and the religion is now in a position to emerge from underground. With the influx of several skilled Cuban musicians, *santería* music is also flourishing in the United States.

Santería is not the only Afro-Cuban religion. A group of slaves roughly equal in number to the Yoruba were brought from the Congo region in

Tropical religion in the barrio: One of New York City's many *botánicas* (photo by Peter Manuel)

Central Africa. The Congolese were Bantu-speaking hunter-gatherers and agriculturalists, whose society was in some ways less sophisticated than that of the Yoruba. Nevertheless, the Congolese contribution to Afro-Cuban culture is probably as substantial as that of the Yoruba, although more influential in the realm of secular music. Congolese religions in Cuba are generically called *palo* (and their practicioners, *paleros*). *Palo* centers in worship of ancestors and anthropomorphic spirits, who are honored in ceremonies with music and dance. The *palo* drums, songs, and rhythms are distinct from those of *santería*. Instead of *batá* drums, *paleros* generally use single-headed *ngoma* drums, which developed into the familiar conga drum, whose name derives from its ethnic origin. The *palo* rhythms are simpler and fewer than those of *santería*, and the dances are more vigorous; *palo* also has a stronger component of black magic. Like *santería*, *palo* flourishes in New York City and elsewhere.

Another distinctive Afro-Cuban music and dance tradition is that associated with the *abakuá* secret societies, whose founders came from the Calabar region in modern Nigeria. In Cuba, their descendants and others formed all-male secret societies, based mostly in and around Havana and Matanzas, especially among dockworkers. *Abakuá* is not a religion, but in ceremonies, *abakuá* members (also called *ñáñigos*) perform music and dance that reenact events from their mythological history. *Abakuá* societies still flourish, and their remarkable dances, like those of *palo* and *santería*, are often performed in folkloric contexts. The *abakuá* dancers are easily recognizable by their hooded costumes, which closely resemble those still used by their relatives in Calabar today. Two other African-derived sects are the Dahomeyan *arará* and the Yoruba offshoot *iyesá*. The distinctive ceremonies and musical traditions of *arará* and *iyesá* still survive in *cabildos* in the city of Matanzas.

Batá drum (atop a timpani) (photo by Peter Manuel)

RUMBA

By far the most famous and influential Afro-Cuban secular music and dance genre is rumba. The word "rumba" has long been used rather loosely in the realm of commercial dance music and salsa. Properly speaking, however, rumba denotes a traditional genre in which one or two dancers are accompanied by an ensemble consisting of three congas, two pairs of tapped sticks, and a lead singer and chorus. In the absence of any European melodic or chordal instruments, rumba sounds very African, and it appears to derive from secular dances cultivated by the Congolese slaves in Cuba. But unlike *santería* music, rumba is a distinctly Cuban creation, not a retention of an old African genre.

Rumba seems to have emerged in the late 1800s as an entertainment genre performed at parties, mostly in urban, lower-class black neighborhoods. While several different kinds of rumba once flourished, since the mid-twentieth century, only three have persisted. Of these, the most popular is the *guaguancó*, which is distinguished by its particular rhythm and dance styles.[1] (The basic *guaguancó* pattern is shown in Musical Example 2.) In the *guaguancó*, an ostinato (recurrent pattern) is played by either one or

MUSICAL EXAMPLE 2

two drummers on two differently tuned congas; another player taps an interlocking pattern with hard sticks (*palitos*) on the side of one drum. The lead singer strikes two short hardwood sticks together to provide another pattern; these sticks and the standardized pattern played on them are both called *clave,* the importance of which as an underlying rhythmic concept we discuss below. Meanwhile, another conga player (playing the higher-pitched *quinto* conga) improvises throughout. Over this intricate composite rhythm, the lead vocalist, after singing a few introductory nonsense syllables, performs an extended text, perhaps loosely improvising melodies and lyrics. The rumba lyrics can be about anything—love, politics, cockfights, or neighborhood events and people. This section of the rumba, the *canto,* can last a few minutes; sooner or later, the lead vocalist cues the other singers to commence singing a short refrain, and they then proceed in call-and-response fashion. This part is called the *montuno* (a word we will encounter later).

As soon as the *montuno* starts, a couple begins to dance in a pantomime game of coy evasion on the woman's part and playful conquest on the man's. While the female dancer undulates gracefully about, the man, without touching her, performs a variety of improvised, constantly changing steps and gestures around her, alternately importuning her, pretending to ignore her, mimetically cajoling her, and then, when he senses an opportunity, performing a *vacunao,* which consists of a pelvic thrust or even a graceful kick or swat in the direction of the woman's groin. A sense of fun and humor prevails throughout, and the sophistication, variety, and suppleness of the dance save it from being vulgar. Indeed, rumba dance is a difficult art and is only attempted by Cubans who have really cultivated an interest in it.

Of the two other types of rumba still performed, the *yambú* is like a slower, more restrained *guaguancó,* while the *columbia* is a solo male dance, stressing the dancer's acrobatic grace and virtuosity. The *yambú* is often traditionally played on wooden boxes (*cajones*) instead of congas.

As an informal fiesta dance, rumba is no longer very common. It is, however, often performed in folkloric contexts, which should not be regarded as "artificial." Any group of amateur *rumberos* can form a folkloric group to perform in various competitions or variety shows held throughout the island. Winning groups could even try to get regular gigs at a tourist venue. Meanwhile, in New York barrios, rumba caught on in its own fashion in the 1950s, and on weekends Spanish Harlem and Central Park have since resounded to the intricate pounding of conga drums. From there the rumba spread to Puerto Rico and elsewhere, and it continues to flourish among Latino communities outside Cuba, although the emphasis tends to be more on flashy conga playing than on the dance and singing.

Abakuá dancer

A MUSIC FESTIVAL IN
SANTIAGO DE CUBA

For a final look at Afro-Cuban music, I will describe an evening I spent in
Santiago de Cuba in the 1980s. Santiago is the largest city in the eastern
part of the island (Oriente) and has quite a different flavor from Havana.
There are no skyscrapers there, and the atmosphere is more provincial and
laid-back; however, the region is renowned for its rich Afro-Cuban cultural
heritage and for its proud, independent populace, who were leaders both in
the anticolonial wars and in the Revolutionary struggle. When I visited
Santiago de Cuba, there was a music festival in progress. Various groups
from other Caribbean countries were performing, along with some European acts. The one country conspicuously absent was the United States,
which would never have sent a cultural delegation to its sworn enemy, Communist Cuba. The Cubans, of course, would have welcomed a troupe from
the United States, and Michael Jackson's song "Thriller" was then a big hit
on the island. But there was no shortage of performances to choose from. I
ended up at a sort of Afro-Cuban variety show in a courtyard.

The first act represented a tradition unique to eastern Cuba, called *tumba
francesa*. The *tumba francesa* societies were social clubs formed by the more
than thirty thousand Haitians who fled to eastern Cuba around 1800 during the Haitian Revolution; several thousand more Haitians immigrated in
the early 1900s. The main *tumba francesa* activities are nightlong social
dances in which call-and-response singing is accompanied on a set of three
large *tumba* drums, a log (*catá*) struck with sticks, and metal rattles
(*chachas*). At present, only two dances survive. In one of these, the *masón*
(from French, *maison*), elegantly dressed couples perform graceful steps in
stylized imitation of French colonial dances (in that sense, like the Afro-
American cakewalk). The music, however, consists not of dainty minuets
but of vigorous Afro-Haitian drumming. In the other surviving dance, the
yuba, a solo male dancer improvises acrobatic steps in a sort of a duel with a
drummer, who plays straddling the largest *tumba* drum, which is laid
lengthwise on the floor.

Nowadays, the *tumba francesa* societies no longer fulfill important functions, although the government encourages their arts by hiring them to play
at events like this one. The *tumba francesa* may have become "folkloric" in
that sense, but for these musicians and dancers, it was just another party
which happened to be on a stage, as they were clearly having a wild time. I
noted that several of the performers were young, and many audience mem-

bers were singing along with the songs, which are in Haitian creole, not Spanish. Others standing near me were conversing in creole as well. In fact, the Franco-Haitian immigrants have contributed a special flavor to Oriente's culture.

The next act was an amateur rumba group, consisting mostly of black teenagers. Their performance was loosely structured in the form of a skit set in the pre-Revolutionary days, when rumba parties and *santería* ceremonies were often harrassed by the police. In the skit, they reconstructed a rumba party, which came to an abrupt halt when a lanky black policeman appeared and broke up the festivities. They pleaded with him and then offered him a few pesos, which he furtively accepted. The dancing resumed with a lively solo rumba *columbia*. After a few minutes, however, the policeman, who had been watching from the side, looked around to make sure his superiors were not watching and then, pushing the dancer aside, stepped into the ring and proceeded to perform his own virtuoso *columbia*. The audience roared with delighted applause and laughter.

After the rumba group came another set of Afro-Cuban teenagers, doing congas. Conga, as mentioned above, is the Congolese-derived drum used in dance bands; but it is also a kind of Afro-Cuban traditional dance and music, somewhat like rumba but less complex. Congas are usually performed in connection with Carnival processions, and the dancing generally consists of simple steps accompanying percussive music provided on slender conga drums, iron bells, and a marching-band-type bass drum (called *bombo* or *galleta*). This group, shunning the low stage, started performing fast congas in the middle of the courtyard, and the drummers were playing as if possessed—but of course they were not, because conga, like rumba, is a secular entertainment form and has no particular connection with Afro-Cuban religion. However, a problem soon arose, as within minutes a few hundred people had pressed into the small space, laughing, dancing, and shouting (and flattening our correspondent against a wall). There was clearly only one solution—and so the crowd, performers and all, burst out into the street, where more revelers joined in a wild, wriggling procession that gyrated about energetically for another hour.

This conga event turned into a sort of miniature version of Carnival, which is celebrated on a vast scale in Cuba. Carnival originated as a Christmastime fiesta held, elsewhere in Cuba, on Three Kings Day (*el día de Reyes*, January 6), during which all the Afro-Cuban *cabildos* were allowed to form street processions, with drumming and dancing (and often, fighting). Eventually, the processions came to be organized by competitive clubs with traditional titles and themes (the Gardeners, the Dandys, etc.). The clubs, after months of practice and preparation of elaborate costumes, floats, and ambulatory dances (mostly versions of the conga), would form *comparsa* processions, parading through streets lined with onlookers and, at one locale, a panel of judges. The Santiago Carnival had always been held in July, and Fidel Castro wisely timed his initial revolutionary escapade—the 1953 attack on the Moncada barracks—to coincide with the festivities and prevailing inebriation. The attack was a fiasco, but after the eventual triumph of the Revolution in 1959, Carnival throughout the island was shifted to July in order to commemorate the event. With a combination of state funding and avid grass-roots participation, the event soon grew to be more extravagant and lavish than ever.

EUROPEAN-DERIVED MUSICS

The various kinds of Afro-Cuban music were generally confined to a social underground until the mid-twentieth century, by which time they had come to pervade commercial dance music and had been celebrated by scholars like Fernando Ortiz. They have since come to be recognized as among the most dynamic parts of Cuban popular culture. But they represent only half the story of Cuban music, as the best-known forms of Cuban music—especially the country's dance-band music—have been formed as much by European influences as by African ones.

As we mentioned, Cuba's population has consisted of relatively equal proportions of whites, blacks, and mulattoes since the early 1800s. Spanish and Canary Island settlers continued to come even through the early 1900s. The Spaniards brought their own musical traditions with them, from rustic peasant songs to genteel aristocratic dances. In Cuba, all these musics gradually acquired a distinctively national flavor, in some cases due to a clear Afro-Cuban influence. With the advent of Cuban nationalism in the late 1800s, these creole forms became symbols of Cuban patriotism, as opposed to the perceivedly stuffy and stiff "peninsular" (i.e., pure Spanish) forms of music and dance.

The music of white Cuban farmers, who are called *guajiros,* derives primarily from Spanish and Canary Island origins, as is reflected in its reliance on guitars and mandolin-like instruments and its frequent use of the *décima.* The *décima* is an old Spanish-derived verse form, based on ten-line stanzas usually in the *espinela* rhyme scheme *abbaaccddc.* In Cuba and Puerto Rico, the *décima* is as familiar as limericks are in the United States, and students and literati have long learned to recite and compose them. Cuban peasants developed a variety of styles of singing *décimas* (under the label *punto*) and

would hold frequent contests at rural fiestas, especially in the white-popu-
lated tobacco-growing regions of the island. Singers would often be expected to compose impromptu *décimas,* perhaps using a fixed last line (*pie
forzado;* literally, "forced foot") given to them on the spot. Such informal
performances often take the form of a duel (*controversia*) between two
singer-poets, who trade off *décimas,* attempting to outdo each other in their
clever rhymes and witty insults (which are more important than ability to
sing well). Here is a famous *décima* from around 1900; it expresses the
ambivalence of Cubans toward the United States, which had invaded Cuba
in 1898, finishing off the already-collapsing Spanish rule and establishing its
own pattern of intervention in the island.

	(rhyme)
La tierra del Siboney	a
que da el tabaco y la caña	b
de la tutela de España	b
nos liberó McKinley.	a
Dale vivas, que es del ley	a
a nuestros buenos hermanos	c
¡Vivan los americanos!	c
sin cesar repiteremos,	d
pero también les diremos:	d
¡Cuba para los cubanos!	c

[U.S. President] McKinley has liberated the land of Siboney,
with its tobacco and sugarcane, from Spanish rule;
Let's sing the praises of our good brothers.
"Long live the Americans!" we'll ceaselessly repeat.
But we'll also tell them, "Cuba is for the Cubans!"[2]

The *Punto Cubano*

The Cuban *punto* is sung in a variety of styles throughout the island. The predominant style in the western part of the island is the so-called *punto libre,* in which the
verses are rendered in free rhythm in a stock, invariable melody. In between the sung
lines, the ensemble of string instruments and percussion plays a simple chordal ostinato, with flashy improvisations on the *laúd* (a mandolin-like instrument). The *décima* given above would be sung roughly as in the transcription shown in Musical
Example 3. To non-Hispanic ears, it may sound as if the tonic were C major, but, in
accordance with Andalusian harmonic conventions, the tonic is really G (mixoly-
dian), which is stressed in all cadences.

To perform or read this *décima* (which is a bit hard to transcribe clearly): the first
four lines (*abba*), notated in the example as (1) proceed to the end, leading to (2)
(lines *ac*), which, after the ensemble interlude (second staff), segues to (3) ("vivan

MUSICAL EXAMPLE 3

. . . repetiremos"), which goes directly to the last two lines ("pero . . . ") without an ensemble interlude.

Another kind of Hispanic-derived folk-style music is the *guajira,* a song form that has flourished from the early 1900s. The *guajira* is accompanied by the same sorts of instruments as the *punto,* which generally reiterate a simple I–IV–V progression. Its texts praise the beauty of the Cuban countryside and the simple, happy life of the Cuban peasant, as imagined and romanticized by urban songwriters. In that sense, many early *guajiras* represented a kind of fake country music, sort of like North American commercial cowboy music. But, as with cowboy music, rural people grew quite fond of these songs, which thus acquired their own sort of authenticity. The most famous *guajira* is "Guantanamera," which uses a patriotic text by Cuban nationalist José Martí (d. 1895).

In the 1800s, while the Cuban *punto* styles were evolving in the countryside, the white and mulatto populations of the island's towns and cities were cultivating their own lively musical culture. In the early 1800s, most dance music in urban white society consisted of European genres such as the waltz, the minuet, the gavotte, and the mazurka. Over the course of the century, however, these gradually came to be replaced by distinctively Cuban forms, which thus became nationalistic symbols in a time of growing resentment against Spanish colonial rule.

Many Cubans were growing increasingly frustrated by the economic restrictions and corrupt and inefficient government Spain imposed on Cuba.

Both culturally and politically, the Cuban middle classes became attracted less to backward, feudal, and repressive Spain than to the liberal bourgeois cultures flourishing in other European countries. The Franco-Haitian immigration from Haiti around 1800 brought cosmopolitan French culture to eastern Cuba; similarly, the melodramatic Italian style of vibrato-laden bel canto singing, popularized by the operas of Donizetti and Bellini, became widely popular in Cuba and elsewhere in Latin America. Alongside Italian operas and European concert music, particularly popular were Spanish-language light operas, called *zarzuelas,* and the less formal *tonadillas,* both of which were often locally composed. Cuba's urban cultural scene became one of the liveliest in the hemisphere, and indeed, by 1800, Havana was the third largest city in the Americas (following Mexico City and Lima and well ahead of provincial Boston and New York). As Cuban author Alejo Carpentier observed, both the refinement of this bourgeois culture and the cruelty of its economic base could be seen in such newspaper classified advertisements as one in 1794 that offered for sale a spinet piano, a colt, and a seven-year-old negro boy.[3]

Musically, the most important genre in the emergence of nineteenth-century Cuban creole national culture was the *contradanza habanera* (Havana-style contradance), which in Cuba was generally referred to simply as *contradanza* (or, less often, as *danza*). In the late 1700s and early 1800s, various kinds of related dances (e.g., the English country-dance and French *contredanse*) had been popular among the European middle classes. Cubans were familiar with the Spanish *contradanza,* which, like the early northern European styles, featured group-style dancing directed by a caller, in a fashion similar to the Virginia reel. Over the course of the nineteenth century, the Cubans came to regard the Spanish style as stuffy and archaic, and so they adopted the contemporary French and British trends, gradually dispensing with the collective character of the dance and turning it into an intimate couple dance. At the same time, the Cubans gave it a bit of Afro-Caribbean spice, in the form of syncopated rhythms (especially the pattern: x--xx-x-, also distinguishing the early Argentine tango). Although most *contradanza* patrons were white or mulatto, audiences preferred to hire dark-skinned musicians, prompting one writer to proclaim with alarm in 1832, "The arts are in the hands of people of color!"

Accordingly, while the *contradanza* was cultivated as a light-classical form to be played by pianists or chamber groups in aristocratic salons, more animated versions were also performed by various ad hoc ensembles (e.g., guitar, flute, and fiddle) at all manner of middle- and working-class fiestas. By the 1830s, this *contradanza habanera* had become popular in Europe, where

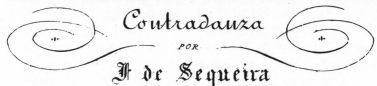

A typical nineteenth-century contradanza for piano

it was known as "habanera" (or, incorrectly, as "habañera"). Georges Bizet used a contemporary habanera melody in his opera *Carmen,* and another habanera, "La Paloma," became one of the most popular songs in Latin America. Both songs use the basic ostinato shown in the previous paragraph.

In the 1850s–60s, Cuban urban musical life was enlivened by the presence of Louis Moreau Gottschalk, a composer and virtuoso pianist from New Orleans. In his extended visits to Cuba, Puerto Rico and elsewhere, Gottschalk inspired local composers and audiences with his flashy compositions using contemporary Caribbean melodies and rhythms.

In the 1880s, especially through the influence of composer Miguel Faílde, the *contradanza* was eclipsed by a new form, the *danzón,* which reigned as the national dance of Cuba until the 1930s. The *danzón* retained a European light-classical orientation in its use of rondo-like sectional structure (often *abac*), written scores, sophisticated harmonies, and instrumentation. But if Afro-Cuban rhythmic flavor was hinted at in the *contradanza,* it was unmistakable in the *danzón* (much to the horror of negrophobic stuffed shirts), especially in the persistence of the *cinquillo* ostinato (Musical Example 4). This ostinato is found in a variety of Afro-Caribbean musics, includ-

MUSICAL EXAMPLE 4

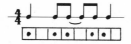

ing Haitian *vodou* drumming, *batá* music, and West Indian calypsoes like "Yellow Bird."

Through about 1910, for outdoor occasions the *danzón* was generally played on a horn-dominated *orquesta típica* ensemble, sounding a bit like early New Orleans jazz, with which it had some ties. By 1920, however, this tropical ragtime *danzón* ensemble had been largely replaced by a sweeter, indoor-type ensemble called *charanga,* in which a wooden flute and two violins were backed by piano, string bass, *güiro* scraper, and *timbales* (small, metal-framed drums with a crisper sound than the timpani). The *charangas* and their favored idiom, the *danzón,* retained a certain bourgeois character, but their suave mixture of "fire and grace," as John Storm Roberts put it in his book *The Latin Tinge,* ensured their vitality through the 1950s.

While the *danzón* was a popular dance idiom, it was also a sophisticated light-classical salon genre whose composition and performance required training in European art music. Since the mid-nineteenth century, Cuba had been producing many skilled classical performers, and in the early twentieth century, some of its composers achieved international renown. Amadeo Roldan (1900–1939) and Alejandro García Caturla (1906–1940) were two remarkable modernists who synthesized Afro-Cuban rhythms with bold, Stravinsky-like sonorities. Both died in their thirties; Caturla, a magistrate, was murdered by a criminal he had paroled. Representing a somewhat more populist vein was composer and pianist Ernesto Lecuona (1895– 1963), remembered for his zarzuelas, tuneful ballads such as "Siboney" and "María la O," and impressionistic piano pieces such as the still-popular "Malagueña."

Finally, in discussing the more European-oriented Cuban musics, we should also mention the bolero, which evolved in the early twentieth century as a popular slow-dance song. The bolero's lyrics, sung in European bel canto style, are unabashedly sentimental and romantic, celebrating eternal love, wallowing in the sweet pangs of unrequited longing, or lamenting the fickleness of faithless women. The bolero became widely popular as a voice-and-guitar idiom throughout much of Latin America by the 1920s. While the original Cuban style was sung solo or duet, Mexican groups like the Trío Calaveras popularized the practice of singing it in suave, smooth, three-part harmony, which then became the norm in Cuba, Puerto Rico, and elsewhere. Although heavily influenced by Italian song, the bolero also accommodates subdued Afro-Cuban rhythms and sometimes segues into a faster *montuno* section, in which case it might be called *bolero-son* or *bolero-chá*.

THE *SON* AND
MODERN CUBAN DANCE MUSIC

The twentieth century constituted a new chapter in Cuban history. With Spain out of the picture, Cuba developed closer economic, political, and cultural ties with the United States. At the same time, many Cubans, fiercely nationalistic as always, resented the growing North American domination of the island and especially the humiliating occupations by the U.S. Marines in 1906–1909, 1912, 1917–1920, and 1933–1934. Meanwhile, Cuban society was modernizing and transforming. Slavery was over, although most black people continued to face dire poverty and overt discrimination until the Revolutionary reforms of the 1960s. One important challenge for the country was the need to develop a national cultural identity that would unite the entire population—white, black, and mulatto. Insofar as this goal has been achieved, music has played an important role in the formation of such an identity. From the 1920s on, hostility to Yankee domination and corrupt dictators like Gerardo Machado fueled the growth of a vibrant cultural nationalism that gradually came to embrace Afro-Cuban culture as well, as is reflected in the work of intellectuals like Fernando Ortiz and poet Nicolás Guillén. Perhaps most important for our purposes was the emergence of dance-music genres that synthesized European and Afro-Cuban elements.

We have suggested how the *contradanza* and *danzón* became symbols of creole national identity by departing from Spanish traditions and acquiring a distinctively Cuban flavor. Much of this flavor came from the incorporation, whether subtle or overt, of Afro-Cuban syncopations. But the medium-tempo *danzón*, for all its once-controversial rhythmic "oomph," was still a rather genteel and restrained form, far removed from the rumba loved by lower-class blacks. The genre that was to succeed in creatively fusing equal amounts of white- and black-derived musical features was the *son*, which subsequently came to dominate musical culture not only in Cuba but in most of the Spanish-speaking Caribbean as well.

The *son* originated in eastern Cuba in the first decades of the century. From the start it represented a mixture of Spanish-derived and Afro-Cuban elements. In the early *son,* the European features were somewhat more prominent, as is reflected in the predominance of string instruments (guitars and the guitar-like *tres*), the rather moderate tempo, and a "song"-like first section (the *largo*) that had an extended harmonic progression and a melody often sung in suave bel canto style. At the same time, Afro-Cuban influence was present in several aspects, notably in the use of bongo drums and the *marimbula* (a bass instrument derived from African "thumb-pianos" like the *mbira*) and in the extended *montuno* section (following the *largo*), in which vocal call-and-response patterns were sung over a simple harmonic ostinato. In the *largo–montuno* structure and the use of *clave* sticks and associated ostinatos, the *son* thus also had structural similarities to the rumba. Finally, most *soneros* themselves were black or mulatto, and their song texts were rooted in Afro-Cuban street life.

By 1920, the *son* had become popular in Havana, where most ensembles added a trumpet, making the standard format a septet. Recordings by the Sexteto Habanero and Ignacio Piñeiro's Septeto Nacional became popular throughout the island and outside Cuba as well (where their music was often confusingly labeled "rumba"). The *son* managed to achieve commercial appeal without losing its barrio flavor, relected in its song texts dealing, like rumba lyrics, with all manner of topics, from romance to neighborhood events.

The subsequent evolution of the *son* was marked by increasing sophistication, featuring, on the one hand, the inclusion of more complex, jazz-influenced harmonies and European instruments (horns and piano) and, on the other hand, the gradual adoption of faster tempos and a more percussive, rhythmic sound. In that sense, the mature *son* was as much an heir to the proletarian rumba as to the suave and genteel *danzón*.

The most dramatic change came in the 1940s, especially in the music of the Conjunto Casino and of bandleader Arsenio Rodríguez (d. 1970), a *tres* player, composer, and arranger. Arsenio, who had lost his sight in childhood after being kicked by a horse, came to New York (which had by this time become a center for Cuban music) to pursue his career and, he hoped, cure his blindness. Like the Conjunto Casino, he enlarged the *son* ensemble, adding a conga, a piano, and a second trumpet (a format called *conjunto*). Most important, all the instruments were to play regulated parts: the horn players played precomposed sectional arrangements while the rhythm section (piano, bass, and percussion) played standardized accompaniment patterns (as shown in Musical Example 13, below). This modernized *son* gave up some of the informal, collective looseness of the traditional *son*, in which, for example, the bongo player improvised throughout the song. But it provided a tight, composite rhythm that had a unique drive and an electrifying appeal to dancers. These innovations laid the foundation for salsa, which was taking the Latin music scene by storm at the same time as Arsenio, still blind, was dying in poverty.

The basic two-part formal structure of the *son* has remained the same from the 1920s to the present, and the vast majority of salsa songs (which Cubans would call *son* or *guaracha*) also follow this pattern. The first part is like a closed "song" in itself, usually lasting less than three minutes. Often it uses the thirty-two-bar *AABA* format typical of Euro-American popular songs, in which the *B* section is a modulating bridge. The *montuno* is usually much longer than the "song" section. It can include extended instrumental solos as well as short, precomposed horn sections (in salsa terminology, mambo or *moña*), which punctuate the call-and-response vocals.

One of the most distinctive features of the composite rhythm of the modern *son* (including most salsa songs) is the bass pattern. In most North American and Afro-American popular musics, from rock and rap to disco and doo-wop, the bass emphasizes the downbeat, falling strongly on the "one" beat of the four-beat measure. In the *son*, by contrast, the bass usually omits the downbeat entirely, in a pattern known as the *anticipated bass*. You can get the feel of this rhythm by repeatedly counting "one–two–three–one–two–three–one–two" and clapping on the underlined "ones" (not the first "one"!). The pattern is called "anticipated" because the note of the last "one" indicates the chord of the following measure. The resulting effect is quite different from the steady "thump-thump-thump" of such musics as disco, merengue, and most rock. Instead, the rhythm seems to glide along in a fluid manner reflected in the dance style. At fast tempos, it is not too hard for gringos and the uninitiated to get lost (if that happens, listen to the bell part—or seek private therapy from a *salsero*). Jazz trumpeter Dizzy Gillespie used to relate with amusement and awe how he once became completely disoriented in a jam session with Cuban musicians, shouting helplessly, "Where's beat one?!" The anticipated bass pattern is found, with some variation, in most salsa songs; together with the characteristically syncopated piano and percussion parts, it forms an essential cog in the intricate machinery of Latin rhythm (and is illustrated in Musical Example 13, below).

Another important development of the 1940s was the invention of the mambo. Essentially, the mambo was a fusion of Afro-Cuban rhythms with the big-band format adopted from swing jazz. The key to big-band music—aside from its ability to fill a dance hall with sound—was the concept of sectional writing for contrasting instruments, in which distinct trumpet, trombone, and saxophone sections would play interlocking, often responsorial lines. Typically, the saxes might play *guajeo*-type ostinatos adapted from *tres* patterns of the *son,* while the other sections would toss melodic fragments back and forth, occasionally all joining in for climactic bursts. Mambos were primarily instrumental dance music, with vocal parts, if present, generally restricted to short nonsense phrases.

Although bands in Cuba like Orquesta Riverside were already playing mambo-style arrangements in the 1940s, the invention of the mambo is usually credited to Cuban bandleader Pérez Prado, who spent most of his years touring in Mexico and elsewhere outside the island. The advent of microphones enabled bandleaders like Beny Moré to combine mambo format with the *son* and *guaracha* (a similar up-tempo dance genre). The mambo reached its real peak in New York City in the 1950s, where bands led by Machito (Frank Grillo, with his brother-in-law Mario Bauzá) and the Puerto Ricans Tito Puente and Tito Rodríguez incorporated jazz-influenced instrumental solos and more sophisticated arrangements. The bands of these "Big Three" played both for Latino and Anglo audiences, outshining corny crossover orchestras like Xavier Cugat's and setting the stage for the salsa boom of the 1960s. With Prado based chiefly in Mexico and the New York mambo bands developing their own styles, Cuban music had already taken on a life of its own outside the island.

A Word about *Clave*

We have mentioned that *clave* (literally, "key") refers to the pair of hardwood sticks used in rumba and *son,* as well as the pattern played on them. *Clave* is actually a rhythmic concept that underlies most forms of Afro-Cuban dance music, from rumba to salsa; for musicians and, on an intuitive level, dancers and listeners, *clave* really is a "key" that makes the music fit together. Musicians swear by the importance of *clave*, and it is worth describing here, even if it is a somewhat technical matter.

In Cuban dance music, there are basically two *clave* patterns, the "three–two" *clave* and the more common "two–three" *clave*. Those familiar with early rock 'n' roll will recognize the three–two *clave* from its use in Bo Diddley songs like "Not Fade Away" (Musical Example 5a). The two–three *clave* is the same, but reversed (Musical Example 5b). A given song will be set in one or the other of these patterns (as is generally indicated on the sheet music chart).

MUSICAL EXAMPLE 5a

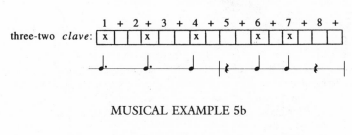

MUSICAL EXAMPLE 5b

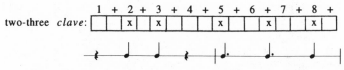

In the traditional rumba and *son*, these patterns are clearly played on the *clave* sticks (although the rumba pattern, as shown in Musical Example 2, above, is slightly different). In *conjunto,* mambo, and salsa bands, the *clave* sticks are often absent, and so the basic pattern is not sounded. However, in all of these forms, the *clave* pattern is always present in the minds of the musicians and, in a composite, subtle manner, in most of what they play. Thus the arranger composing the horn parts, the trumpeter or pianist improvising solos, the lead vocalist singing lines in the call-and-response *montuno*—in short, everyone—must have the *clave* pattern going in his head and be following it, however subtly, in his music. (I say "his" because there are precious few women in Latin music.) The idea is not to be slavishly and mechanically beating out the *clave* pattern—that would be obtuse. Instead, for example, if a piece (or a section of a piece) is in two–three *clave*, the musicians will try to suggest that pattern and, above all, to avoid playing or composing lines that suggest three–two *clave*.

Irregularities in *clave* can happen in different ways, aside from the case of a hopelessly amateurish band. Perhaps a guest soloist is present, in the form of some gringo jazz trumpeter who likes Latin music but doesn't really understand *clave*; or perhaps, after a long percussion solo in the middle of the song where the *clave* is especially

Güiro **player (Ethnic Folk Arts Center)**

subtle, the musical director of the band cues the horns to reenter on the wrong measure. There have also always been some popular songs written with what hard-core musicians would regard as incorrect or *cruzao* (crossed) *clave*. An example is the 1989 hit "Cali Pachanguero," by the Colombian band Grupo Niche. Chris Washburne, a New York salsa trombonist, relates, "That's a catchy song, and audiences love it, but most musicians hate to play it, because the *clave* is all messed up. Another thing that can really screw things up is when some misguided zealot in the audience starts clapping *clave—the wrong way*—and everyone else joins in."

If, for whatever reason, a band starts playing out of *clave*, knowledgeable musicians will exchange despairing glances at one another as they play, and some veteran dancers on the floor may sense, however intuitively, that the sound is somehow jumbled and confused and perhaps this is a good time to take a break and have another beer.

You can get some idea of how *clave* is observed in the *montuno* refrains shown below. The first, "La esencia del guaguancó" (Musical Example 6), is from a *son* by Puerto Rican composer Tite Curet Alonso (recorded by Johnny Pacheco and Pete "El Conde" Rodríguez on "La Perfecta Combinación" [Fania 4XT-SLPC-380]); the

MUSICAL EXAMPLE 6

2-3 clave

3-2 clave
(wrong)

MUSICAL EXAMPLE 7

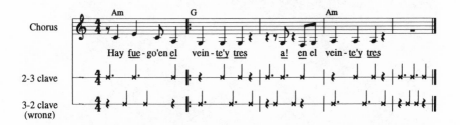

second, "Hay fuego en el veinte y tres" (Musical Example 7), is from a *son montuno* of Arsenio Rodríguez. Both are in two–three *clave*. In each case, some of the *clave* beats (as shown by the underlined syllables) coincide with structural beats of the melodies. Try singing these patterns (with help, if need be) while clapping the *clave*. Then try doing the same thing over the "incorrect" three–two pattern. Ideally, you should be able to hear that the "incorrect" *clave* is clearly out of sync with the melody. However, your reaction might still be, "What's so bad about that? It sounds OK to me." But if you listen to a lot of Latin music, you will reach a point where such incongruities sound messy and inappropriate to you (and the rest of the music will sound even better).

While the mambo and *conjunto* bands were in full flower, the *charangas*, with their quaint yet soulful flute-and-violin sound, were surviving by changing with the times and making their music hotter and more Afro-Cuban. Since José Urfé's "El bombín de Barreto" of 1910, *charanga* band-leaders had been enlivening *danzones* by adding vamp-like *montuno* codas. In the '30s and '40s, Antonio Arcaño's group codified this practice and shortened the opening, more "European" sections; Arcaño called his inno-vation "mambo," although it sounded quite different from the big-band genre of the same name. Other *charanga* groups, like the famous Orquesta Aragón, started playing up-tempo *son* and *guaracha*, effectively Afro-Cu-banizing the *charanga* repertoire (even if its audiences and peformers re-mained mostly white). Then, around 1950, *charangas* got a big boost when bandleader Enrique Jorrin popularized the *chachachá*, a funky, medium-tempo song form with unison vocals and a simpler, "one–two–chachacha" choreography. The *chachachá* enjoyed its own craze in the United States, but its accompanying commercialization and Arthur Murray–style dilution also guaranteed its decline. As John Storm Roberts puts it, "A few years of lumpy rhythm sections, mooing sax section, and musicians raggedly chant-ing CHAH! CHAH! CHAH! were enough."[4]

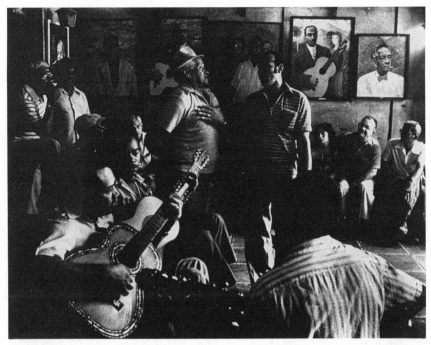

Old *trovadores* (María "Marucha" Haya, courtesy of Center for Cuban Studies)

Commercial or not, it was through such syntheses of Euro-American and Afro-Cuban elements that these fresh forms, especially the modernized *son*, became the favorite dance music of Cubans of all ages, classes, and races. Meanwhile, the success of the synthesis was reflected internationally, as the *son* and mambo became widely popular in the United States, Africa, and Latin America and provided the basis for what later came to be known as salsa.

In the late 1940s, New York became the crucible for another dynamic Afro-Cuban spin-off when jazz trumpeter Dizzy Gillespie teamed up with Cuban conga-player Chano Pozo to form a Latin big band. Although jazz influences had already come to permeate Cuban dance music, Dizzy's band was the first to present mambo-style big-band pieces like "Manteca" not as dance music but as listening music, emphasizing jazz-style solos. Thus began the subgenre known as Latin jazz, which has come to denote listening-oriented, predominantly instrumental music, usually played by a combo rather than a big band and featuring sophisticated improvised solos.

Cuban dance music reached a peak of sorts in the 1950s. The *son*, mambo, and *chachachá* were in full flower, with New York and Havana as the twin poles of a Latin dance empire. Havana had become America's bachelor entertainment center, with its glittery world of casinos, cabarets, and over two hundred brothels. Bands led by Miguelito Cuní, Felix Chappotin, and Benny Moré were in constant international demand.

Nueva trova singer Pablo Milanés (María "Marucha" Haya, courtesy of Center for Cuban Studies)

But the revelry and merriment of the fifties could barely mask the deep tensions in Cuban society that were in the process of exploding. More and more Cubans were growing disgusted with the corrupt U.S.-backed dictatorship of Fulgencio Batista, the prostitution, the poverty and alienation of the lower classes, and the continued domination of the Cuban economy by Yankee businesses and mafiosi. People of various political leanings began to sympathize with the earnest urban guerrillas and with the ragtag band of bearded revolutionaries off in the Sierra Maestra, led by one Fidel Castro.

"SOCIALISM WITH *PACHANGA*"

Whether or not a Communist dictatorship was what most Cuban supporters of the anti-Batista struggle had in mind, that was the direction in which

Machito and vocalist Graciela (at left) at the Savoy Ballroom (Photographs and Prints Division, Schomburg Center for Research in Black Culture, New York Public Library, Astor, Lenox, and Tilden Foundations)

Poster for 1973 festival of political song (courtesy of Center for Cuban Studies)

the Cuban Revolution was driven by events, including hostility from Washington, D.C., Soviet friendship, and Fidel Castro's personal vision. The Revolution had profound effects on every aspect of Cuban life and culture, including music. One change was that because of the U.S. embargo against Cuba, North Americans and Puerto Ricans were cut off from musical activities on the island. Cuban groups and their records were not allowed into the United States, and so a myth began to spread in this country that communism had killed Cuban music. In fact, whatever the merits or demerits of the Revolution as a whole, music has done quite well since 1959. The communist government has treated the arts and culture as high priorities, and music has received particularly generous support. Revolutionary leader Che Guevara envisioned Cuban communism not as a drab work regime but as a dynamic program of economic justice and lively popular culture, or, as he put it, as "socialism with *pachanga*" (referring to a popular dance rhythm of the 1950s).

To a considerable extent Guevara's vision was achieved, although with some shortcomings. The performance of the record industry—a nationalized bureaucracy since the early sixties—has been particularly undistinguished. The records produced have often been too few and too late, their sound is uneven, and they have had little international distribution (partly due to the U.S. embargo). Because the mass media in Cuba do not disseminate any music by defectors, Cubans have had to tune in to Miami radio stations to hear the music of expatriates like Celia Cruz. Perhaps the most frustrated musicians have been Latin jazz superstars like trumpeter Arturo Sandoval and saxophonist Paquito d'Rivera, who were unable to tour the United States because of the American embargo; both eventually defected and now live in New York. Critics also argue, with some legitimacy, that the extraordinary musical vitality of the 1950s has not been matched since—perhaps, some say, because the whole colorful lumpen underworld of casinos, brothels, and bohemian artists was eliminated (with the musicians becoming salaried state employees and the prostitutes given respectable jobs).

It may be true that the Revolutionary period did not foster any extraordinary stylistic developments and that its impact has been more in how music is produced and consumed than in the nature of the music itself. With the nationalization of all aspects of the music industry—from clubs and conservatories to the manufacture of *batá* drums—all forms of commercialism were removed from musical culture. After some initial government reservations about jazz and rock were overcome, musicians were free to experiment, and they have not been pressured to politicize their art (although they would also be ill-advised to criticize the basic goals of the Revolution in public). In accordance with the generous state support of music, until the economic crisis of the 1990s, most full-time professional musicians enjoyed leisurely work schedules and cradle-to-grave security (in the United States, by contrast, most dance-band musicians have to work full-time day jobs in order to survive). In the 1980s, Antonio, a pianist in a hotel dance band, told me, "I play three hours a day, and for that I get full salary, a month's vacation, and of course free health care. The rest of the time I practice, hang out, and watch American TV, which I pick up via my homemade antenna." (That kind of low productivity is exactly what is wrong with Cuban socialism, say some critics.) Meanwhile, the state has continued to support all kinds of old and new music, from *punto* contests to the avant-garde experiments of guitarist Leo Brouwer and the pyrotechnics of jazz pianist Gonzalo Rubalcaba.

For folklorist Rogelio Martínez Furé (a director of the Conjunto Nacional Folklórico), the biggest improvement resulting from the Cuban Revolution was the integration of lower-class Afro-Cubans and their culture into the mainstream of Cuban society. This was achieved partially through raising the lower class's standard of living (at the expense of the rich); through eliminating the racial discrimination that pervaded pre-Revolutionary clubs, beaches, hotels, and restaurants; and through generous state support of Afro-Cuban culture and music and the fostering of a new, integrated Cuban sense of identity. The Revolutionary government, in spite of its atheistic Marxism, made no attempt to repress the Afro-Cuban religions, and it is not uncommon to see statuettes of *orishas* Yemayá or Changó alongside a photo of Fidel in a Cuban home.

In general, the fervent nationalism, invigorated sense of purpose, and state support fostered by the Revolution unleashed tremendous creative energy, manifesting itself in all aspects of Cuban life, from music and cinema to sports and medical research. For that matter, the vitality of music in Revolutionary Cuba must also be viewed in relation to changes in society as a whole. Communist Cuba, for example, has been the only country in the Americas with a music industry free from under-the-table payoffs, liquor company sponsorship, narco-dollars, advertisements, and commercialism in general; for that matter, it has also been the only country in the region with no homelessness, drug addiction, and malnutrition (until the present crisis, which owes much to a crippling U.S. embargo). Insofar as these aspects of modern Cuba have influenced musicians, audiences, and cultural life in general, they have been relevant features of the Cuban musical milieu.

Aside from such sociomusical developments, the Revolutionary period has fostered some innovative bands and styles. In the realm of dance music, the two most influential groups have been Los Van Van, a sort of enlarged *charanga* ensemble that popularized the *comparsa*-influenced *songo* beat, and Irakere, a brassy supergroup known for its jazz-influenced innovations. Recent years have seen the rise of hot dance bands like NG La Banda and a variety of combos blending modern Cuban sounds with reggae, rock, *santería* music, and heavy metal. Even rumba dancers keep up with the times, mixing elements of break-dancing into their acrobatic *columbia* steps.

The most distinctive new music associated with the revolution has been *nueva trova,* the Cuban variety of Latin American *nueva canción* (new song), which is itself loosely related to North American "protest music." *Nueva trova* emerged in the early seventies, and since then, its leading performers, Pablo Milanés and Silvio Rodríguez, have become international stars, especially among educated, politically progressive Latin American youths. Some *nueva trova* songs make self-conscious use of traditional Cuban elements, but most are in the singer-songwriter vein of Bob Dylan, Joan Baez, and their ilk.

Much *nueva trova* sounds essentially like soft-rock ballads, leading some critics to disparage it as bourgeois, bland, commercial-sounding, and lacking the punch of Afro-Cuban music. However, *nueva trova*'s fans enjoy its sophisticated lyrics, its often beautiful melodies, and the progressive politics of its singers. Most *nueva trova* songs are about love, but many deal with contemporary sociopolitical issues. As one singer relates, "We are free to be controversial; we do songs about housing shortages, pollution, how vacation spots give priority to foreigners."[5] The early 1990s have seen singer Carlos Varela voice the sentiments of disgruntled youth in oblique antigovernment jibes—including in occasional concerts funded by the state itself. More typical are songs that implicitly endorse the ideals of the Revolution; these generally avoid vulgar slogan-mongering, preferring the pensive yet committed affirmation of Pablo Milanés's "I don't live in a perfect society" or Silvio Rodríguez's "Little Daytime Serenade," a subtle, poignant tribute to the martyrs of the Cuban Independence Wars and the Revolution:

> I live in a free country,
> which can only be free in this land, in this moment
> and I'm happy because I am a giant. . . .
> I'm happy, a happy man
> and I wish to beg pardon for this day
> from all those who died for my happiness.[6]

In an unusually militant but no less lyrical vein is Pablo's "Son de Cuba y Puerto Rico" (*Son* of Cuba and Puerto Rico), written in the 1970s heyday of the Revolutionary period when morale was high and Cubans looked hopefully at Puerto Rico's independence movement:

> When my banner is raised, yours should be raised too
> for that time [the anti-colonial struggle] it was raised first
> that together we might fly.

Later a beloved voice cried with much truth,
"Cuba and Puerto Rico are the two wings of one bird."[7]
Puerto Rico, wing that fell to the sea, that couldn't fly,
I invite you to my breast, that we might fly together. . . .
Following the same path, we return to meet and together demand
that your destiny change.
And if they try to deny you by force that which is your right,
I invite you to fly with me with a machete under your wing.

Since 1990, unfortunately, it has been the Cuban economy that has essentially fallen into the sea, due to the loss of the Soviet umbilical cord, the inflexibility of hard-line Communist policies ("Castro Inconvertible"), and, above all, a tightened American embargo designed either to provoke civil war or to starve the country (children and all) into submission.[8] As of early 1995, the situation is dire, and the government is more concerned with providing basic nutrition than with funding nightclubs. But even though many of the top groups have based themselves abroad, the state still stages performances, from little campesino fiestas to mega-concerts drawing two hundred thousand people to Havana's Revolution Square. Meanwhile, Afro-Cuban cult music and religion seem to be flourishing more openly than ever, with evident state tolerance. Above all, Cubans have had to draw from the heritage of nationalism, rebelliousness, and heroic perseverance that fueled the independence struggle, the toppling of the Machado dictatorship, and the Cuban Revolution itself. Whatever form the new chapter in Cuban culture and history may take, two constants will surely remain: the indomitable Cuban spirit and its rich expression in music. As the slogan defying the embargo proclaims, *¡Cada día más cubano!*—"Every day more Cuban than ever!"

BIBLIOGRAPHY

Cuban writers have produced many excellent books on all varieties of Cuban music, but these are in Spanish and are generally unavailable even in Cuba, not to mention elsewhere. Spanish-language books available (with a bit of hunting) in the United States include Alejo Carpentier's dated but still peerless *La música en Cuba* (Mexico City: Fonda de Cultura Económica, 1946); Cristobal Diáz Ayala, *Música cubana del areyto a la nueva trova* (Hato Rey, P.R.: Editorial Cubanacan, 1981); and Elena Pérez Sanjurjo, *Historia de la música cubana* (Miami: Moderna Poesía, 1986).

English-language books include Peter Manuel, *Essays on Cuban Music: Cuban and North American Perspectives* (Lanham, Md.: University Press of America, 1990); Steve Cornelius and John Amira, *The Music of Santería: Traditional Rhythms of the Batá Drums* (Crown Point, Ind.: White Cliffs Media, 1992); and John Storm Roberts, *Black Music of Two Worlds* (New York: Praeger, 1972) and *The Latin Tinge: The*

Impact of Latin American Music on the United States (New York and Oxford: Oxford University Press, 1979).

RECORDS AND FILMS

TRADITIONAL GENRES: *The Cuban Danzón* (Folkways FE 4066); *Cuban Counterpoint: History of the Son Montuno* (Rounder CD 1078); *Caliente = Hot: Puerto Rican and Cuban Musical Expression in New York* (New World 244); *Afro-Cuba: A Musical Anthology* (Rounder CD 1088).

MODERN DANCE MUSIC: *Cuba Classics 2: Dancing with the Enemy* (Luaka Bop 9 26580–2); *Arsenio Rodríguez* (Ansonia ALP 1337); *Cuba Classics 3: Diablo al infierno* (Luaka Bop 9 45107–2); *Al Santiago's "The Best of Cuba"* (Funny CD-507).

ANTHOLOGIES: *A Carnival of Cuban Music: Routes of Rhythm vol.'s 1 & 2* (Rounder CD 5049)

FILMS: *Routes of Rhythm, with Harry Belafonte (vols. 1–3);* by Eugene Rosow and Howard Dratch (Cultural Research and Communication, Inc., 1989).

3

Puerto Rico

Much of urban Puerto Rico looks more or less like parts of the mainland United States; and, after all, in its "commonwealth" status, Puerto Rico, although not a state, is politically and economically part of the United States. Its culture is also a mixed bag of the indigenous and the imported. Certainly, there is plenty of mainstream Stateside culture there, from Madonna to McDonald's. And for that matter, in speaking of Puerto Rican society, it is ultimately impossible to separate the island from the mainland United States, where two-fifths of the people of Puerto Rican descent live. Likewise, New York is the largest Puerto Rican city and has been the biggest center for Puerto Rican dance music since the 1930s. But there are many aspects of Puerto Rican culture that really flourish only on the island, especially its rich heritage of folk musics, from campesino songs to the lively, percussive *plena* and *bomba*.

In my first trip to Puerto Rico, I visited an Anglo friend, Al, who had married a Puerto Rican woman and lived in San Juan.

"How do you get along with your in-laws?" I asked.

"It's been fine since I learned to dance," he replied. "That was a big problem at first. It seemed that every time I was over there, at the drop of a hat someone would put on a record, and then it's party time, and I have to dance with the mother, the grandmother, the aunts, you name it. But I didn't know how to dance Latin-style, so I felt like a real *pendejo* [not a nice word]. Then I actually took lessons for almost a year and learned to dance the *guaracha*, merengue, bolero, all that stuff. Since then it's been great. Man, these people just love to dance."

"Do you ever hear *plena?*"

"Only every day. There's a business being picketed by striking union workers across from my apartment, and the protesters sing *plena* most of the day."

"Sounds more like a party than a picket line," I mused.

"Well, that's certainly how some people felt in New York, when it seemed to them that the Puerto Rican contingent in street demonstrations was turning them into fiestas. But that's how they use *plena* down here. No student protest is complete without it."

"What about *bomba?*" I asked, eager to see the island's oldest Afro-Caribbean dance.

"That's a bit harder to find. But if we're lucky we'll see some at the *fiesta patronal* in Loíza next weekend."

And indeed we did. But before telling you about that, let's review some of the historical background of Puerto Rican music.

CUBA AND PUERTO RICO: "THE TWO WINGS OF THE SAME BIRD"

In its history and culture, Puerto Rico has much in common with Cuba, its sister colony under Spanish rule until 1898. As in Cuba, the Spanish conquistadors claiming Puerto Rico in 1493 found a thriving Taino Indian population, whom they enslaved and soon effectively exterminated. Taino culture also died out, but as in Cuba, many Taino words survive, especially food and place names—including the island's original name, Borinquen (Borikén). This name and the image of Taino culture in general live on as symbols of national identity and of a free and independent Puerto Rico. Like Cuba, colonial Puerto Rico became populated by substantial numbers of Europeans from Spain and elsewhere, and by slaves brought from Africa.

In the nineteenth century, as more and more Puerto Ricans grew frustrated with backward and oppressive Spanish rule, a nationalistic creole culture developed on the island in tandem with its Cuban counterpart. From the early 1800s until today, Puerto Ricans have avidly borrowed and mastered various Cuban music styles, including the Cuban *danzón, son, guaracha,* rumba, and bolero. Indeed, the richness of Puerto Rican musical culture derives in large part from the way it has adopted much of Cuban music, while contributing its own dynamic folk and contemporary popular musics. The major Puerto Rican music genres can also be seen as counterparts to Cuban ones; thus, for example, the Puerto Rican *seis* and *danza,* which we discuss below, can be regarded as parallels to Cuban campesino music and the *danzón,* respectively.

But Puerto Rico should not be regarded as simply a miniature Cuba, especially since genres like the *seis, bomba,* and *plena* are distinctly Puerto Rican creations, owing little to Cuban influence in their traditional forms. Beyond that, there are significant historical, cultural, and political differences between the two islands, which are reflected in their distinct musical heritages. One difference is that while Cuba's sugar-plantation economy occasioned the massive importation of African slaves, Puerto Rico's main agricultural products in the Spanish period were tobacco and coffee, neither of which required large amounts of slave labor. As a result, proportionally fewer Africans were brought to Puerto Rico, and the institution of slavery as a whole was far less widespread and culturally significant than in Cuba (or in the United States, for that matter). Perhaps partly as a consequence of this, neo-African music and religion are less prominent in Puerto Rico than in Cuba.

The islands' political fortunes also diverged after 1898. While both came under the domination of the United States, in Puerto Rico this took the form of direct colonial rule. Since the institutionalization of the commonwealth arrangement in 1952, Puerto Rico has achieved the highest material standard of living in Latin America, but North American rule has been a mixed blessing. Most Puerto Ricans lived in wretched poverty until the 1950s, when Governor Luis Muñoz Marin's combination of socialist public works and capitalist investment incentives uplifted the economy. However, industry and agribusiness brought pollution and ended the island's former self-sufficiency, so that it has since exported most of its products to the mainland and imported most of what it consumes. Most of the rural population has been effectively dispossessed, driven to seek work in San Juan, New York City, and throughout the United States. Puerto Rican migrants developed an acute sense of marginalization and alienation, while many on the island came to resent the dominance of mainland corporations and the inundation of cheap American commercial culture.

Under such conditions, Latin music and, especially, indigenous genres have taken on a special role in Puerto Rican culture as symbols of an independent national identity. There has been a resulting tension between those Puerto Ricans who identify with American culture, including middle-class, predominantly white *rockeros* (rock fans), and those more inclined toward island culture, including the cultural-nationalist left and lower-class black and mulatto fans of Latin music, sometimes called *cocolos* (loosely, "coconut-heads").

EUROPEAN-DERIVED MUSICS

The Hispanic-derived musical forms that evolved in Puerto Rico reflected the class stratification of colonial society. Classical and light-classical musics flourished in the salons of the small but culturally significant elite, which consisted mostly of agricultural landowners, or *hacendados*. Most *hacendados* had natural cultural ties to Spain, but as in Cuba, autocratic and economically repressive colonial dictatorship bred increasing discontent. One colonial governor declared, "The locals can be ruled with a whip and a violin," while another banned beards because they looked subversive to him. Frustration with such misrule fed nationalistic sentiment and conditioned the development of an aristocratic creole culture.

The primary urban base for this culture was the southern town of Ponce rather than the capital, San Juan, whose own cultural and intellectual life was restricted by the colonial bureaucracy and the reactionary church. The musical form that came to embody the spirit of emerging bourgeois nationalism was the *danza,* which appears to have derived, appropriately enough, not from Spain but primarily from the Cuban *contradanza.* However, as with other styles adopted from Cuba, Puerto Rican musicians turned the borrowed idiom into something new and distinctly local. This kind of creative appropriation is most evident in the ensemble *danzas* of Juan Morel Campos (d. 1896), and especially the piano *danzas* by Manuel Tavárez (d. 1895), which combine a Chopinesque sophistication with a hint of jaunty Afro-Caribbean syncopation. Like the Cuban *contradanza,* the *danza* came to be adopted by petit bourgeois artisans and merchants and by peasants, all of whom interpreted it in their own livelier, more accessible fashion (leading the colonial governor to attempt to ban it in 1849). By the 1920s, the *danza* had become archaic; although no longer popular at dance halls, it is still often heard at weddings, and the unofficial Puerto Rican anthem, "La Borinqueña," is a suave *danza* rather than a pompous martial air.

More resilient and widespread forms of creole music were developed by the island's small farmers, the *jíbaros.* The *jíbaros,* white peasants who accounted for the vast majority of the population until the 1930s, have been regarded as the epitome of traditional Puerto Rican identity. In literature and song, they have long been celebrated, however paternalistically and nostalgically, for their legendary hospitality, individuality, self-sufficiency, and love of the simple pleasures of nature, coffee, fiestas, and homespun music. Accordingly, *jíbaro* music has been regarded as a quintessential symbol of island culture, however diminished its actual popularity is now.

The most distinctive feature of *jíbaro* music is its typical ensemble of *cuatro* (a guitar relative with five doubled strings), guitar, and assorted percussion instruments (usually *güiro* scraper and maracas). The *jíbaro* music repertoire today includes several forms of obvious European origin, such as the waltz and the mazurka, along with the Cuban-derived *guaracha* and the occasional Dominican merengue. But the backbone of the *jíbaro* repertoire consists of the purely local *seis* and *aguinaldo.* Both the *seis* and the *aguinaldo* have several subvarieties, distinguished by stock melodies and harmonic progressions. They are named variously after places of origin (*seis fajardeño, aguinaldo orocoveño*), musicians (*seis andino*), or formal features (*seis con décimas*). *Aguinaldos* are particularly associated with the Christmas season, when roving bands of amateur musicians (*parrandas*) stroll from house to house, singing, accepting snacks and drinks, and partying.

Both the *seis* and the *aguinaldo* can accompany dance, especially at informal *jíbaro* fiestas, and they are often fast and lively. The Spanish origin of the instrumentation and Andalusian harmony is clear, although in the twentieth century, *jíbaro* music has incorporated an Afro-Caribbean flavor in the form of bongos, syncopated bass, and Cuban rhythms. While using stock harmonic-melodic forms, the *seis* and the *aguinaldo* are very rich musically in their alluring melodies, catchy rhythms, and often flashy *cuatro* playing.

The most important aspect of the *seis* and the *aguinaldo*, however, is the lyrics, which for over a century have constituted a rich body of oral literature chronicling the joys and sorrows of the Puerto Rican people. It is important to remember that, as in Cuba, poetry and, especially, the *décima* have not been purely aristocratic forms but idioms widely cultivated by ordinary folk. Partly as a result of the low literacy prevailing until the mid-twentieth century, oral culture has been particularly vital in Puerto Rico, and it is safe to say that poetry in general has been much more widely cultivated on the island than in the United States. Particularly prized is the ability of the poet-singer (*trovador*) to improvise *décimas* on the spot, whether on a given *pie forzado* (forced foot) or in response to a competitor in a *controversia*. Accordingly, the lyric content of the *seis* and the *aguinaldo* is rich, dealing with a wide variety of topics. The timeless themes of love, patriotism, maternal devotion, and religion are prominent, along with all manner of topical sociopolitical commentary. Often lyrics relate the cruel misfortune of the singer, who laments, *triste y olvidado*—sad and forgotten. Other *décimas* are humorous and satirical, particularly in the case of *controversias,* such as this one between the famed *jíbaro* singer Chuito (Jesús Sanchéz) and his son, Chuitín:

Chuitín:
Come with me, my friend, let's go hear Ejío's band,
it's a hot party, and they say it'll go on till dawn.
My wife is so proper, she'll stay at home.
Don't say no, let's go party,
and I'll show you that I'm the boss in my house.

Chuito:
I won't go there with you,
because it's known that your wife is fearsome and disliked by all.

Jíbaro musician, with *cuatro* (Ethnic
Folk Arts Center)

If she finds out you're planning to drink,
God bless you, she won't let you go.
She won't let you move from the plaza to the corner,
because I know that she's the boss in your house.

Chuitín:
You're all wrong, you know that I'll go by car
and I'll spend the whole night dancing.
When I get a little tipsy, I even dance the *guaguancó*.
The dance has started, so let's go and boogie,
I'll show you who's the boss at my house.

Chuito:
You're a fool if you go there,
because your wife has you boxed up in a coffin.
She'll give you a black eye, listen Chuitín, you'll see.
In the morning when you return she'll be as hot as a coal,
because I know in your house she's the boss.[1]

Within the first half of the twentieth century, Puerto Rican society changed beyond recognition under the impact of U.S. rule. As American agribusiness acquired most of the arable land, most *hacendados* were bankrupted and the *jíbaros* were dispossessed. Deprived of livelihood, they migrated en masse to cities, especially San Juan, where they congregated in

Jíbaro musicians (Ethnic Folk Arts Center)

slums like La Perla. The rate of urbanization was dramatic—in 1900, roughly 95 percent of the population was rural; by 1970, it was 60 percent urban. From the 1940s on, hundreds of thousands of *jíbaros* emigrated to the mainland United States in search of work. As a result, *jíbaros,* along with their lifestyle, have all but disappeared, although their music lives on.

Many *seises* and *aguinaldos* chronicle the migrant experience, which we discuss below. Some focus on the problems of adjusting to modernization:

> The first shoes I got, I used to wear them on the wrong feet.
> When I came to Mayagüez, *caramba,*
> what a spectacle I caused.[1]

Others, like this poignant *décima* sung by Ramito (Flor Morales Ramos), the most brilliant *jíbaro* singer of the century, nostalgically lament the passing of an entire way of life:

> My Borinquen has changed so much,
> and for me it's a surprise.
> It causes me great pain,
> that the past is so transformed.
> You've become so modernized,
> in a way I can't explain.

Today, while I sing, I'll tell you,
I feel an emptiness in my soul,
because they've changed my hut
for a house made of cement.

There is no one to shoe
either the mare or the stallion,
and in preparing his vegetables,
the peasant doesn't even want to do it by hand anymore.
He no longer listens intently
to the song of the rooster,
and to feel at home,
he can no longer walk about in the morning
when the river and brook
are replaced by a cement canal.[3]

While the decline of *jíbaro* culture is chronicled in such song texts, it is also clear in the reduced popularity and importance of *jíbaro* music in Puerto Rican culture. Most young Puerto Ricans regard *seis* and *aguinaldo* as "hick" music, preferring the contemporary sounds of salsa, merengue, and hip-hop. Mainland Puerto Ricans have little exposure to *jíbaro* music, except perhaps via their grandparents' record collections.

But if *jíbaro* music has declined, it is far from dead. Some *jíbaro* migrants to the cities have tried to maintain their traditional music, and there are many commercial recordings, however jazzed-up with Cuban rhythms and nontraditional instrumentation. The records document the range of vocalists, from amateur poet-crooners to the late Ramito. Most Puerto Rican towns and villages (*pueblos*) hold annual festivals in honor of their patron saints, during which *controversias* are featured (along with salsa bands). There are several skilled *trovadores* and instrumentalists among the younger generations. A few salsa songs make self-conscious use of *jíbaro*-music mannerisms like singing the vocables "le-lo-lai." On a more general level, *jíbaro* music and culture, however deprecated by aspiring city sophisticates, remain for many Puerto Ricans symbols of a vital, self-sufficient, and independent Puerto Rican culture, rooted firmly and proudly in an ancestral homeland.

Seís and Aguinaldo Structure

Around fifteen or twenty forms of *seis* and *aguinaldo* are in common usage today. Each has its own standardized accompaniment pattern and melody. The verses, which are sung solo, are usually in *décima* form or, less often, *copla* (couplet) form. In between the verses, the *cuatro* player performs improvisations, which may be quite flashy. A few of the most common and easily recognizable accompaniment

MUSICAL EXAMPLE 8

MUSICAL EXAMPLE 9

MUSICAL EXAMPLE 10

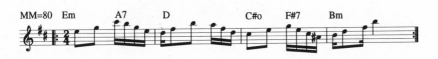

MUSICAL EXAMPLE 11

patterns are *seís mapeyé* (Musical Example 8), *seís fajardeño* (Musical Example 9), *aguinaldo orocoveño* (Musical Example 10), and *aguinaldo jíbaro cayeyano* (Musical Example 11).

THE *FIESTA DE SANTIAGO APÓSTOL* AT LOÍZA ALDEA

For a look at Puerto Rico's African-derived musical heritage, we can visit the town of Loíza Aldea, some twenty miles east of San Juan. The district of Loíza, which consists of a few adjacent villages (notably, Medianías Alta, Medianías Baja, and Loíza Aldea), is populated mostly by black descendants of slaves who worked at nearby sugar plantations. Along with a few villages on the southern coast, Loíza is renowned as a cradle of Afro-Rican culture, especially music and dance.

For three days every August, Loíza comes alive for the festival of its patron saint, Santiago (Saint James), whose cult invigorated the Spanish war against the Moors (the *reconquista*). The core religious events are processions on three successive days, in which three statuettes of Santiago are carried between the towns. In the accompanying parade, townspeople symbolically reenact the Christian–Moor conflict by dressing either as swashbuckling mounted Spaniards (*caballeros*) or as the pagan adversaries. The latter include ghoulish *viejos* (old men), satanic *vejigantes* wearing grotesque African-derived spiked masks and bearing bladders mounted on sticks, and *locas* (crazy women), who are actually men in drag, all behaving outlandishly. In addition, some participants wear various K-Mart costumes (Bart Simpson, Batman, etc.), while others have designed their own clever outfits. After the parade, there are usually stage concerts and informal parties which may feature *bomba*.

It is 1991, and some friends and I have come to Loíza to enjoy the spectacle and, we hope, to see some *bomba* as well. The road between Loíza and Medianías is lined with spectators, and in the early afternoon, the ragtag parade appears. The first thing I notice is that the "Spaniards" are far outnumbered by *vejigantes, viejos,* and ludicrous *locas.* My Puerto Rican friend comments, "Of course—it's much more fun to be a pagan. Besides, most of these people are black, and if anything, they identify with the Moors, not with the Spaniards who enslaved them."

Indeed, whatever religious significance the event may have once had or may still have for some people seems to be largely inverted. The *vejigantes* are running amuck, bopping women on the head with bladders and extorting change from them, and the *locas* are dancing and strutting lasciviously; one, dressed in a bridal gown, walks calmly down the center of the street, flanked by attendants, smiling beatifically at admirers and looking angelic except for his thick moustache. Meanwhile, following the three Santiago figurines is a group of giggling, beer-quaffing men carrying a similar statuette, which on closer inspection turns out to be a Mickey Mouse doll mounted on a toy horse. And to make the entire event quintessentially Caribbean, there are intermittent torrential downpours in which everyone is thoroughly drenched.

A few musical groups also pass by, including two or three trucks carrying brass bands playing *danzas.* Following them comes an impromptu *plena* group consisting of a dozen or so young men, some of whom play *panderos (panderetas),* the jingleless tambourines that are the basic instrument in the genre. They pause in front of a house while one of them runs and fetches a trumpet. *Plena,* which emerged in the early 1900s, is informal music, performed at parties, street protests, and processions like this one. Its lyrics, set to sing-songy verse-and-refrain tunes, can be about news, barrio gossip, or anything at all. Aside from the obligatory *panderos,* which play a steady four-beat pulse, a *plena* group could include whatever instruments are handy, whether a guitar, an accordion, or nothing at all. This group in Loíza is singing "Santa María," one *plena* that everybody in Puerto Rico knows (Musical Example 12).

The next day the parade is even larger and is followed in the afternoon by a stage competition of "Afro-Antillean musics" in Loíza's central plaza.

MUSICAL EXAMPLE 12

San - ta Ma - rí - a If - bra-nos de to - do mal am -

pa - ra - nos se - ño - ra de'es - te te - rri - ble a - ni - mal

This consists of about three hours of nonstop *rumba guaguancó* conga drumming, with occasional vocal accompaniment and no dancing. At one point, the organizers invite audience members to come up to the stage and dance *bomba*; one man casually walks up and does a few indifferent steps, thereby winning a liter of beer, as he is the only contestant. I am starting to wonder if derivative rumba has overrun the local *bomba* scene.

In the evening, the plaza fills up with people who have come to hear the dance bands. First comes a local professional *plena* band, Los Pleneros de Loíza, who, like a few other groups on the island, add trumpets, keyboard, and bass to the *plena* format while retaining the genre's typical rhythms, melodies, and *panderos.* Then follows the real attraction, a series of merengue and salsa bands, which are responsible for the traffic jam now ensnarling the area as people flood into town. Actually, there are few salsa clubs in Puerto Rico, since many people prefer to go to free concerts in the *fiestas patronales* like this one.

On the final day, the parade is bigger still, and there is another concert at Loíza. However, acting on a hunch, we decide to pass the evening at a

Plena on stage: New York's Los Pleneros de la 21 (photo by Peter Manuel)

Plena on the streets of New York

humble barrio by the beach in Medianías. (If you visit, eat at Chicho's.) Around dusk, a small steel band sets up by the side of the dirt road and starts to play "Sopa de caracoles," a Honduran *punta*-rock ditty that has become a pan-Caribbean hit. A small crowd of schoolgirls materializes and starts doing the jerky, twist-like *punta* dance. The same tune and indefatigable dancing go on for almost an hour.

Then, just as we are contemplating leaving, a few men appear carrying two squat *bomba* barrel drums and, seating themselves on benches in a café open to the road, start to play. Another man, playing a cowbell, assumes the lead-singer role, and the women standing by energetically join in singing the responsorial choruses. But the real focus is the dancing, which is done by a solo dancer directly in front of the drummers, with the singers and onlookers forming a dense ring around them. While one drummer, along with the bell player, provides a steady ostinato, the lead drummer mimics and follows the dancer, who performs a variety of stock, improvised movements. For some reason, men no longer seem to be interested in dancing *bomba*, so the dancers are all female; several of them are children no more than eight years old. They take turns, each dancing a few minutes before the drummer, while the onlookers cheer, clap, and sing the choral refrains in a spirit of riotous fun.

Bomba, the most vital Afro-Rican music and dance idiom, is a product of the slave barracks and was described in chronicles dating as early as the 1820s. I had previously been led to believe that *bomba* was a near-extinct form, done only by doddering octogenarians or in lifeless stage renditions by folkloric groups, such as I had seen. In fact, it is still alive, although only in a few towns such as Loíza. Outside of such locales it is rare, and most Puerto Ricans have no exposure to it.

At this point, it seems possible that the thin strands of the living tradition could break. Locals say the Catholic priests in Loíza have consistently campaigned against *bomba*, denouncing it as pagan and vulgar. In fact, *bomba* is a secular dance with no particular religious overtones, although it is true that the lyrics are often uninhibitedly spicy (leading a 1960s study to conclude that *bomba* is "unsuitable for use in secondary school choral groups").[4] As for the dance, like most Latin dancing it is indeed erotic, but when well done, it is too expressive, fresh, and downright beautiful to be vulgar (except perhaps to someone who has sworn to celibacy). Fortunately, there are enough young performers that, should conditions permit, a revival of this dynamic art could still take place.

PLENA AND *BOMBA*
IN THE DANCE HALL

Since the 1920s, *plena* and, to a lesser extent, *bomba* have been performed and commercially recorded, in modified forms, by professional dance bands. The challenge for these genres has been that since the early twentieth century, the realm of commercial dance music in Puerto Rico (and among "Newyorican" communities) has been dominated by Cuban-style music (and, more recently, by the merengue). Moreover, even when Puerto Rican dance bands adapt *plena* and *bomba,* there has been a marked tendency to use Cuban-style rhythms, arrangements, and instrumental mannerisms, so that the commercial *plena* and *bomba* tend to lose their local flavor. The story of urban *plena* and *bomba* is in part a chronicle of the interaction of native Puerto Rican forms with imported Cuban genres, which Puerto Ricans have adopted as their own.

The first bandleader to popularize *plena* in a dance-band format was Manuel "Canario" Jiménez, whose recordings and performances brought a modernized *plena* to large audiences in New York and Puerto Rico in the 1930s. Canario retained much of the traditional *plena*'s character by using the *pandero,* simple melodies, topical texts commenting on current events, mixed male and female choruses, and alternating verse-and-chorus structure (as opposed to the *canto-montuno* format of the *son*). At the same time, he filled out its traditionally sparse instrumentation with piano, bass, and trumpets. In the 1940s, bandleader Cesar Concepción brought the *plena de salon* to new levels of popularity and bourgeois "respectability" while further Cubanizing it with mambo-style big-band arrangements, which thoroughly diluted the traditional proletarian character of the genre.

In the 1950s, Rafael Cortijo, a bandleader from Loíza, together with singer Ismael "Maelo" Rivera and a similar band led by Mon Rivera, burst onto the Puerto Rican music scene with a raw, revitalized *plena* and *bomba,* successfully adapted to standard Cuban *conjunto* format. While the *bomba* of Cortijo and Rivera was far removed from its folk model, their renditions of both *bomba* and *plena* retained the original earthy, barrio vitality and the distinctly Puerto Rican character. Cortijo's songs, often dealing with barrio life and strongly Afro-Rican in flavor, constituted a new sort of urban folklore and placed black music squarely in the mainstream of island culture. Similarly, Rivera's "Alló, ¿Quién ñama?" dramatizing a contemporary textile workers' strike, linked the commercial *plena* with the genre's traditional usage in proletarian protests.

After Cortijo's band broke up in 1962, *plena* and *bomba* receded from the dance arenas, which have since been dominated by salsa and merengue.

Plena is still performed by quasi-folkloric bands such as the Pleneros de Loíza and New York's Pleneros de la 21. Meanwhile, throughout the trendy rise and fall of dance-band *plena* and *bomba,* the genres in their traditional forms have continued to thrive as vehicles of popular expression, completely independent of the commercial record industry.

MUSIC AND
THE PUERTO RICAN DIASPORA

Since the 1920s, Puerto Rican music has been as much a product of New York City as of the island itself, due to the fundamental role that the migration experience has come to play in Puerto Rican culture. The diaspora has been massive; about 40 percent of people of Puerto Rican descent live on the mainland. Moreover, many of those still residing on the island visit the mainland, and of course, the mass media, visits by mainland relatives, and the effects of international capital make island society even more intertwined with that of the greater United States. As a result, Puerto Rican culture cannot be conceived of as something that exists only or even primarily in Puerto Rico; rather, it has become inseparable from "Newyorican" culture, which itself overlaps with black and other Latino subcultures in New York and, for that matter, with mainland North American culture as a whole.

Migration to the greater United States had been a steady trickle through the 1930s, and handfuls of Puerto Ricans had settled as far away as Hawaii to market their skill at growing sugarcane. In the 1940s, the trickle turned into a flood as hundreds of thousands of Puerto Ricans took advantage of cheap air tickets to try to escape poverty and find better fortunes abroad. Many moved to rural New Jersey and Connecticut to work in migrant labor camps. However, more than half settled in New York City and, especially, in East Harlem, which subsequently became known as Spanish Harlem or simply "the barrio." *Newyorican* (*Nuyorican*) subsequently became a convenient term, however problematic, for all migrants (many of whom, however, refer to themselves simply as Puerto Rican or "Spanish"). Altogether, some 2.6 million people of Puerto Rican descent now live on the mainland, as opposed to 3.7 million living on the island.

As migrants found themselves in the alien, English-speaking, stressful, and often violent milieu of New York's tenements, it was natural for them to try to make their surroundings more familiar by transplanting as much of island culture as possible to the barrio. Hence taverns and clubs formed where migrants from island villages and barrios like La Perla could regroup themselves and socialize. Enterprising Newyoricans built flimsy yet gaily decorated shacks (*casitas*) on vacant lots to serve as clubhouses. One recent migrant relates, "I cannot live in Puerto Rico because there's no life for me there, so I'll bring it with me bit by bit; four land crabs from Vacía Talega, in the trip before, two fighting cocks, in my next, all of Cortijo's records."[5]

Music has been an important source of solace and recreation for the migrants, and Puerto Ricans have tried to maintain their traditional musics, whether they have settled in Harlem or in Hawaii (where their songs are called "kachi-kachi" music). Conditions favored the transplantation and flourishing of certain genres more than others; thus trios and quartets playing Cuban-style *guaracha* and bolero at parties and clubs proliferated through the 1940s, while *jíbaro* music and *bomba* do not seem to have thrived outside the island.

As can be imagined, the migration experience most often has been difficult, if not traumatic. Migrants have been gouged by landlords, victimized by thugs, ruthlessly exploited by sweatshop employers, and harassed or, at best, neglected by police. Even those eligible to vote in New York were disenfranchised by gerrymandering and English literacy tests until the mid-1950s. These and other features of tenement life exacerbated the tendencies toward family disintegration, crime, and drugs. The travails of migration have been described in many books, but they are also extensively chronicled in the oral folklore of *plenas*, boleros, and *seises*, such as this 1927 song of Rafael Hernández:

> I came to New York hoping to get ahead,
> but if it was bad back home, here it's worse.
> Sometimes it's hot, and other times freezing cold,
> sometimes I look like a bundle sliding around on the snow.
> I don't like this, I'm going back to my hut.[6]

Coping with the language barrier and the unfamiliarity of the city was a perpetual frustration, especially for former *jíbaros* who had migrated straight from the countryside to the concrete jungle of the barrio. The travails of the *jíbaro* in New York are the subject of innumerable *seises:*

> One morning I went out to get medicine
> for my friend who was suffering with pneumonia,
> but since I didn't know how to get around in New York,
> I took the wrong subway, and it took me five days to get back.[7]

Another *seis* relates:

> I came to New York thinking that they spoke as much Spanish
> as English, but here they told me, "No you're quite mistaken,
> when you want *bacalao,* you have to say 'co'fi'" [codfish] . . .

I feel so ridiculous in the restaurant, when they ask, "Wha' you wan'?"
and I have to point with my finger.[8]

Feelings of nostalgia and homesickness are particularly intense during
Christmas season, which is an occasion for family reunions and celebration
in Puerto Rico, as elsewhere. An *aguinaldo* consoles migrants:

You don't suffer in vain even if you're far away
as long as the memory of your beloved homeland
shines in your heart and remains there your entire life.
If someday you may return, come with a kiss;
your country, Borinquen, awaits you at Christmas.[9]

While the material problems of poverty, climate, and harsh work conditions have been formidable, the psychological stress of the diaspora experience has been equally painful. Many Puerto Ricans, whether black, white,
or mulatto, were exposed to humiliating ethnic discrimination on the mainland. The migration experience has heightened the long-standing identity
problem felt by some Puerto Ricans, already self-conscious of their status as
perpetual colonial subjects. In a conformist society where schoolchildren
were punished for speaking Spanish and the mass media excluded any people of color, it was natural for the first generations of migrants to feel
ashamed of their ethnicity. Many Newyoricans did their best to assimilate
and to raise their children without any sense of their Latino cultural heritage. For many such parents, it was a cruel irony to see their children being
socially rejected despite their best attempts to Anglicize them. (Indeed, it
was a different sense of identity that inspired Newyorican *salsero* Mark Anthony to thank his parents, on the liner notes to his 1993 record, for making him speak Spanish at home.)

We saw in the previous chapter how by the 1940s, New York City had
become a second center for the development of Cuban music. The city also
came to be a center for Puerto Rican/Newyorican culture, but in a somewhat different sense. It was not that Puerto Rican music per se took New
York by storm but rather that Puerto Rican musicians and audiences came
to dominate the city's Latin music scene. One music historian describes the
resulting paradox: "The bulk of what we today call popular Puerto Rican
music was written and recorded in New York. Puerto Rico is the only Latin
American country whose popular music was mainly created on foreign soil.
The curious thing about this phenomenon is that it was precisely in those
years that the popular Puerto Rican song became more Puerto Rican than it
has ever been before or since."[10]

Such was the case particularly with the music of Afro–Puerto Rican composer Rafael Hernández (d. 1965) and his contemporary Pedro Flores, both of whom spent many years living, composing, performing, and recording in New York (while doing menial jobs to survive). Although most of their hundreds of compositions are boleros in more-or-less standard Cuban style, their songs dominated Puerto Rican popular music in the 1930s and 1940s and still warm the hearts of the older generations. Most of these pieces are sentimental love songs; some of the best-known ones obliquely address the migrant experience by combining nostalgia for the homeland with the memory of a loved one left behind. Flores's "Bajo un palmar" is typical:

> I had a blissful dream, which I wanted to make into a song
> I took my guitar and put all my heart into it, concentrating on you. . . .
> It was on a beach in my homeland so beloved
> by the waters of the sea,
> It was there that we were picnicking under a palm tree. . . .
> You were so precious . . . you were my love
> and I felt you breathing nervously in my arms.[11]

New York City became a center for Puerto Rican music largely because of its recording studios, its media infrastructure, and its concentrated market; indeed, New York has been the largest Puerto Rican city for several decades. But perhaps more important, it was in New York that musicians and audiences alike were exposed to broader cultural horizons. The Cuban *son, guaracha,* and bolero, which had already taken root in Puerto Rico,

Rafael Hernández

were the dominant styles in New York's Latin music scene, and it was natural for Puerto Rican musicians to form or join trios, quartets, or larger ensembles playing such music. Cuban music or diluted versions thereof were also gaining popularity among Anglo dance fans, especially after the hit success of Don Azpiazú's 1930 ditty "The Peanut Vendor" (El manicero), a catchy *son* popularized under the misnomer "rhumba." To some extent, a "downtown–uptown" dichotomy emerged between the hotter, more authentic Latin music played for Puerto Ricans and Cubans in East Harlem and the slicker, smoother sounds played for Anglos in swanky lower Manhattan ballrooms. The most popular downtown-style bandleader was the Spanish-born, Cuban-raised Xavier Cugat, who commented, "To succeed in America I gave the Americans a Latin music that had nothing authentic about it."[12]

The Latin bands, whether small or large, "authentic" or "commercial," soon became filled with Puerto Rican musicians, many of whom had acquired formal music training in municipal bands back home. However, as the writings of John Storm Roberts and Ruth Glasser have shown, the "downtown versus uptown" model is a bit of an oversimplification. For instance, the Palladium (then on 52nd Street, nominally "downtown") became a center for the hottest and most vital Latin music, frequented by blacks, Anglos, Latinos, Jews, Italians, and even Chinese. And Puerto Rican musicians found themselves playing in all sorts of bands (including black, Mexican, and Anglo) for all sorts of situations, at times providing Anglo music

Pedro Flores

for Latin audiences, at others, Latin music—whether real or stereotyped—for Anglo audiences.[13] Puerto Rican musicians thus became highly versatile and, in their own way, cosmopolitan, while adopting Cuban-derived styles as a basic musical lingua franca. By the 1940s, Newyoricans like *timbalero* Tito Puente and vocalist Tito Rodriguez had become the top bandleaders and innovators, and the Latin dance music scene in New York came to outstrip that on the island. (Even today, there are more salsa bands and clubs in New York than in Puerto Rico.)

As Newyorican culture has developed in its own directions, it has been natural for a gap to widen between it and island culture. Hence some Newyoricans have come to regard islanders as provincial, while some islanders deprecate their mainland cousins as decultured half-breeds who cannot even speak Spanish properly, if at all. The history of emigrant Puerto Ricans has been, in part, the slow, painful process of establishing enough self-confidence (or righteous indignation) to take pride in their distinct ethnicity and culture and to assert its right to exist in a multicultural society. Such a conception of identity goes beyond merely establishing a beachhead enclave of transplanted traditional culture, an "island in the city"; rather, it involves building a new cultural identity that at once embraces island tradition and engages actively with mainstream society. In the words of scholar Juan Flores: "The Newyorican experience is showing how it is possible to struggle through the quandary of biculturalism and affirm the straddling position."[14] At that stage, it is the borders of the "island in the city" that become the fluid sites of the most dynamic and progressive forms of cultural creation.

In this transition from Puerto Rican to Newyorican (or "AmeRícan"), music has played a particularly crucial role. But it was really not until the late 1960s that Newyoricans on a mass level began to recognize and affirm the uniqueness and vitality of their culture. This new self-consciousness demanded a new form of musical expression—or perhaps, a reinterpretation of an older form. That music, called salsa, is the subject of the next chapter.

BIBLIOGRAPHY

Spanish-language books include Pedro Malavet Vega, *Del bolero a la nueva canción* (Ponce, P.R., 1988) and *Historia de la canción popular puertorriqueña, 1493–1898* (Ponce, P.R., 1992); María Luisa Muñoz, *La música en Puerto Rico* (Sharon, Conn.: Troutman, 1966); Francisco López Cruz, *La música folklórica de Puerto Rico* (Sharon, Conn.: Troutman, 1967).

For literature in English, see Peter Bloch, *La le-lo-lai: Puerto Rican Music and Its Performers* (New York: Plus Ultra, 1973); John Storm Roberts, *The Latin Tinge:*

The Impact of Latin American Music on the United States (New York and Oxford: Oxford University Press, 1979); *Centro de estudios puertorriqueños bulletin* (Spring 1991); and articles by Jesus Quintero-Rivera, Juan Flores, and Jorge Duany in Vernon Boggs, *Salsiology* (New York: Greenwood 1992).

RECORDS AND FILMS

JIBARO MUSIC: *The Music of Puerto Rico, 1929–1946* (Harlequin HQ 2075); *Return on Wings of Pleasure: Pedro Padilla y su conjunto* (Rounder 5003). See also the records cited in the notes to this chapter, as well as any records by Ramito and Chuito (available on the Ansonia label).

COMPILATION: *Caliente = Hot: Puerto Rican and Cuban Musical Expression in New York* (New World 244).

FILMS: *Salsa: Latin Music of New York and Puerto Rico* (from the series "Beats of the Heart") by Jeremy Marre (Harcourt Films, 1979); *Plena Is Work, Plena Is Play* by Pedro Rivera and Susan Zelig (Center for Puerto Rican Studies, Hunter College, New York).

4

Salsa and Beyond

THE *SON* SIRES A SON

The 1960s did not commence as an auspicious period for Latin music in the New York City area. The advent of small amplified ensembles and rock 'n' roll had contributed to the decline of big bands, and the mambo craze had fizzled out accordingly. The big Latin ballrooms, which had hosted the mambo bands of Machito and Tito Puente, were no longer profitable, and the closing of the Palladium in 1966 marked the definitive end of an era. There was little Cuban-style dance music on the media, except for a few programs deejayed by Anglo enthusiasts. A few major record companies (notably RCA) were producing some Latin music, but they seemed to regard it as ethnic throwaway music, to be packaged with cheap covers featuring a sexy woman and a conga and dumped in barrio grocery bins. Only two small record companies, Tico and Alegre, were marketing Latin dance music with any creativity and energy. Finally, the embargo against Cuba, designed to strangle the rebellious island and isolate it culturally, cut off influence from the most dynamic center of Latin dance music. But the decade ended up being an extremely fertile one for Latin music in the United States, and for American music in general. Indeed, the 1960s constituted a period of dynamic upheaval and reorientation for American culture.

The sociopolitical ferment for which the 1960s are remembered was to a large extent a phenomenon of white bourgeois youth. Frustrated by the stifling social conformism of the 1950s, empowered by allowances, cars, and the growing economy, and emboldened by their purchasing power and sheer demographic mass, middle-class baby-boomers symbolically rejected much of their parents' culture and values, cultivating new styles of music, dress, art, politics, and recreation. The focal point for countercultural dissent was the Vietnam War, in which the government killed some two million Asians in trying to prop up a series of right-wing dictatorships.

Some of the causes and products of the 1960s counterculture had little resonance with Latinos and other minorities. While white middle-class youths seemed to be rejecting the American house-and-two-car dream as boring, minorities still wanted to achieve that dream and resented being denied it. And in many respects, the barrio remained a closed, Spanish-speaking world, where the Beach Boys, the Beatles, and legions of white pseudo-bluesmen were essentially irrelevant.

But the 1960s were also a period of upheaval for minorities, and there were significant areas of overlap between their turmoil and the middle-class youth revolt. Minorities had made some economic progress, which at once empowered them and heightened their resentment of social discrimination. Opposition to the war united whites and minorities, and to the extent that the white youth counterculture constituted a genuine protest against social injustice, it marched hand in hand with the civil rights movement. Most important, the sixties saw the intensification and increased militancy of the Black Power movement. Latinos were profoundly affected by this and started to conceive of themselves as more than just the "other" that was neither Anglo- nor Afro-American. Inspired by the Black Panthers, the Young Lords, a group of socio-political activists, mobilized Newyoricans to demand fair treatment and better social services for their city's large but previously neglected Latino population. The Young Lords achieved several of their material goals, but the most significant development was a new sense of pride in being Latino. For the first time, Latinos on a mass scale rejected the Anglocentric assimilationist goals that had led so many Newyoricans to feel ashamed of their language and culture. The model of the civil rights movement, the new interest in "roots," and, indirectly, the still-smoldering Puerto Rican independence movement made the barrio a cauldron of militant assertiveness and artistic creativity.

The new social consciousness called for a new musical movement that could at once embrace Puerto Rican tradition and capture the spirit of the barrio in all its alienated energy and heightened self-awareness. The logical musical vehicle for this was not the perceivedly quaint and provincial *seis* or *plena* but modernized Cuban dance music—especially the *son,* which had for decades been the favored idiom of urban Puerto Ricans and Newyoricans. In the process, the *son*'s Cuban origin, like that of the rumba now so avidly played by barrio street drummers, was de-emphasized, and the genre became resignified as a symbol of Newyorican and, by extension, pan-Latino ethnic identity.

The rise of salsa was tied to Fania Records, which had been founded in 1964 by Johnny Pacheco, a bandleader of Dominican parentage and Cuban musical tastes. Fania started out as a fledgling independent label, with Pacheco distributing records to area stores in the trunk of his car. From 1967, Fania, then headed by Italian-American lawyer Jerry Masucci, embarked on an aggressive and phenomenally successful program of recording and promotion. Fania's early roster included established performers such as "boogaloo" king Ray Barretto and Pacheco himself, who performed in a standard *típico* (loosely translated, "traditional") style of 1950s Cuban bands like the Sonora Matancera, using the *conjunto* format of two trumpets and rhythm section.[1] But the characteristic Fania sound came to be defined by the barrio-based groups that the label sought out and promoted.

Particularly influential was composer-arranger Willie Colon, a Bronx prodigy discovered and signed by Fania at the age of fifteen. Colon's early albums, with vocalists Hector Lavoe, Ismael Miranda, and Ruben Blades, epitomized the Fania style at its best and captured the fresh sound, restless energy, and aggressive dynamism of the barrio youth. As modern *salsero* Sergio George describes it, "In my opinion, the true salsa sound of that era was the musical fusion of New York with Puerto Rico, with Cuba and with Africa; that whole fusion was for me the true roots of salsa in the late '60s, early '70s. It came out of a street sound, a barrio sound. People jamming in the park with the congas and somebody coming to sing. . . . That was the raw street salsa sound."[2]

Every commercial music genre needs a catchy label, and there was a natural desire for a handier one than "recycled Cuban dance music" or "the son/mambo/rumba complex." Hence Fania promoted the term *salsa* (literally, "hot sauce"), which was already familiar as a bandstand interjection (and as the name of a Venezuelan radio show). To many, the term has always seemed to be an artificial, commercial rubric, designed partially to obscure the politically inconvenient Cuban origin of the music. The label seems especially meaningless when applied to *típico* musicians like Pacheco or to Tito Puente and Celia Cruz, whose musical styles evolved twenty-five years before the label was coined. (While Puente has reconciled himself to the term, he has also said, "The only salsa I know comes in a bottle. I play Cuban music.") Even mainstream salsa still follows the basic styles and formal structure of 1950s Cuban dance music. In defense of the term, however, one could point to various innovations that distinguished the new subgenre, such as the greater use of trombones, the use of *timbales,* and the occasional Puerto Rican elements (like singing "le-lo-lai"). Such innovations are especially prominent in the music of the salsa "vanguard," whose outstanding figures have been Eddie Palmieri and Ruben Blades. Palmieri is a unique bandleader whose best music combines dramatically original arrange-

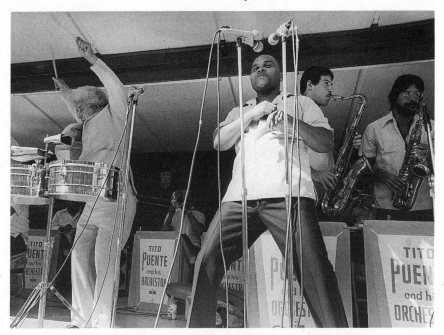

Tito Puente (left), with singer Frankie Feliciano (Fran Vogel)

ments, modern jazz-influenced solos, and an ineffable drive and power. Blades, whom we discuss below, is quite a different sort of character, whose brilliance is more reflected in his eclectic style and intelligent lyrics.

The most significant justification for the new term *salsa*, however, was the way in which the music voiced the militant self-consciousness of the new generation of Latinos, becoming, as in the title of a Los Angeles radio program, *la alma del barrio*—"the soul of the barrio." This spirit was most explicit in song texts. Most songs dealt with love, in more or less traditional manners, but a significant minority openly reflected the new mood of the barrio, becoming soundtracks for early 1970s street protests. Some songs called for pan-Latin solidarity, as in Conjunto Libre's "Imágenes latinas":

Indians, Hispanics, and blacks, we've been mixed into a blend,
with the blood of all races, to create a new future;
we've come to strengthen ourselves, to work and live
within the entrails of the monster, as Martí put it.[3]
From Quisqueya to La Plata, from the Pampas to Havana,
we are blood, voice, and part of this American land;
whether in the land of snow or underneath a palm tree,
Latinos everywhere struggle for their liberty.
We're Latin American, from the center, north, and south,

Eddie Palmieri (Fran Vogel)

with a present of struggle and a future of light.
This is my Latin image, my new song,
to tell you, my brother, to seek and find unity.

Other songs confronted American imperialism, whether directly or obliquely. Most characteristically, several songs portrayed the alienation, violence, and lurking malevolence of barrio life. Typical in this respect are early songs of Willie Colon, who styled himself "El Malo," or "bad." His 1973 "Calle luna calle sol" warns:

Listen, mister, if you value your life,
stay out of trouble or you'll lose it. . . .
Listen lady, hang on to your purse,
you don't know this barrio, here they attack anyone. . . .
In the barrio of *guapos,* no one lives at peace;
watch what you say or you won't be worth a kilo,
walk straight ahead and don't look sideways.
You may have a patron saint but you're not a *babalao* [*santería* priest].[4]

In such songs, there is an ambiguous mixture of attitudinal stances. On one level, these songs are simply "telling it like it is," baring barrio reality in a nonjudgmental way. One could also interpret such lyrics as denunciations of the social system that produces such conditions. Colon's classic dictum "I'm bad—because I've got heart"[5] implies that the Hobbesian world of the barrio obliges a man to be tough in order to defend his sense of justice. But the lyrics also convey a sort of tension-ridden adrenalin high and suggest at

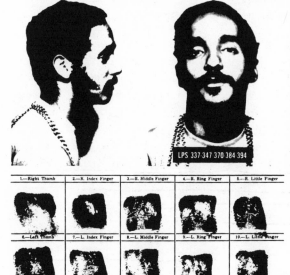

Willie Colón LP cover from the gangster-salsa days (Fania SLP 394)

least a hint of fascination with the ghetto's lawlessness and with the figure of the *guapo,* the macho hoodlum who has achieved power in the marginalized and oppressed world of the barrio. The song "Juanito Alimaña," written by Puerto Rican composer (and postal worker!) Tite Curet Alonso and recorded by Colon and Lavoe, captures this spirit:

> The street is a concrete jungle full of wild animals;
> no one leaves home full of joy anymore.
> Here you can expect the worst, wherever you are.
> Juanito Alimaña swaggers to the cash register,
> nonchalantly draws his knife, and demands the money.
> He takes the bills, takes the pistol,

then he disappears like the wind,
and although everyone saw him, no one saw anything.
Juanito Alimaña commits his daily crime,
drinks his beer, has an orgy;
people fear him because he's careful,
you'd have to be mad to challenge him.
If he gets arrested, he walks free the next day
because a cousin of his is in the police.
If Juanito Alimaña has brains, they're in the form of shrewd deceit.
He's tight with whoever's in power,
and although he steals from half the world
and everyone talks about him, no one betrays him.

In their ambivalent portrayal of ghetto lawlessness, such songs fore-shadowed hard-core rap, although they contain little of the latter's mis-ogyny and celebration of violence for its own sake. Songs like "Juanito Ali-maña" epitomize how distinct salsa's milieu was from that of the glamorous Palladium era or from the Cuban heyday with its songs about quaint and colorful old Havana. From the Puerto Rican perspective, they also contrast the grim and violent barrio with the picturesque and forever-lost world of the *jíbaro*.[6] Salsa captured the new mood of Latinos in the 1970s, reflecting their consciousness of marginalization, their politicization, and their en-hanced awareness of one another, all of which were reinforced by the mass media and the migrant experience. Salsa was rooted in the New York bar-rio, but because the modern urban alienation it described was common to so many other Latin American cities, salsa soon became an international phenomenon, a chronicle of the urban Hispanic Caribbean.

Salsa's international pan-Latin character was, of course, inherent even within the New York context. Both salsa's audiences and its musicians, though dominated by Newyoricans (and some Cubans), included a wide variety of Latinos from other backgrounds. Among New York–based *sal-seros*, one could mention the Dominicans Johnny Pacheco and José Alberto and the Panamanian Ruben Blades (and, for that matter, the Jewish Ameri-cans Larry Harlow and Marty Sheller). More significant, however, was the spread of salsa throughout the Spanish-speaking countries of the Caribbean Basin.

The case of Venezuela is representative.[7] Between 1935 and 1988, the country's population had gone from being 70 percent rural to 85 percent urban. By 1970, salsa, whether performed by local or foreign groups, had become the favored music of the urban lower classes, cherished especially for its barrio-oriented *malandro* (malevolent) edge. Initially, the predomi-nantly white bourgeoisie tended to disparage salsa as *música de monos—*

"music of apes"—just as their Yankee-philic Puerto Rican *rockero* counter-parts deprecated salsa fans by the racist term *cocolos*. But by the mid-seventies, salsa, especially as performed by local superstar Oscar d'León, had won over even the middle classes, and salsa record sales in Venezuela came to surpass those in New York and the Caribbean combined.

Meanwhile, Colombia emerged as another vital center and mass market for salsa and today has come to replace economically declining Venezuela as a transnational hub for salsa, generating its own superstars, Joe Arroyo and Grupo Niche. On a smaller scale, salsa went on to take root beyond the Latin world, especially in Sweden, Denmark, and even Japan, whose slick Orquesta de la Luz raised eyebrows throughout the salsa world in the early 1990s.

Unfortunately, there have been limits to salsa's ability to cross market boundaries. In the 1970s, when the style was at its peak, many had high hopes that it, like reggae, could cross over to the Anglo and world-beat markets. For promoters it would mean a taste of the commercial jackpot, while musicians could find a way out of the exhausting and exploitative club circuit. But salsa, despite Fania's commercially inspired efforts, never did catch on with the mainstream record audience. Carlos Santana's rock versions of Tito Puente songs inspired a few Anglo rock fans to seek out the real thing, but on the whole, the language barrier and competition from disco and rock kept salsa marginalized in its ethnic enclave. Most Anglo buyers had little interest in what looked like corny big-band music played by short-haired slickers in matching polyester leisure suits.

Despite the failure of salsa's crossover dreams, the 1970s were the heyday of salsa and of Fania, which dominated the market. Mainstream acts like El Gran Combo, Willie Colon, and Ismael Miranda churned out hits and kept the dancers on their feet, while innovators like Palmieri, Blades, and Jerry and Andy Gonzalez made the margins of the music scene shimmer with creativity. By the end of the decade, however, salsa found itself on the defensive against an onslaught of merengue and hip-hop and an internal creative decline. But before discussing that situation, let us look at the salsa life in general and at one of its most remarkable artists.

RUBEN BLADES: THE CUTTING EDGE

Most *salseros*, if asked to identify the single most distinguished figure in the field, would probably unhesitatingly name Ruben Blades. While pursuing law, acting, and politics, Blades, in his intermittent periods devoted to salsa, has produced much of the genre's most innovative, ambitious, and socially relevant music.

Blades grew up in Panama City, where he acquired a law degree while singing with local Cuban-style bands. In 1974, he moved to New York and, forsaking the courtroom for the recording studio, joined the roster of Fania Records, which was then at its peak. Blades's charisma, razor-like voice, and boyish good looks might have guaranteed him some measure of success in themselves, but he had much more to offer. Unlike many singers, Blades is a skilled instrumentalist (guitar) and composer; many of the pieces he has authored or coauthored (sometimes in collaboration with Willie Colon) rank among salsa's most memorable and popular melodies and are full of innovative touches. His LP *Siembra* gained both critical acclaim and commercial success, selling over four hundred thousand copies.

Blades's music is particularly celebrated for his intelligent lyrics, which, departing from the normal *telenovela* (soap-opera) doggerel and "hey, let's dance" cliches, embrace a variety of social themes with an incisive originality. Inspired by such writers as Gabriel García Márquez and Carlos Fuentes, Blades has written songs about everything from disarmament to the environment. His 1980 recording of Tite Curet Alonso's "Tiburón" (Shark), an allegorical indictment of American imperialism, along with his denunciation of U.S. economic warfare against Cuba, incurred death threats from right-wing Cubans in Miami, who banned his music from local radio stations. Perhaps Blades's most memorable songs are not the controversial political ones but those in which he strives to create, as he puts it, "a folklore of the city—not of one city, but of all the cities in Latin America."[8] His "Numero seis" is a light-hearted lament about waiting for the subway, while "Te están buscando" is a Willie Colon-esque portrayal of barrio malevolence.

His most famous songs are epigrammatic character studies that personify, with a mixture of criticism and empathy, the vanities and travails of urban proletarian Latinos. The lyrics of "Juan Pachanga" portray a perfumed dandy whose suave exterior conceals an inner emptiness and loneliness; the song is also a driving dance tune, whose title is now the name of a Queens salsa club. "Pablo Pueblo" describes the monotonous, pointless, and joyless life of a proletarian worker:

A man returns in silence from his exhausting work,
his gait is slow, his shadow trails behind.
The same barrio awaits him, with the light at the corner,
the trash in front, and the music emanating from the bar. . . .
He enters the room and stares at his wife and children,
wondering, "How long does this go on?"

He takes his broken dreams,
and patching them with hope, making a pillow out of hunger,
he lies down, with an inner misery.

In "Pedro Navaja," another innovative classic whose text is a sort of existential snapshot of barrio life, a petty gangster and a hooker shoot each other in an incident whose background is unknown and essentially irrelevant:

And Pedro Navaja fell mortally wounded to the sidewalk,
watching this woman who, revolver in hand, tells him,
"I was thinking that this just isn't my day, and I'm sunk,
but look at you—you're really shit out of luck."
And believe me, folks, that although there had been a noise,
no one stopped, no one was interested,
no one asked what happened, no one wept.
Only one drunk, stumbling over the two corpses,
pocketed their pistols, switchblades, and money, and walked on.
And as he staggered merrily along, he sang, out of tune,
the refrain that is the message of my song:
"*Ay Dios,* life is full of surprises!"

Blades has constantly tried to expand the horizons of Latin music. While he dislikes the word "crossover," he has tried to break barriers between the

Ruben Blades (Fran Vogel)

compartmentalized Latin and mainstream markets. Seeking to reach English-speaking Latinos as well as Anglos, he has recorded several songs in English, and his later LP covers include English and Spanish versions of his texts. Stylistically, much of his later music draws eclectically from reggae, calypso, merengue, and rock, and he has collaborated with artists as diverse as Joe Jackson, Linda Ronstadt, Lou Reed, and Elvis Costello. Blades, indeed, is the only salsa-based artist to have broken into the world-beat market, while maintaining his preeminence in the salsa world. Nevertheless, Blades has never really attained superstar popularity, a fact that he accepts stoically: "I will never be a superstar. My role is to be different, to do what others won't do, and as a result, my fortunes will always fluctuate."[9]

Since the early 1980s, Blades has devoted much of his time to interests other than music. In 1984, he left salsa to earn a degree in international law from Harvard, and he has also pursued a moderately successful Hollywood acting career. His most prominent role was in the 1985 film *Crossover Dreams*, in which he portrayed a *salsero* torn between the integrity of *típico* Latin music and his commercial ambition to cross over to the Anglo market and break out of the local club scene. From one perspective, Blades's preeminence as a *salsero* is paradoxical in that his commitment to music has never been more than sporadic and part time, involved as he has been in law, cinema, politics, and other matters. But seen from another angle, his ongoing involvement with nonmusical endeavors may have much to do with his greatness, since it is precisely his broader vision that has distinguished him from the ranks of mainstream *salseros* who, however talented, cannot seem to transcend the provincial club scene. As Trinidadian author C.L.R. James wrote, "What do they know of cricket, who only cricket know?"

In 1989, U.S. President George Bush ordered the invasion of Panama in order to depose his former CIA employee, the dictator Manuel Noriega, who had been involved in drug trading. After the invasion, which caused hundreds of Panamanian deaths and some two billion dollars worth of damage, the nation's presidency fell into the immense lap of Guillermo Endara, a nincompoop under whose rule drug trafficking and corruption increased beyond the level of the Noriega era. Among those incensed by the invasion and its aftermath was Ruben Blades, who in 1993 returned to Panama to run for president, with the goal of rescuing his country from corruption and Yankee big-stick imperialism. His campaign failed, but Blades may yet return to politics. If running for president might seem far removed from singing, for Blades both endeavors have the same ultimate goal: "What I propose is to create what up to this point has been a mythical place: a Latin

America that respects and loves itself, is incorruptible, romantic, nationalistic, and has a human perception of the needs of the world at large."[10]

STYLE AND STRUCTURE

In accordance with salsa's international popularity, the repertoires of some salsa bands have included a few jazzed-up Puerto Rican *plenas* and *bombas*, Dominican merengues, and the occasional Colombian *vallenato* and *cumbia*. Roberto Torres's hit recording of "El caballo viejo" illustrates how salsa can be enriched by creative and eclectic infusions from its stylistic and geographical margins; while the song was written by a Venezuelan, Torres performs it as a Colombian *cumbia*, using a *charanga* ensemble supplemented by *vallenato*-style accordion and trumpet. Nevertheless, some 90 percent of salsa songs can be basically categorized as modernized renditions of the Cuban *son* (or *guaracha*, which is now practically identical). The typical salsa song, then, coheres to the pattern of the modern *son* as described in Chapter 2. Like the *son*, it commences with a songlike first section, followed by an extended *montuno* with call-and-response vocals; instrumental breaks (mambo, moña); and improvised, jazz-influenced solos, all over a repeated harmonic-rhythmic ostinato.

A typical band consists of ten to fourteen people: the leader (who nowadays is usually the singer), two to four horn players, and those who play piano, bass, conga, bongo, and *timbales* (a kit including two drums and a cowbell), and perhaps one or two *coro* (choral refrain) singers. One of the vocalists might also play *clave*, *güiro*, or maracas, and the bongo player typically switches to second cowbell when the *montuno* begins. A variety of different horn instrumentations are found, including the lean, crisp *conjunto* format of just two trumpets (used, e.g., by Johnny Pacheco); a brassy four-trumpet section (Papo Lucca's Sonora Ponceña); or more commonly, two trumpets plus one or more saxophones and trombones.

As in the Cuban *son*, the instrumental parts follow somewhat standardized accompaniment patterns, especially in the *montunos*. The schematized excerpt below (Musical Example 13), loosely taken from Eddie Palmieri's "Ven ven,"[11] illustrates some of these basic features. The rhythmic ostinatos are two-bar patterns fitting into the *clave* structure, which, in this case, is "two–three" *clave*. Accordingly, the piano part hits the downbeat of the odd-numbered (e.g., first) bars while gliding over the even-numbered (e.g., second) bars. The anticipated bass skips, or rather, glides, over the downbeats, playing the chordal roots before the other instruments (here, the piano) reach the corresponding chord. The *coro* (choral response),

MUSICAL EXAMPLE 13

which here is a simple "ven ven" (come, come), is answered throughout the *montuno* by the lead vocalist's semi-improvised "call" or *sonejo*—in this case, "a bailar la rumba buena" ([come, come] to dance the lovely rumba).

THE SALSA LIFE

While salsa is an international music with mass followings, New York City remains its home and creative hub. Most of the big-name groups and record companies are based there, and despite the effects of merengue, hip-hop, and economic recession, New York still hosts the liveliest salsa club and street-concert scene.

In terms of repertoire, prestige, and performance contexts, the New York salsa bands can be divided into two categories. The lower echelon consists of lesser-known bands that play cover versions of other groups' hit songs, performing at private parties, weddings, and at the "*cuchifrito* circuit" of relatively cheap, unpretentious, and sometimes dangerous clubs (whose name derives from the fried snacks sold there). It is hard to estimate how many such bands exist, since they often consist of *ad hoc* ensembles hastily put together by a leader before a gig. More visible, significant, and influential than these groups are the fifteen or so big-name bands, which record, perform their own original songs, and have more fixed personnel. These bands occasionally play at private events, at which they are obliged to play a few covers of hits, including a few merengues like "El compadre Pedro Juan." Mostly, however, they play at city- or corporate-funded free concerts

Salsa LP cover from 1982 (Profono TPL 1403)

in parks and streets and, more regularly, at the ten or so fancy salsa clubs located in various places in the city. If all is going well, every band does two or three gigs a week, each consisting of two sets; occasionally they will be more busy and may even play a "double" or "triple," perhaps zipping off in a rented van to Philadelphia or elsewhere for a late-night gig after an after-noon park concert and a normal club date.

Aside from the musicians, the top bands also employ a "band boy," a sort of gofer-factotum, whose most important job is to whisk the folders of sheet-music charts off the music stands after each set, before they can be stolen by some spy or traitor in the service of a cover band.[12] I asked Chris Washburne, a trombonist who plays in the top rank of bands and studio dates, to describe the typical salsa sideman:

It's hard to describe anyone as typical, since they are so varied. Ethnically, maybe about 80 percent are Newyorican, and the rest are a mixed bag of Dominicans, Cubans, and others, including several Anglo horn players like myself. Some of them, like me, do a fair amount of studio work in the daytime and in that sense could support themselves just playing music. But most of them, aside from the leaders, of course, have various kinds of day jobs.

The need for daytime employment is evident from the wages. Most sidemen get about ninety dollars for a night's work. Even for a successful sideman (working two or three nights a week, forty-some weeks a year), this would translate into only about thirteen thousand dollars a year—and it is very difficult to support a family on that in New York City. Needless to say, working a forty-hour day job plus playing salsa until 4:00 A.M. two or three nights a week can be a grueling schedule. As Washburne relates, "If the music's hot, it's still a gas—but if the music's bad or the band isn't playing well, then it's *death*."

Because work even with the big-name bands can be irregular, many musicians do free-lance work with other bands at the same time. This practice can require a fair amount of telephonic juggling, as one free-lancer relates:

> Bandleader X might call me on Tuesday and offer me a job for Saturday night. If the weekend is open, I may accept, but then perhaps bandleader Y calls me on Wednesday offering work on both Friday and Saturday. So I accept, and call around frantically to get someone to sub for me on X's gig. Then maybe on Thursday Y calls back to say that the Saturday gig has fallen through, so I'm stuck without work that night. Maybe this was Y's fault, and he was just promising two nights of work in order to get me to commit to him. But then, sometimes clubs book popular bands and advertise for them, just to attract crowds, and then they cancel those bands and have a cheaper band play.

Bands also have to put up with other sorts of chicanery. Washburne notes:

> Sometimes we might play one set, and then the club owner tells us to leave, giving us just half-pay. That's understandable if it's a Sunday-night gig, and you can see that there aren't many dancers and the club is losing out, but sometimes it's for no good reason. On other occasions, especially with free-lance gigs, you just don't get paid, and there's nothing you can do about it. I'm owed several hundred dollars that I'll probably never see. But most musicians are so hard up for work they'll go on working for the same people who occasionally rip them off. It's a mess, especially since nothing is written down.

Many such abuses could be rectified if salsa musicians were unionized, but the American Federation of Musicians has always ignored Latin bands, and post-Reagan America is hostile territory for unions in general. Further, salsa musicians, due to the nature of their work, are notoriously difficult to organize, as Ruben Blades found out when he tried to start a union in the 1980s.

Drugs have a certain presence in the salsa world, as they do in most popular music scenes and cash-oriented sectors of the economy. In general, however, drugs are not nearly as pervasive in the salsa world as they were, for example, among jazz musicians in the 1930s and 1940s. Most sidemen are more or less "straight," in accordance with their rigorous work regime and the need to be punctual, well-attired, and well-behaved onstage (and, to some extent, offstage as well). Unfortunately, some bandleaders have had serious problems with drug abuse. Drugs are also part of the salsa scene in another way: some club owners are believed to launder drug money through the cash-dominated club economy, and some groups, whether in New York or Cali, Colombia, are sponsored by drug barons.

Since the 1980s, the business aspect of the salsa scene in the United States has tended to be dominated by a few impresarial moguls—and to a considerable extent, by one man, whom I shall call Ralph Mercado (since that is his name). Mercado manages most of the major bands and controls most club bookings and big concerts. His record company, RMM, has been the biggest salsa label since the mid-1980s, and he allegedly wields considerable influence (I won't say how) over airplay on the two New York radio stations that play salsa regularly. Groups that, for whatever reason, do not work with Mercado may have a hard time getting gigs and recording contracts. Those that do work with him may do well, especially if able to conform to the paternalistic structure of his organization. Washburne likens RMM to Motown, the 1960s soul label run by Berry Gordy in the manner of a family factory, complete with "house" composers (for Motown, Holland-Dozier-Holland) and an authoritarian command structure. RMM's in-house musical wizard is Sergio George, a talented Newyorican who arranges and plays piano on most recordings and who has codified the smooth, brassy sound of modern pop salsa, influenced by R&B groups like Tower of Power. George's arrangements are doled out, Motown-style, to the appropriate artists on the RMM roster, in consultation with Mercado. The result is the slick and commercially successful sound that dominates New York's salsa radio slots.

Much of the crisp, flawless, mechanical slickness of modern salsa records (whose standards are set by RMM) derives from the way they are recorded. In the old days, a band, having played a set of songs for months in clubs, would book a few days in a recording studio and there perform the songs more or less "live" (i.e., without overdubbing). At its best (e.g., recordings of Arsenio Rodríguez), this practice allowed for loose, spontaneous interaction between musicians, quick recording sessions, and reasonably good audio fidelity. But in the modern pop music scene, reasonably good is not good enough—everything has to be seamlessly perfect, and twenty-four-track recording technology makes that kind of perfection possible. So with salsa, as with other forms of commercial music, it has become the norm to record most of the parts separately, by a handful of studio musicians rather than by the band that actually plays the songs in the clubs. (Also, songs are usually recorded before groups start performing them in clubs.) First, the piano and percussionists lay down their track, and then the horn players record their parts. In some cases, two horn players or even a single player will record the three or four parts. These, naturally, have to be recorded sequentially, but this is still generally cheaper than having four horn players record them "live," because that would require more musicians, and the greater likelihood of error would require more retakes.

The studio musicians—a select handful—are perfectionists, able to play a part flawlessly while sight-reading it for the first time. (When they hear the final song later on the radio, they may not even recognize it, since they record so much and often hear only their own parts.) After a day or two, the instrumental tracks for the entire record are completed, and the vocalist can spend another day or two recording his part. Spontaneous interaction is out of the question, which is one reason why some moldy figs (like this author) prefer older records (e.g., Cuban classics or early Fania), recorded more or less "live" in the studio.

But if many modern records tend to sound rather slick and commercial, it should be remembered that the dance club scene is more important than records, both to audiences and to band members. The live version of a song is quite different from its recorded prototype. First of all, it is generally at least twice as long, with an extended *montuno* section incorporating improvised solos. Further, the musicians—especially the rhythm section and, one hopes, the lead singer—need not slavishly follow the record but generally enliven the music with variations and flourishes, whether subtle or bold, which collectively electrify dancers and keep the other musicians grinning and energized.

New York's club scene is the throbbing heart of the salsa world. While many clubs come and go over the years, there are a few, like Manhattan's Copacabana and Club Broadway, that have been fixtures for decades. Admission is usually around fifteen dollars for men and somewhat less for women. To sit at a table, however, with a bottle of hard liquor, costs around two hundred dollars. On an average night, the audience of four hundred or so may include a few wealthy regulars and any number of working-class Latinos for whom this is a special occasion. (Anglos are also welcome, as are paying customers of any ethnicity.) While couples are in the majority, there are many unattached men and women who come to dance and socialize. In terms of club attire, Latinos dress up rather than down, and if you show up in jeans and sneakers, you will be turned away at the door, even if your hair is blow-dried.

Some people may sit and shout conversations, others may stand near the stage watching the band, but most come to dance. Indeed, it is worth reiterating that Latin dance music is designed to accompany dance. To attend a Latin dance club, whether in New York, Havana, San Juan, or Caracas, is to see two-hundred-plus people engaged in an extraordinarily rich and dynamic form of creative, artistic expression. This is not the shapeless shuffling and bobbing of mainstream American pop dance but rather a highly stylized and sophisticated couple dance. The basic foot (and hips!) pattern is fairly standardized, but skillful dancers, with the man leading, combine it with such varied, dazzling, high-speed turns, twists, and spins that it is a wonder to behold. Latin dance clubs also differ from rock clubs and other mainstream American dances in that one sees all ages on the dance floor, from gray-haired septuagenarians to nattily dressed twenty-year-olds—and the older dancers are often the best. There is little need for a youth countercultural dance-and-music movement when a style as rich as the *son* has been around so long. Moreover, blacks, whites, mulattoes, and even Asians are all dancing and mingling together, with an ease and naturalness that reflects the racial synthesis that produced Cuban dance music in the first place.

SALSA LITE?

Since its initial heyday in the late sixties and early seventies, salsa has remained stylistically pretty much the same, in its continued reliance on the modern Cuban *son*. This continuity could be taken to indicate salsa's healthy stability and perseverance in the face of changing social conditions and the music industry's ongoing promotion of inane and ephemeral fads. Alternately, the stasis of the salsa scene could be regarded as a reflection of exactly what is wrong with salsa: its failure to have changed with the times, its inability to expand, and the fact that its performers remain stuck in the exploitative, unremunerative *cuchifrito* circuit. Salsa has not really changed much, and whether one thinks this is good or bad, the fact is that the genre has been on the defensive against merengue, rap, and other musics since the late 1970s. What happened to the brash, youthful music that took the Latin world by storm in the late 1960s?

A complex combination of factors has kept salsa in a holding pattern since the mid-1970s. Some of these factors have been external developments, beyond the control of *salseros*. One problem has been the ongoing process of cultural and linguistic Americanization that has led so many Latino youths to shun salsa for rock, disco, and hip-hop. The Young Lords and their ilk may have persuaded millions of Latinos to be proud of their heritage, but inevitably many second- and third-generation immigrants have been losing their Spanish and assimilating into neighborhood Anglo- or, more commonly, Afro-American culture. For many of them, salsa is the old-time music of their parents' generation or of provincial islanders. Many *salseros*, from Ruben Blades to current RMM crooners like Tito Nieves have tried to rein in such defectors by singing in English, but their success has been limited.

Another problem has been the merengue boom. Since the late 1970s, New York and Puerto Rico have been subject to a massive influx of Dominican immigrants (who now number over half a million in New York alone). The Dominicans have brought with them their national music, the merengue, which has since invaded the bastions of salsa's popularity and won over much of salsa's former or would-be audience. The Dominican bands are cheaper, their showmanship is snappier, the dance style is simpler, and a lot of Latinos—from New York to Venezuela—just like merengue more than salsa, for whatever reason. It is fast, tight, intricate, and danceable, even if hard-core *salseros* deplore it as trivial and monotonous.

A third external problem for salsa has been the influence of the big record companies (the "majors"), which, since the early 1980s, have targeted the Latin market in the United States. Unfortunately for salsa, the majors, in classic monopoly-capitalist fashion, have tried to homogenize the market by promoting common-denominator Latin pop and sentimental ballads, rather than catering to the country's various Hispanic groups (which also include Mexican *ranchera* fans, Central American *cumbia* lovers, and so on). With CBS and other multinational recording corporations pressuring radio stations to play Julio Iglesias and other easy-listening crooners, salsa had become marginalized on the airwaves even in its hometown, New York.[13] (In the 1990s, commercial salsa finally found stable niches on the radio.)

But some of salsa's difficulties seem to relate to the directions the genre has taken since its heyday. By the late 1970s, salsa, whether in New York or Caracas, had largely abandoned its portrayals of proletarian barrio reality and its themes of Latino solidarity in favor of sentimental love lyrics. Of course, salsa is not the first art form to have to confront the dual and often incompatible functions of being educational or, alternately, being escapist entertainment. Some people may always prefer fantasy to social realism, and many Latinos who dress up to go dancing in plush salsa clubs do not want to hear songs about barrio murders—that is what they are trying to get away from. The capitalist entertainment industry has generally tended either to co-opt and neutralize "rebellious" art forms (such as rock or rap) or to ignore and thereby marginalize them. Accordingly, as salsa earned a stable niche in the record market, the music industry—starting with Fania in the mid-1970s—has tended to direct it away from its barrio orientation, to make it into a more bland, depoliticized pop—ketchup rather than salsa.

This trend has continued ever since. Most of what is promoted on radio and records is the slick, sentimental *salsa romántica* of crooners like Eddie Santiago, rather than the more aggressive, proletarian, Afro-Caribbean *salsa caliente*. The change is also reflected in the fact that most of today's band-leaders are not trained musicians and seasoned club performers like Willie Colon but cuddly, predominantly white singers distinguished by their pretty-boy looks and supposed sex appeal. Many of them, like Jerry Rivera, are studio-bred creations of the commercial music industry who, in their occasional live performances, cling timidly to the recorded versions of their songs rather than improvising freely. Puerto Rican–born singer Jorge Man-uel "Giro" López articulates the new ideal: "Salsa used to have a nasty im-age, with its sexuality and rough performers, but my salsa is romantic, soothing, pretty . . . sort of like a rhythmic bolero, and that's today's salsa, which has changed a lot from the original style. Salsa used to be all about the *timbales* and bongó, but now it's about sweet and elegant words, and the girls like it much more than the earlier, macho salsa."[14]

With its new image, *salsa romántica* retains a steady niche in the music scene, while becoming irrelevant to many young Latinos who are drifting away to rock and, especially, to rap, which has replaced salsa as the real voice of the barrio. In the opinion of many, what salsa needs is precisely the creative input of these alienated youths, who could rejuvenate the genre and take it beyond the *cuchifrito* circuit.

Problems notwithstanding, salsa remains essentially alive and well, within its limited sphere. Its market has grown in Latin America and Spain, and if some Newyoricans have failed to learn Spanish, New York remains full of newer immigrants—including Dominicans—who fill the salsa clubs. And indeed, there appear to be many salsa fans who have returned to Latin music after being lured away by the mainstream media's rock and rap hit parade. The 1990s have even seen former hip-hop singers La India (Linda Caballero) and Marc Anthony return to Latin music as part of the new wave of salsa stars, attracting young followers with their updated images

(India with her cigar, and the long-haired, denim-clad Anthony with his pop-balladeer style). Critic Enrique Fernandez opines, "*Rockeros,* you see, are a phase Latinos go through on their way out of underdevelopment. *Cocolos* are forever."[15] Another commentator, Pablo Guzmán, writes, "New York still gets cold in winter. Latinos are still third-class citizens. Puerto Rico is still a colony. Which is why, in spite of the petty capitalists and those in media who block it from greater exposure, salsa will not die. It keeps us warm. And along with soul, country, rock, and jazz, it is one of the great kick-ass people's musics of the Americas."[16]

LATIN RAP

While salsa is simply too dynamic to die out, in increasingly opting for the *romántico* route, it has lost the attention—and creative input—of many urban Latino youths who seek a meaningful expression of the proletarian barrio experience. Among English-speaking Newyoricans in the 1980s who were growing up with ghetto blacks and inundated with hip-hop culture, there developed a widespread tendency to adopt contemporary Afro-American dress, mannerisms, and music. In the ethnic mosaic of New York City, the kindred rhythms of Jamaican–New York dancehall reggae have exerted a similar sway, especially as they had already been working their way into rap songs and island airwaves. But because going hip-hop could mean forsaking Spanish language and identity, an inevitable development was the emergence of Latin rap, mixing Spanish and English languages and musical identities in various proportions. The modern mass media have played crucial roles in Latin rap's evolution, as radio programs crisscross the English- and Spanish-speaking islands in the Caribbean night and satellite dishes bring MTV International to the entire region. Latin rap thus emerges as the expression of a common urban identity, especially as experienced in New York, where Latinos, Jamaicans, and Afro-Americans have spliced their musics together like a set of patchwork designer jeans.

Gerardo's late 1980s "Rico Suave" was the first Spanish-language rap hit, and in its wake, various forms of Latin rap emerged in Los Angeles, New York, and the Caribbean Basin. Like salsa, it has developed as an international genre, with offshoots and margins that lie outside the realm of Caribbean culture. For example, although we might wish to delimit a "Caribbean rap" category, it would be artificial to separate the music of Chicano-oriented rapper Kid Frost from that of his Havana-born collaborator Mellow Man Ace or both artists, for that matter, from their Newyorican colleagues Latin Empire. Accordingly, Latin rappers come from all sorts of backgrounds; Gerardo's is Ecuadorian, Mangú's is Dominican, and El General hails from Panama.

Much Latin rap remains heavily derivative of Afro-American hip-hop; most of Gerardo's recordings, for instance, have little Caribbean flavor in their lewdness, boastful swaggering, and funk-rock samples. However, a lot of Latin rap does fall unambiguously into the category of Caribbean music. The most obvious Caribbean element—although not a Latin one per se—is the use of Jamaican dancehall accompaniment and declamation style, as in the music of El General or Puerto Rico's Lisa M and Rude Girl (La Atrevida). The latter seems to share Jamaican homophobia (consider her song "Lesbiana"), while her "Si el hombre quiere" echoes hip-hopper Roxanne Shanté ("the pussy ain't free") by telling men they have to pay for their "piece." If such notions may not exactly cohere with North American bourgeois feminism, it should at least be noted that rap has offered considerably more space to female performers than has Latin dance music.

On the whole, Latin rap shuns dancehall's firearm fetishism and gangster rap's misogyny, anger, and nihilistic glorification of violence for its own sake. Latino culture is certainly patriarchal in its own way, but male Latin rappers do not seem to need to denigrate women as "bitches and 'ho's." What is more characteristic of Latin rap is humor, a delight in Spanish–English wordplay, and a self-conscious, eclectic, often postmodern borrowing and juxtaposition—all combined with an inclusive, rather than chauvinistic, affirmation of Latin identity.

Gerardo's "It's a Latin Thang" is an exemplary barrio product, with its "Spanglish" text, funky boogaloo vamp, and whimsical urban-life interjections, such as a neighbor shouting, "¡Para esa mierda allá!" (Turn that shit off!):

> Why is it cool to be Ecuadorian?
> porque soy Latino [because I'm Latino], don't need a DeLorean.[17]

Currently the most popular rapper in Puerto Rico, Vico C celebrates cultural fusion in his slick and witty use of dancehall, merengue, rumba, rock, and "boogaloo" accompaniments and in his explicitly eclectic lyrics:

> Puerto Rico has *bomba* to bounce, Venezuela has *bomba* to grab you,
> Colombia has *bomba* to enjoy. . . .
> I like to dress up, looking good in my rasta clothes,
> I want to include my chino, to unite all our blood,
> Mixing a little salsa with calypso, making a magic.[18]

A 1994 Latin rap release, "La playa" by Mangú (Freddy Garcia), typified Latin rap's self-conscious eclecticism in both its Spanglish text and its combination of hot Latin piano playing with samples of everything from Pérez Prado grunts to *santería* chanting. As his polyglot lyrics put it:

It's something diferente con esta canción [with this song],
real mambo sound with the chat español,
this unique style que traigo [that I bring] es extraordinario,
move Latin groove with the flow from el barrio. . . .[19]

Latin flavor notwithstanding, the Spanish-language rap audience can be seen from one perspective as constituting defectors from the Latin dance-music scene, and many elders worry that it establishes new avenues of influence for the nihilism and sexism found in hardcore rap and dancehall. Spanish rappers themselves, however, tend to see their music as bringing hip-hop- and reggae-oriented Latino youth back into the realm of Spanish-language music. Latin Empire rappers note that their audience consists largely of wanna-be-black youth who, by way of Latin rap, have rediscovered their ancestral language: "All the Puerto Ricans here, they want to buy English [-language] stuff. You know, but hopefully as more Latin rappers come out doing Latin-reggae, Latin-this, Latin-that, hopefully they'll start to have Latin sections in certain stores and everybody will be proud again of speaking their language."[20]

As of 1995, it remains to be seen if Latin rap will become more than a footnote in the history of Caribbean music. Whether or not it replaces salsa as the new pan-Latino genre, its self-conscious eclecticism reflects the increasingly widespread and culturally significant internationalization of capital, migrant labor, and media networks.

NUEVA CANCIÓN

In addition to salsa and, now, Latin rap, there is one other relevant kind of Latin music with a distinctly international origin and appeal. *Nueva canción*—"new song"—started to emerge in the late 1960s in Chile and Cuba as a sort of self-conscious Latin American "protest music," emphasizing highbrow, progressive verses rather than dance rhythms and *telenovela* lyrics. Although to some extent inspired by the early Bob Dylan and other North American neo–folk artists, *nueva canción* has been motivated in part by an opposition to Yankee imperialism and to the torrent of North American commercial music. With most Latin American governments consisting of right-wing regimes closely tied to North American political and economic interests, *nueva canción* emerged as a persistent, if marginal, voice of leftist opposition, advocating Latino and working-class solidarity and cultural renewal. Throughout Latin America, regional *nueva canción* styles have differed, as artists have made self-conscious use of local folkloric musics; but all have been united by an underlying opposition to imperialism, sexism, and exploitation and a commitment to the creation of a just, humane society.

Perhaps above all, the *nueva canción* movement has sought to avoid and counterbalance the cultural deformations caused by the capitalist music industry, with its sordid machinery of under-the-table payoffs, advertisements, narco-dollars, liquor and tobacco industry sponsorships; its vested interest in maintaining the socioeconomic status quo; and its tendency to reduce all art to entertainment rather than enlightenment. The movement is thus distinct from commercial salsa, *balada,* and rock.

The *nueva canción* movement has its own local efflorescences in the Spanish Caribbean. We discussed Cuban *nueva trova* in Chapter 2, noting how it has been actively supported by the Revolutionary government. The marginal status of the *nueva canción* movement in the Dominican Republic has been more typical of its presence in Latin America. Dominican *nueva canción* emerged in the Joaquín Balaguer years as the most explicit and outspoken music of dissent. As elsewhere, it has been an internally diverse movement, incorporating, for example, the quasi-folkloric group Convite, which reinterprets Afro-Dominican traditional musics, and the sui generis Luis Díaz (also a former Convite member), with his idiosyncratic fusions of rural music and rock. As elsewhere in Latin America, Dominican *nueva canción* musicians have at times been harassed and jailed, although, as ethnomusicologist Deborah Pacini notes, they have also enjoyed a certain degree of protection and media exposure due to their predominantly middle-class backgrounds.[21]

A local variety of *nueva canción* has also flourished in Puerto Rico, loosely allied to the independence and socialist movements. Roy Brown, Silverio Pérez, Andrés Jiménez, and the groups Taoné and Haciendo Punto (with some overlapping members) have, since the 1970s, established followings, especially among university-educated, left-of-center youth. While they have not had to endure direct repression, they have been largely marginalized, like their counterparts elsewhere, by a music industry devoted to profit rather than edification.

As a means of promoting cultural nationalism in opposition to Yankee commercialism, *nueva canción* artists in the Caribbean, as elsewhere, have made deliberate use of local folkloric musics, from the *merengue típico* to the *seis* and *aguinaldo.* The borders of the genre are thus blurred, insofar as performers of mainstream commercial genres also address sociopolitical themes; for example, Johnny Ventura has recorded several progressive sociopolitical merengues, and he participated in a 1974 *nueva canción* conference in Santo Domingo. Similarly, *salsero* Ruben Blades, for his consistent anti-imperialism and sophisticated lyrics, could be considered an honorary member of the movement.

If the workings of the corporate music industry are in some ways contradictory, the *nueva canción* movement has its own ideological and aesthetic dilemmas and contradictions. At the heart of these is the fact that, despite the sincere celebration of proletarian and folkloric values and concerns, most *nueva canción* artists and audiences are from the educated bourgeoisie. From one perspective, their self-conscious usage of folk styles lacks the "authenticity" of its models, and there are only a few performers, like Puerto Rican neo-*jíbaro* singer Andrés Jiménez, who can comfortably straddle both genres. Another subject of controversy is that the search for a pan-Latin medium often leads to the use of Yankee-style singer-songwriter soft rock as a musical lingua franca. When Puerto Rican journalist and scholar Edgardo Díaz pointed out the irony of Pablo Milanés's singing "Canción para la unidad Latinoamericana" (Song for Latin American unity) in rock style,[22] he set off a furor that raged for weeks in local newspapers. Such paradoxes and contradictions may be inherent to the goal of challenging imperialism and capitalism from within, and they will no doubt continue to be the subject of internal polemics. Meanwhile, however, *nueva canción* continues to attract its own small but significant audience and to function as a sort of liberated conscience of the Latin music scene.

BIBLIOGRAPHY

The best book on salsa is Cesar Rondón's classic study *El libro de la salsa* (Caracas, 1980), which, aside from being somewhat dated and in Spanish, is quite hard to find. The early years are also summarized in John Storm Roberts, *The Latin Tinge: The Impact of Latin American Music on the United States* (New York and Oxford: Oxford University Press, 1979). Other articles and interviews can be found in Peter Manuel, ed., *Essays on Cuban Music: Cuban and North American Perspectives* (Lanham, Md: University Press of America, 1990); and in Vernon Boggs, *Salsiology* (New York: Greenwood, 1992). Also see Rebeca Mauleón, *Salsa Guidebook for Piano and Ensemble* (Petaluma, Calif.: Sher Music, 1993).

RECORDS AND FILMS

See the film *Salsa: Latin Music of New York and Puerto Rico* (from the series "Beats of the Heart"), by Jeremy Marre (Harcourt Films, 1979). For records, see recordings by artists mentioned; also *Dancehall Reggaespañol* (Columbia CT 48526).

5

The Dominican Republic

The music and culture of the Dominican Republic pose what might seem a fundamental paradox: How could a country with a history of such oppression, poverty, and instability produce a national music of such manic exuberance as the merengue? Our attempt to answer this question requires situating Dominican music in the context of the nation's history and culture and exploring the relation between the merengue and other local musics. In the process, we will see how the music of this troubled country has come to enjoy its own extraordinary vogue, interacting with the musics discussed in the previous chapters.

The early colonial history of Santo Domingo, as the Spanish half of the island of Hispaniola was called, superficially resembles that of Cuba and Puerto Rico. As in those islands, Christopher Columbus's arrival and Spanish rule led to the rapid extermination of the Taino population (who called their homeland "Quisqueya"), the importation of enslaved Africans, and, after the exhaustion of the island's scanty mineral reserves, ensuing neglect and indifferent misrule by Spain. In other respects, however, Dominican history followed a different and, in many ways, more tortuous trajectory. Spanish sovereignty, earlier interrupted by French conquest in 1795, basically ended in 1822 when the newly independent Haitian government invaded Santo Domingo, occupying the region until 1844. With colonial rule over, Santo Domingo never developed an extensive plantation-based economy, and slavery never played a central role in the region's society. Nominal independence in 1844 failed to bring prosperity or stability, as the country remained undeveloped, insolvent, and divided among regional strongmen (*caudillos*). Occupation by the U.S. Marines from 1916 to 1924 established a certain sort of stability, while paving the way for the despotic dictatorship of Rafael Trujillo.

One of the legacies of the country's chaotic history and fragile sovereignty has been the failure to develop a strong and coherent sense of ethnic or national identity. Despite the fact that three-quarters of the population is mulatto, there is little public acknowledgment of the country's Afro-Caribbean heritage. The middle and upper classes have traditionally identified with Spain, and even the black and mulatto lower classes euphemistically refer to themselves as *indios* or *indios oscuros* (dark-skinned Indians) on their identification cards. In general, African heritage and blackness are associated with Haiti, which is still demonized. Local historians have portrayed the Haitian occupation—in which slaves were freed and Afro-Dominican culture thrived—as a brutal nightmare. Accordingly, Dominican nationalism developed in opposition not to Spain but to Haiti and is still animated by fear and denial of Afro-Caribbean culture. The *negritud* movement, so influential elsewhere in the Caribbean, had little impact in the Dominican Republic, and there are few local counterparts to the innumerable Cuban and Puerto Rican popular songs celebrating Afro-Latin identity.

Nevertheless, the country's African heritage is quite evident, particularly in the realm of folk religion, in which West African and Congolese spirits (*misterios*) like Yemayá and Kalunga are worshiped and importuned. Afro-Dominican folk religion (which has no particular name) bears obvious affinities to Haitian *vodou* and Cuban *santería*, especially in the importance of fiestas (called *velaciones*) in which music, sung and played on *palo* drums, can lead to spirit possession. Dominican *velaciones*, however, are rather more festive than *vodou* or *santería* ceremonies, as they accommodate drinking, social dancing, and uninhibited fraternization between men and women.

Another Afro-Dominican music tradition is *gaga*, a sort of local version of Haitian *rara*. *Gaga* flourishes along the western border areas, which are heavily populated by Haitian migrants. In *gaga* celebrations, members of *vodou*-related Rada cults form rowdy processions, playing interlocking rhythmic parts on bamboo tubes called *vaksin*, which they blow trumpet-style and strike with sticks.

THE EMERGENCE OF MERENGUE

Despite the prevalence of such neo-African traditions, the Dominican Republic's most important musical genre, the merengue, is clearly a product of syncretic creolization, like other mainstream Caribbean musics. *Merengue* (French *meringue*), of course, like the English "meringue," means whipped egg whites and sugar, and it is uncertain how that word came to be applied to the musical genre. The early history of the merengue is also obscure, although as reconstructed by Dominican writers and by ethnomusicologist Paul Austerlitz,[1] it seems clear that the genre developed in the mid-1800s as a creole variant of the family of interrelated, syncopated couple dances variously called *contredanse, contradanza, danza,* and merengue in Cuba, Hispaniola, and Puerto Rico.

This early merengue, like its counterparts elsewhere, may have been predominantly European in origin, but when cultivated as a folk and popular idiom, it acquired a marked Afro-Caribbean flavor in its lively rhythms and call-and-response final section. Merengue texts dealt with all manner of topics, serving as a rich oral tradition of social commentary. Like the Cuban *contradanza* and *danzón,* the nineteenth-century merengue was denounced as vulgar and barbaric by negrophobic aristocrats, although it thrived in regional variants as a folk genre throughout the country.

Typically, the merengue was played by an ensemble of guitar (or the guitar-like *cuatro*), *güira* scraper (which looks like a cylindrical cheese grater), double-headed *tambora* drum, and marimba. The marimba used for merengue is not the xylophone of Central America and Mexico but an African-derived instrument consisting of a wooden box with plucked metal keys; like the Cuban *marimbula,* it is a bass instrument and is much larger than its African *mbira*-type ancestors. The *tambora* is a barrel drum rested horizontally on the musician's lap; the left head, played with the palm of the left hand, is made from a male goatskin, while the other head, made from a female goatskin, is struck with a stick. (As Dominican poet Manuel del Cabral rhapsodized, "Caribbean man, look at your dead goat singing.")[2] From around the 1870s, the button accordion, brought by German immigrants, came into vogue, largely replacing the softer and less durable string instruments.

THE *MERENGUE TÍPICO* OF CIBAO

While merengue has always differed from region to region, it was the style of the densely populated Cibao Valley that came to be by far the most influential. By the 1920s, the *merengue típico* (loosely, "traditional merengue") of Cibao had acquired a somewhat standardized, classic form, especially as popularized by band leaders Toño Abreu and Nico Lora. This style uses the standard ensemble of accordion, *güira, tambora,* and marimba. The *tambora* mostly plays a short roll leading up to the downbeat. The most important instrument is the accordion, which, in the hands of good players, provides a dazzling, shimmering, and constantly varying barrage of crisp, staccato accompaniment figures (better rendered on button accordion than on keyboard accordion). Many *típico* ensembles also came to incorporate a saxophone, playing fast arpeggios in harmony with the accordion.

Most merengues would start out with a short, march-like *paseo*, leading to a "song"-like section, itself called "merengue," with a topical text; like the Cuban rumba and *son*, the piece would then segue to an extended call-and-response section called *jaleo*. The *merengue típico*, however, differs from the contemporary *son* in its instrumentation, its simpler harmonies (often only alternating tonic–dominant chords), and its relentlessly fast tempo. Its choreography is also simpler, consisting of a basic two-step pattern, with or without variations.

This *merengue típico cibaeño* came to thrive as folk entertainment in Cibao, performed especially at Sunday-afternoon fiestas (*pasadías*) and in red-light bars in Santiago de los Caballeros, the provincial capital. The name of one of these taverns, the Perico Ripiao (Ripped Parrot), became adopted as a sobriquet for the Cibao merengue. While horn-based merengue subsequently went on to blare its way into international popularity, *perico ripiao* has continued to thrive in Cibao and especially in Santiago, which functions as a sort of Dominican Nashville. Today, *perico ripiao* is generally played in a style called *merengue típico moderno*, with electric bass replacing the marimba. The accordion remains at the genre's heart, however, and Cibao has continued to produce flashy and innovative players. Foremost among the latter in recent years have been Francisco Ulloa, El Ciegito de Nagua, and even a few women, especially the indomitable Fefita de la Grande, who shows that women as well as men can embody the aggressive feistiness, called *tigueraje* ("tigerness"), that Dominicans prize.

THE MERENGUE AS NATIONAL SYMBOL

From the Spanish–American War of 1898 through the Panama invasion of 1989, the U.S. government has undertaken a series of military interventions and occupations in the Caribbean Basin designed to establish and maintain economic and political control over the region. From 1916 to 1924, it was the Dominican Republic's (first) turn, as U.S. Marines occupied the country in order to keep menacing European creditors at bay. The best that can be said about the occupation is that it generated an unprecedented degree of nationalist solidarity, in which Dominicans of all classes came to resent Yankee rule. On the popular level, the occupation provoked prolonged guerrilla resistance and inspired several nationalistic merengues, including Nico Lora's "La protesta," which is still performed today:

The Americans came in 1916,
trampling Dominican soil with their boots . . . .
The Yankee intruders, we'll drive them out with machetes.

Of greater lasting significance was the belated adoption of the merengue by the bourgeoisie of Cibao, which had hitherto shunned it in favor of dainty European waltzes, minuets, and the like. Caught up in the nationalistic fervor, the provincial elite soon came to close their foxtrot and *danzón* parties with salon versions of the local merengue, as played by professional, sax-dominated big bands led by Juan Bautista Espiñola, Pavin Tolentino, and others. This trend laid the foundation for the genre's subsequent emergence as a national music.

Another foundation laid during the U.S. occupation was that of military dictatorship, as the Marines set up a National Guard and prepared collab-

Asa Dife brings Afro-Dominican music to New York, playing the long *atabales* drums (photo by Peter Manuel)

orator Rafael Trujillo to lead it. In 1930, Trujillo seized the presidency in a coup d'état and commenced a thirty-one-year dictatorship that colored every aspect of Dominican culture, including merengue. Trujillo brutally stamped out dissidence and promoted a culture of fear, sycophancy, and propaganda; even in front of the Nigua city insane asylum, a sign proclaimed, "We owe everything to Trujillo." Meanwhile, "El Benefactor" turned the country into his own private enterprise; by 1961, he and his cronies owned over half the nation's assets, and he had become one of the world's richest men—with the tacit support of Washington, D.C., which, until the late 1950s, regarded him indulgently as "a son of a bitch, but *our* son of a bitch."

With the backing of the Catholic church, Trujillo repressed Afro-Dominican religion and culture and revived anti-Haitian phobias. In 1937, he had some twenty thousand Haitians on the border regions massacred and tried to get himself awarded the Nobel Peace Prize for settling the boundary.[3] While his land expropriations uprooted thousands of peasants, he prohibited large-scale urbanization and even tore up a railway in order to discourage travel. Under the guise of nationalism, he limited foreign investment (so that he and his family could monopolize the economy) and discouraged international musics like rock 'n' roll.

Of particular significance was Trujillo's influence on merengue. Trujillo was of humble origins, and he resented the elite sophisticates who had earlier barred him from their social clubs. In turn, Trujillo promoted the Cibao-style merengue, of which he was an enthusiast, as a populist symbol. Merengue groups accompanied him on his campaigns and tours, and hundreds of songs were commissioned to sing the praises of his policies and activities. Urban dance bands were henceforth required by Trujillo to incorporate merengues into their repertoires. The Santiago-based band of Luis Alberti, renamed Orquesta Presidente Trujillo, was brought to the capital as a state ensemble, and its 1937 hit "El compadre Pedro Juan" established the merengue's popularity in the urban salon. Such *orquestas* were heavily influenced by swing big-band jazz, using mambo-like sectional arrangements highlighting the trumpets and especially the saxophones, which have retained their importance until the present. At the same time, Alberti's occasional use of *típico* elements like the *güira, tambora,* and accordion bridged the gap between folk and salon merengues. Meanwhile, Trujillo's brother Petán, another merengue lover, inundated the public with merengue over the radio and television, which he dominated.

In effect—and by a 1936 decree—Trujillo turned the Cibao merengue into the country's national music and dance genre. While the *perico ripiao* and *orquesta merengue* remained tied to their separate social classes, the modernized Cibao-style merengue became what is still the single most significant unifying cultural entity in the nation.

THE MODERN MERENGUE

In 1961, the Central Intelligence Agency, fearful that Trujillo, like his neighbor Fulgencio Batista in Cuba, might be ousted by a popular insurrection, helped local conspirators assassinate El Benefactor. For months, the most popular merengue in the country was "El muerte del chivo"—"The Death of the Goat"—celebrating the event. Popular elections held the following year led to a landslide victory for the liberal PRD (Partido Revolucionario Democrático), headed by intellectual Juan Bosch, who promulgated civil liberties, land reform, and labor-union rights and tried in general to dismantle the dictatorship.

Unfortunately, to Washington, D.C., these reforms smacked of communism, and after a right-wing military coup ousted Bosch in 1963, the administration of Lyndon Johnson endorsed the new dictatorship. By spring of 1965, however, the Dominican people had taken to the streets and were on the verge of ousting the junta. At this point, Johnson sent twenty-two thousand Marines to invade the island, routing the popular forces and supervising rigged elections in which Trujillo's former right-hand man, Joaquín Balaguer, assumed the presidency. (This is called "making the world safe for democracy.") Thus began the next chapter in Dominican history—a semi-dictatorship that has continued, with one inconclusive eight-year interruption, through the mid-nineties.

In some ways, the Balaguer regime has been a continuation of the previous dictatorship—Trujilloism without Trujillo. The power of the Trujillo elite and the military has remained intact, labor unions were smashed, and right-wing death squads terrorized the slums. Balaguer maintained his dictatorial power by regularly rigging elections, including those of 1994 (by which time he was blind and eighty-nine years old).

In other respects, the Balaguer years have constituted a new era, with marked effects on music. One change has been the dramatic urbanization of the country, fueled by the land acquisitions of multinational corporations like Gulf & Western, which uprooted tens of thousands of peasants. Most of these peasants flooded into the urban shantytowns, especially in Santo Domingo, whose population doubled between 1961 and 1970. The character of the nation's culture has naturally changed, as a population that in 1960 was 70 percent rural is now predominantly urban.

Perico ripiao merengue group (José Quesada), with *güira*, sax, *tambora*, and accordion (© Vicente Fernandez/City Lore)

Balaguer, in accordance with the wishes of his backers in Washington, D.C., dismantled Trujillo's barriers to foreign investment and opened up the country to multinational corporations. Urbanization thus became coupled with internationalization, as foreign businesses, consumer products, and media networks came to pervade the country. The foreign presence was particularly visible—or rather, audible—in the realm of music, as merengue, which had previously been able to monopolize the music scene, found itself in cutthroat commercial competition with rock, pop ballads, and salsa. Whereas the latter were backed by powerful multinationals, as of the early 1960s, the Dominican record industry scarcely existed, because Petán Trujillo's dilettantish involvement in records and radio had scared off any would-be competitors, while failing to produce more than a handful of records. Merengue and other local musics were thus at a distinct disadvantage in competing with foreign musics. On another level, the competition between local and foreign musics involved the development of new sorts of national identity, now conceived in relation to the broader world. As we shall see, a spiffed-up merengue, invigorated by the very foreign influences that threatened it, eventually came to triumph not only in its homeland but abroad as well.

Rock music, in full flower-power by the mid-1960s, soon made significant inroads into the Dominican music scene and has occupied a stable niche ever since, especially among bourgeois youth. But the language barrier, anti-Americanism (heightened by the 1965 invasion), and the love of Latin-style dancing have saved the Dominican Republic from disco domination. A different sort of foreign competitor has been the pop *balada,* the international genre of sentimental love songs crooned by Julio Iglesias, José José, and others. The *balada* can to some extent be seen as a relative of the bolero and Latin American *canción* (a generic term for romantic songs that are not composed for dance), but it is best regarded as a Spanish-language counterpart to the mainstream, commercial Euro-American ballads of Barbra Streisand, Englebert Humperdinck, and their like. In its pristine avoidance of sociopolitical flavor, its orientation toward fantasy, its dissemination by mass media rather than in live performances, its generally passive consumption, and its dependence on multinational capital, the *balada* is regarded by critics as subtly but profoundly alienating. Whatever its effects may be, the *balada* continues to compete with merengue and, as we mentioned in Chapter 4, with salsa on the airwaves, although it seldom functions as dance music.

The most immediate competitor to merengue has been salsa. Salsa emerged in the late 1960s as Cuban-style music played primarily by Puerto Ricans as an expression of the New York City Latin experience. Salsa soon became an international phenomenon, marketed and cultivated throughout cities of the Hispanic Caribbean Basin. However, salsa's role in Dominican national culture has been inherently ambiguous. On the one hand, it is a pan-Latin music and a dynamic symbol of Latino cultural resistance to North American "Coca-Colonization." On the other hand, while most Dominicans like salsa, they regard it as foreign in comparison to the indigenous merengue.

For those involved as performers or businesspeople in the Dominican music industry, the 1970s were a period of an intense musical war. Until the late 1970s, the merengue was definitely on the defensive, as the airwaves and record stores were dominated by North American pop, weepy *baladas,* and hard-driving salsa. By 1980, however, the tide was turning. For one thing, the Dominican recording industry was coming into its own; with Petán no longer intimidating entrepreneurs, several local record companies and sophisticated studios had emerged, able to produce slick, professional recordings that could stand their ground against the foreign imports. Dominican producers were also better poised to sway local radio disc jockeys with "incentives" (i.e., payola) than were foreign-based competitors.

Further, salsa had lost much of its youthful vigor and freshness, and the trend toward bland, commercial *salsa romántica* was well underway. The most important factor, however, was the emergence of a new, revitalized merengue, that managed to combine the sophistication of the big-band salon merengue, the raunchy intensity of *perico ripiao*, and the best and most appropriate influences from its foreign competitors. The most innovative and significant figure in this development was bandleader Johnny Ventura. Starting in the 1960s, Ventura broke from the "sweet" sound of salon big bands like Alberti's, paring down the ensemble to a lean *conjunto* of two saxes and two or three other horns. The key instruments were the saxes, which played crisp, staccato arpeggio patterns, interlocking percussively with the newly highlighted *tambora* to produce tight (*apreta'o*), machine-gun-like composite rhythms. Some of Ventura's songs perpetuated the merengue's tradition of social commentary, and his outspoken support for the PRD illustrated how the merengue easily shed its negative associations with Trujillo.

While maintaining some traditional aspects, Ventura enlivened the merengue with a variety of select foreign influences. He incorporated the sophisticated arranging style of salsa and adopted from disco the use of the bass drum, whose steady, crisp "thump-thump-thump" became a standard feature of merengue. Together with his partner and manager, William Liriano, Ventura, inspired by soul singer James Brown's revue, outfitted his band in flashy costumes and had them perform snappy dance steps on stage, turning every performance into what came to be known as a "combo show." Meanwhile, Liriano aggressively promoted the band on the island's concert circuit, realizing that this was one arena in which foreign musics could not compete. The band itself was packaged as a commodity, embodying a new image of merengue as glamorous and extravagant but, at the same time, indigenous. In effect, Ventura's band managed to refashion the merengue as a music that combined the best of the local and the international, the traditional and the modern, while becoming an embodiment of Dominican *tigueraje*. Ventura's band soon became the model for commercial merengue groups (now called *orquestas*), and he continues to enjoy the status of a Tito Puente–like Dominican music doyen.

THE MERENGUE INVASION

By the early 1980s, the merengue, revamped by Ventura, Wilfrido Vargas, and their followers, had definitively triumphed in its homeland, dominating the TV music programs and the playlists of the country's more than two hundred radio stations. More remarkably, the exuberant merengue went on to invade salsa's own homelands of Puerto Rico and New York City, putting salsa on the defensive and writing a new chapter in the history of Latin music.

To a large extent, the merengue has been personally carried abroad by the massive wave of Dominican migrants pouring out of the country, especially into New York City, since the 1970s. While Trujillo's policies had restricted emigration, the Balaguer regime has encouraged it. Political opponents and dissidents have been given the option of emigration or "disappearance," and the continued concentration of land ownership has driven thousands of dispossessed peasants into exile; other young Dominicans are simply *loco para irse*—"obsessed with leaving"—motivated by consumerism and an adventurist urge to see the Big Apple. Because of the expense of emigration, many emigrants have been members of the educated petty bourgeoisie, seeking better opportunities abroad.

In all, well over 10 percent of the Dominican population has migrated to the United States since 1961, including around half a million in New York and over two hundred thousand in Puerto Rico. Many come illegally, especially by small boats plying the turbulent Mona Passage between the island and neighboring Puerto Rico; many boats have capsized in the white-capped, shark-infested waters, with hundreds of lives lost. Modern merengue bandleader Wilfrido Vargas has warned would-be emigrants in one song:

Puerto Rico may be close, but go by air,
if you get a visa you won't have problems with immigration;
don't go in a *yola* [launch], don't kid yourself,
because in the Mona Passage, the sharks will devour you.[4]

Once in the United States, some immigrants have ended up on welfare and some have enriched themselves as drug traffickers, but most have found service-sector jobs. New York City's Washington Heights—now nicknamed Quisqueya Heights—has become dominated and economically revitalized by "Dominican Yorks," as they are called, who have also taken over many of the city's innumerable *bodegas* (or *colmados*—Latino mom-and-pop stores). On the whole, the Dominicans have distinguished themselves by their aggressive industriousness and their willingness to do hard work for little pay (incurring mixed feelings among Puerto Ricans and others with whom they find themselves in competition). Meanwhile, the city's cauldron of crime and drugs has taken its toll; as Sandy Reyes sang:

Here your life isn't worth a rotten guava;
if the hoodlums don't kill you, the factory will.[5]

Johnny Ventura (Fran Vogel)

Wilfrido Vargas (Fran Vogel)

As merengue bands followed the Dominican migrants, dance clubs sprang up throughout Upper Manhattan and the Bronx, from plush venues like Club 2000 to funky, Third Worldy, hole-in-the-wall joints featuring *perico ripiao*. But merengue's popularity soon spread beyond the Dominican community to pervade the Latin music scene. Many salsa musicians, promoters, and fans have watched with dismay as their favorite clubs and radio stations have switched to merengue formats, barrios came to resound to the beat of the *tambora*, and it seemed that Upper Manhattan was being consumed by a giant lemon meringue pie.

Some of merengue's success has been due to the willingness of the Dominican bands to play longer for less money. Moreover, the Dominican bands, true products of the MTV generation, wear garish outfits and perform flashy and often gimmicky choreography that most salsa musicians would scorn as silly. As one Dominican described the merengue bands in Puerto Rico, "They are musical guerrillas, who go to Puerto Rico and place bombs where they play."[6] But the fact remains that a large portion of former or would-be salsa fans, whether in New York, Puerto Rico, or elsewhere, have simply come to prefer merengue. For one thing, the two-step merengue dance is considerably easier than the basic salsa footwork, and many younger Latinos and fumble-footed *rockeros* intimidated by virtuoso salsa dancers can easily boogie to the Dominican beat. Moreover, fads have their own logic, and just as salsa was getting stale, merengue appeared on the scene—spicy, hot, and eminently danceable.

Delfín Pérez, a composer and musicologist, offered the disparaging perspective that "Merengue has taken over just the way the aggressive, hardworking Dominicans have taken over entire neighboorhoods of New York. And the commercial merengue itself, in its flashiness, machismo, and consumerism, reflects mostly the lower aspects of Dominican culture." Some Dominican critics have similarly assailed the merengue's perceivedly glib superficiality, trivial lyrics, and commercial orientation toward a relatively uneducated, lowest-common-denominator audience.[7] It is certainly true that the merengue's harmonies, choreography, and rhythms are simpler than those of salsa and that its frenetic beat does not lend itself to a wide variety of textual sentiments; hence any social commentary in the lyrics inevitably assumes a rather light-hearted flavor. But after all, merengue, like salsa, is dance music, and lyrical profundity may be less important in that sense than the intricate rhythms and the exuberant arrangements.

As of the early 1990s, the merengue invasion appears to have slowed down, and *salseros* seem to feel that the situation has stabilized somewhat. A portion of the salsa audience may have been irretrievably lost to merengue, but salsa is now holding its own, especially as an increasingly formulaic merengue accommodates itself to commercial success. Moreover, most Dominican clubs alternate salsa and merengue bands, and as second- and third-generation Newyoricans forget their Spanish and defect to rock and rap, the ranks of salsa fans are to some extent being replenished by Dominican immigrants.

Meanwhile, the international merengue boom has to some extent inverted the whole Dominican commercial music scene, so that its center of gravity, like that of Puerto Rican music, is now New York City (which Wilfrido Vargas refers to as "a province of the Dominican Republic"). As record executive Juan Hidalgo observes, "The capital of Dominican music? New York, of course." While a hit record may sell ten thousand copies on the island, in New York it can sell one hundred thousand.[8] Several major bands are based in New York, and some never bother to tour the island itself. In some respects, New York has become the tail that wags the dog, in accordance with the island's penetration by international capital and, for that matter, the fact that since 1961, Dominican political and economic policies have ultimately been determined in Washington, D.C., that is, by the International Monetary Fund and the U.S. State Department.

There are other aspects, both positive and sordid, of the linkage of merengue to commercial capital. As to some extent with salsa, drug money is said to subsidize the merengue scene in various ways. More openly, many bands on the island are supported by ties (*patrocinio*) to businesses, especially beer, rum, and cigarette companies, who sponsor tours and concerts in exchange for exclusive contracts and advertising rights. Such sponsorship may seem natural and harmless enough, except when one considers that, according to one broad survey, Dominicans spend some 30 percent of their income on liquor and cigarettes and that they have the second highest per capita consumption rate of alcohol in the world (next to former Yugoslavia).[9] Moreover, commercial merengue's image of glitter and extravagance, especially as presented on Dominican television, has embedded it in an alienating media world that systematically excludes the poor and any sort of oppositional discourse. But that's show biz—at least, under capitalism.

MERENGUE STYLE AND DANCE

The essence of merengue is its intricate, composite rhythm, which combines frenetic speed with crisp, controlled instrumental parts. Typically, while the *tambora* roll highlights the downbeat of every other bar, the *güira* provides a steady "chick-chicka-chick-chicka" pattern, and the bass plays a steady half-note pulse. Meanwhile, the melodic instruments typically play fast arpeggio ostinatos, as in the excerpt from a *perico ripiao* by Fefita la Grande ("Tengo un lio") shown in Musical Example 14.

MUSICAL EXAMPLE 14

Variations on these patterns are common: the bass player, for example, may play a Cuban-style anticipated pattern for variety, and the *tambora* roll can straddle the downbeat. At a fast tempo, such variations can make the beat anything but simple. When combined in different ways, different songs and sections of a single song may exhibit considerable rhythmic variety within the basic framework. We should also mention the reemergence of the guitar-based merengue, popularized by artists like Blas Duran, who feature a trebly sounding electric guitar in place of a horn section.

The formal structure of the modern merengue often resembles that of the *son* in having an initial "song"-like section (itself called "merengue") with a text, followed by a longer *jaleo* section, which, like the *montuno*, contains call-and-response patterns over a repeated chordal ostinato, punctuated by precomposed horn passages (called "mambo," as in salsa). In many cases, the harmonies to the entire song consist of alternating tonic–dominant (I–V) chords, so that the first and second parts are not as distinct as in *son* and salsa. Some merengues consist only of a *jaleo*, such as Wilfrido Vargas's hit "Abusadora" and the subgenre of merengue known as *pambiche*.

Many songs with more varied chord progressions were not originally merengues. In the 1980s, it became common for bands to take various popular songs, especially slow *baladas*, and perform them as merengues, adding snappy *jaleos* and, of course, doubling or tripling the tempo. Wilfrido Vargas did several such cover versions of French Caribbean *zouk* and *compas* *(konpa)* songs; his hit "Jardinera" was originally a Mexican *ranchera*. This practice is known as *fusilamiento,* which literally means "firing." The implications of the term are ambiguous; for fans, it can imply that a song has been "fired up" and energized when done as a merengue; for critics, however, it implies that the original version has been butchered.

The basic merengue dance step is quite simple, consisting of rocking back and forth between the left and the right foot in time with the bass and bass-drum beats. Partners can embrace loosely or more intimately—*brillando hebillas* (polishing belt-buckles), as they say. The two-step pattern is considerably easier than the basic salsa choreography, which, for men, could be schematized as right–pause–left–right/left–pause–right–left, and so forth (the opposite for women). In both salsa and merengue, dancers can combine the basic step with a variety of turns, spins, and breaks. Many merengue dancers, however, restrict themselves to the basic step, so that it often seems that they are barely moving, or are doing so in some sort of viscous medium. Also, the embellishing turns can be done at slow tempo, unlike in salsa dancing, where the delight lies in their dizzyingly rapid and yet smooth execution. Thus, although merengue as music is celebrated as *subido*—fast and intense—its accompanying dance is often *bajado*—cool, subdued, and restrained.

BACHATA: SONGS OF BITTERNESS

Merengue's role as national music is undisputed, as it remains beloved by Dominicans of all classes, colors, ages, and backgrounds. At the same time, however, if *perico ripiao* remains a Cibao-based folk music, the modern *orquesta merengue* has its own image of glamor and glitter that orients it toward the bourgeoisie and the upwardly mobile working class. Most Dominicans seldom see live merengue, which usually takes place in expensive urban clubs with restrictive dress codes. Those clubs are for the local elite, like the residents of the affluent suburb stretching up the gentle hillside overlooking Santo Domingo's Avenida de los Mártires.

Looking directly across from this suburb, one sees another barrio and, indeed, another Dominican reality. This neighborhood, Villa Miseria, is one of the vast shantytowns that ring Santo Domingo and that house half a million or so rural migrants. It is a world of mud alleys, open sewers, rat-infested garbage heaps, and flimsy shacks clinging precariously to the slopes of a ravine. It is also a world essentially ignored by the Balaguer regime, which has preferred to devote its attention and the nation's resources to projects like the $250 million Columbus lighthouse monument overlooking the harbor.

The shantytown residents enjoy merengue, but they also have their own music, called *bachata*—a music until recently ignored by the mainstream media and deplored by the bourgeoisie but cherished by the poor (and well documented in Deborah Pacini Hernandez's book, *Bachata*). If merengue is music for the feet and hips, *bachata* is music for the soul—the battered Dominican peasant soul, driven by poverty from rural Cibao to urban slums and often on to Puerto Rico and Upper Manhattan. *Bachata's* original milieu was the sector of society that Dominicans compare to *concón*, the burnt rice at the bottom of the pan—the poor who are exposed to the heat of poverty, toil, and oppression and who are unable to develop as well as the rest.

Stylistically, *bachata* is distinguished by the use of guitar-based ensembles, as opposed to the accordion-led *perico ripiao* or the sax-dominated *orquesta merengue*. *Bachata's* roots lie in the informal, guitar-led folk groups that played merengue and other genres in the nineteenth century. By the 1880s, accordion-based groups had become more popular, but the guitar ensembles, rather than disappearing, continued as a somewhat marginalized folk tradition. By the 1950s or so, these groups typically consisted of one or two guitars, maracas, and perhaps bongo and marimba, accompanying a solo male singer. Their repertoire consisted of Cuban *sones,* Mexican *rancheras,* local merengues, and, above all, weepy boleros. The music was predominantly romantic, used by suitors to serenade their ladies, to accompany dancing at rural parties, and to soothe the sentiments of jilted lovers at neighborhood taverns. Many songs were full of ribald double entendres and made no pretensions to bourgeois respectability.

In the 1960s, as dispossessed peasants flooded into urban shantytowns, they brought with them their guitar-based *canciones de amargue* (songs of bitterness), as they were then called, and the music came to express the frustrations and longings of male slum dwellers. As disseminated on cheap, poorly produced 45s and cassettes, the music found new homes in tavern and brothel jukeboxes and in tape players in neighborhood *colmados* and on street corners.

As we have seen, peasant music in Puerto Rico and Cuba has enjoyed a certain idealized status in national ideology; but the Dominican lower-class guitar songs have enjoyed no such paternalistic support. Dismissed by the bourgeoisie as *cachivache* (trivial, worthless), in the early 1970s the music came to be called *bachata,* the word for a rowdy lower-class fiesta. However derogatory in origin, the term stuck, and by the early 1980s, *bachata* music, though largely shunned by television and radio and marketed mostly by humble street vendors, had come to rival merengue in record sales and popularity. As *bachata* singers like Luis Segura, Leonardo Paniagua, and Julio Angel popularized the genre, its relationship to merengue took on aspects of a symbolic class war, pitting the homemade guitar against the noisy saxophone, and the humble *colmado* against the elite club.

As Pacini illustrates, however, *bachata*'s originally proletarian character lay not in the presence of overtly political songs (of which there are few) but in the ways that its sentimental lyrics expressed the concerns of its core audience, the male shantytown dwellers. About half the songs are sentimental boleros, like boleros elsewhere in the Caribbean. Many songs seem particularly suited to express the frustrations of devalued, discouraged barrio men, in a milieu where men are often unemployed or dependent on working women and where transient liaisons between men and women outnumber stable marriages. Women, semi-liberated by enforced economic self-reliance and the breakdown of kinship relations, come to be regarded with ambivalence by men who feel socially and economically marginalized and superfluous. *Bachata* songs express these feelings of bitterness (*amargue*). Like innumerable boleros and Mexican *rancheras,* they often portray the man drowning his sorrows, cursing perfidious women, and offering bitter advice to other men, as in Confesor Gonzales's "No te amargues por ella":

> I've lost my illusions about all women
> Because I saw what happened to a friend of mine
> He trusted his wife, he would have given her his life
> And he trusted her so much, she betrayed him with another. . . .
> My friend, come sit at my table
> I'm going to offer a toast of liquor
> Don't get bitter for her
> A man is worth more than a woman.[10]

Other songs lament the perceived corruption of urbanized women:

> I'm going to tell you about women who come to the capital
> After three days she gets so you can't put up with her
> And she starts to walk in the streets alone
> And she even deceives you with your own best friend.
>   (Manuel Chalas, "Aquí la mujer se daña")

When not denouncing the perfidy of women, men boast of their sexual prowess:

> I'm like the dollar, valued all over the world
> And wherever I go, I get what I want.
> I wander here and there, seducing women
> And because of the way I am, I get what I want.
>   (Manuel Chano, "Yo soy como el dólar")

In a more light-hearted vein are the *doble sentido* (double entendre) songs, with their thinly disguised sexual metaphors:

I have a little car, that's a delight
If I'm with women it goes faster. . . .
I keep my car in the carport,
But I take it out for the woman next door.
(Tony Santos, "El carrito")

I have a very strong tree, no one can knock it down. . . .
More than three hundred women came to the challenge
They sawed for a while, but not one succeeded.
(Juan Bautista, "El serrucho")

Most *bachata* songs are boleros performed at a somewhat faster tempo than elsewhere in the Caribbean, and a solo male singer rather than a vocal trio is the norm. Still, the sophisticated guitar playing, the standardized rhythm, and the unabashed sentimentality link *bachata* to the broader bolero tradition, and since the mid-1980s, the genre has largely shed its lower-class stigma. Nowadays everyone likes *bachata*, regardless of social class. *Bachata* has become the nation's romantic music of choice, and macho origins notwithstanding, it is especially popular among women, many of whom prefer its sentimentality to merengue's manic glibness. To some extent, this development is due to the singer, songwriter, and bandleader who has emerged as the nation's most versatile and popular musician and who merits special attention in this chapter.

JUAN LUIS GUERRA

Juan Luis Guerra, like Ruben Blades, is a sui generis musician—in a class by himself. On the one hand, his music is too unique to be typical, but on the other hand, it illustrates the internationalization and growing sophistication of Dominican music. Guerra's training was somewhat unusual by Dominican standards; after leaving the Dominican national conservatory, he went on to study at Boston's Berklee College of Music, where he was trained in jazz and exposed to a wide variety of international musics. Returning to Santo Domingo, he formed a vocal quartet called 440, which performed original jazz-oriented songs in a style inspired by the U.S. group Manhattan Transfer. 440's music was oriented primarily toward urban intellectuals and university audiences, although his subsequent recordings have managed to retain this orientation while enjoying genuine mass appeal. Guerra's success derives both from his musical talent and his refined and sensitive lyrics, with which he has taken both *bachata* and merengue to new levels of profundity and expressiveness.

In the early 1990s, Guerra moved beyond the Latin-Manhattan-Transfer stage, foregrounding his own somewhat effeminate, often strikingly original singing and incorporating diverse styles and influences. His output has included several merengues, which set new standards for harmonic and vocal sophistication. His "A pedir su mano" is a sort of merengue to end all merengues, with its brilliant and eclectic orchestration and searing chorus.[11] In his neoclassical version of the venerable standard "Mal de amor," he at once tips his hat to the 1950s bands of Luis Alberti and Papa Molina and reinterprets the song in an idiosyncratically modern fashion.

Guerra's biggest hits, like "Burbujas de amor," have been sentimental love songs in a sort of prettified *bachata* style, through which he has out-Julioed his way to international renown as one of the leading Latin pop crooners. Such songs fit comfortably into the "Latin pop" category of MTV International (which excludes salsa and merengue). Other of his songs might be classified as a sort of neo–*nueva canción*, in their singer-songwriter lyricism and their frank confrontation of social themes. His "Visa para un sueño," for instance, is a poignant portrayal of the desperate aspirations of visa applicants at Santo Domingo's U.S. embassy, while his *bachata* "Frío frío" draws from themes of Spanish poet Federico García Lorca. In other pieces, Guerra uses a *son*-salsa format, inviting comparison with the music of Ruben Blades.

Literary allusions and self-conscious eclecticism aside, Guerra's mass appeal can be attributed especially to his tuneful melodies and inventive arrangements. One reviewer summarizes his talent: "If we were part of an award committee, we'd have to give the highest honors to Guerra for the diversity of his themes, the incisive yet balanced social criticism, the philosophical depth, and for the taste and intelligence of the author, as much in the music as in the poetry."[12] The eclecticism and sophistication of Guerra's music illustrate how Dominican music has come of age, at once transcending and retaining its earthy folk roots and becoming an international art in its own right.

BIBLIOGRAPHY

See Deborah Pacini Hernandez, *Bachata: A Social History of a Dominican Popular Music* (Philadelphia: Temple University Press, 1995) and Paul Austerlitz, *Dominican Merengue in Regional, National, and International Perspectives* (Philadelphia: Temple University Press, forthcoming).

6

Haiti and the French Caribbean

MUSIC IN THE STREETS OF PORT-AU-PRINCE

On a hot, sunny January day in Port-au-Prince, my friend Tony, a flute player, invites me to visit a rehearsal of a new popular music group he just joined. We walk to the street and Tony lets out a loud "psst" sound, flagging down a local bus. Called a *tap-tap*, our bus is really a half-ton flatbed pickup truck with an elaborately painted wooden frame covering the cargo area. Piled atop our *tap-tap* are bags of charcoal used for cooking food, some fruits and vegetables, and a young man carrying two chickens. *Tap-tap* are decorated with paintings of Roman Catholic saints, important people like Malcolm X, movie stars (Rambo is a popular choice), and other people who display unique and admirable qualities. Slogans painted on the *tap-tap*, such as "Dieu qui décide" (God decides) and "Psaume 34" (Psalm 34), serve to protect us from a fatal traffic accident, while other slogans like "Miami Beach" and "Min Nou!" (Here we are!) are expressions of the *tap-tap* owner's taste and personality.

We board the *tap-tap* on Avenue J. J. Dessalines, the main thoroughfare in Port-au-Prince. Since the vehicle is completely full, we opt to hang off the back of the truck, holding onto the roof rack for balance. We are in a superb position to observe the many types of musical activity found on the streets of Haiti's capital. Our *tap-tap* is mounted with large speakers that blare Haitian dance music called *konpa;* a few of the passengers sing along with the recordings. As we pass the Mache Fè (Iron Market), young men peddle soft drinks by beating rhythms on *kola* bottles, using their metal can openers. Other vendors use similar techniques to draw attention: the ice-

Chapter 6 was written by Michael Largey.

117

cream vendor uses three bells suspended from a piece of wood to announce his arrival, while the shoeshine man rings a single bell. The meat-pie vendor sells his wares by singing the "hot meatpie," and the peanut-brittle seller sings, "Praline"; both sellers hope to make passersby hungry with their not-so-subliminal messages.

On a street corner, two *twoubadou* (troubadors) perform for shoppers. The singer of the group sits on a large, empty tin can and taps out a rhythm on a small plastic bowl with a piece of wood. His partner beats out rhythms on an assortment of cans, tubs, buckets, and scraps of metal. On the next corner, another *twoubadou,* also known as a *mizisyen ambilan* (walking musician), gives a performance as a "one-man band." He strums a homemade guitar pasted with photos from discarded magazines while playing a kazoo that has a car stereo speaker attached to its end. Strapped to his legs are two *tcha-tcha* (maracas), and his foot is beating out a rhythm on a *tanbou* (single-headed drum).

Our *tap-tap* turns up Avenue Delmas, heading toward Pétionville, a suburb of Port-au-Prince. I push the buzzer attached to the back of the truck, signaling the driver to stop while Tony and I jump off the back of the *tap-tap*. We pay our fare of eighty-five centimes apiece (about $0.18 U.S.) and begin the descent to Tony's rehearsal. We are the last to arrive, and some of the musicians have already begun to rehearse by the time we finish greeting everyone present.

Tony introduces me to Théodore "Lolo" Beaubrun, the leader of the group; Lolo's wife, Mimerose; his cousin Daniel "Dadi" Beaubrun; and the rest of the band. Lolo explains that the group's name is Boukman Eksperyans; they take their name from the *vodou* priest Boukman, who in 1791 made a blood pact with a group of *mawon* (runaway slaves) to overthrow the French colonial system. Lolo explains that their music derives its inspiration from the *vodou* ceremony, where worshipers dance to songs and ceremonial drumming meant to communicate with the *lwa* (spirits) of Africa.

Lolo steers me toward a stool in their cramped rehearsal space in the living room. From my vantage point, I can see the entire ensemble, including two female singers, Lolo on keyboard synthesizer, his cousin Dadi on the bass and drum machine, and several drummers playing a set of *vodou* ceremonial drums from the Rada nation of spirits. Lolo asks the band to rehearse their new number, "Se Kreyòl nou ye," a song that uses a familiar *yanvalou* rhythm of "short–long–long–short–long–long–long." The words of the song are striking, since they call for all speakers of *Kreyòl* (the national language of Haiti) to take pride in their native language and culture.

HAITIAN CULTURAL CROSSROADS

Haiti, like Cuba, is place where musical expression reflects the mixture of several different cultural influences. While most historians look at the history of colonial Haiti as a process of replacement of indigenous populations of Native Americans with Europeans and enslaved Africans, in reality, the heritages of all three groups endure in present-day Haiti, albeit in different forms and to varying degrees.

Before Christopher Columbus's arrival in 1492, Haiti was populated by several Native American groups, including the Taino (the largest group), Carib, and Guanahatabey (sometimes referred to as Ciboney) peoples. The Taino groups were led by *caciques* (chiefs) and spoke a language called Arawak; other Taino groups existed in nearby Cuba. Within the first twenty-five years of Spanish rule, about 90 percent of the Taino population of the island was wiped out by Spanish guns and diseases. Nevertheless, some Arawak words are still used in Haiti: for instance, "Quisqueya" (the Taino word for the island) and even "Haiti" itself, which means "mountainous land."

The Spanish ruled Quisqueya, which they renamed Hispaniola (Española), from 1492 until 1697, when, in the Treaty of Ryswick, Spain ceded the western portion of the island to France. The French called their new colony Saint-Domingue and turned it into one of the most profitable economies in the Western Hemisphere, leading Europeans to dub the colony "the pearl of the Antilles." French colonists, especially those who owned and operated the large sugarcane plantations, brought their European entertainments to Saint-Domingue, opening up theaters for musical performances and sponsoring productions of popular French operas. There were over three thousand European dramatic and musical performances in Saint-Domingue between 1764 and 1791, most of which were imported from the theaters of France.

The colony's economic successes were, however, borne on the backs of Africans brought to Saint-Domingue as slaves. Working long hours at the arduous tasks of harvesting and processing sugarcane into molasses, rum, and sugar, Africans enjoyed few of the popular entertainments available to the French planters. Slaves were forbidden by law to attend French entertainments as audience members, but they were drafted as entertainers for wealthy planters. European accounts from the colonial period indicate that many slaves were adept on European instruments such as the violin, clarinet, and French horn.

While African slaves were familiar with several of the musical traditions of their French captors, most of their music making was based in West and Central African traditions of music. Slaves were brought to Saint-Domingue from as far north on the west coast of Africa as Senegal and as far south as Angola. Haitian historian Jean Fouchard claims that many Africans were brought to Saint-Domingue from the east coast of Africa, especially Mozambique and Madagascar. During their perilous voyages as human cargo across the Atlantic, Africans were not able to bring any physical artifacts from home. The *tanbou* drums were carved from Caribbean wood but used designs from drums made back in Africa. Other instruments, like the *ogan* (a struck piece of metal), were adapted by African musicians in Saint-Domingue. Africans also adapted instruments from Taino music, including the *tcha-tcha*, which functioned much like the West African *shekere* (gourd shaker covered with a beaded net), and the *lanbi* (blown conch shell), which was an adaptation of the Akan *abeng* or blown cow's horn.

In addition to the planter and slave classes, there was a significant population of mostly light-skinned free persons of color, called *afranchi*. As the offspring of white French men and African women, the *afranchi* had some legal advantages over the slave classes. *Afranchi* could attend some of the French colonial entertainments and could own land. They were forbidden, however, to hold administrative posts, work as lawyers or doctors, and wear clothing that resembled the styles favored by the wealthy white colonists. Despite the limitations placed on their participation in French planter society, many *afranchi yo* identified themselves culturally with France.

Each of the social groups in Saint-Domingue (French planters, *afranchi* landholders, and African slaves) was interested in breaking free from French governmental control, although their reasons differed. The planters wanted to be free of the tribute they were forced to pay to the French government for the privilege of owning land. The *afranchi,* eager to be rid of the French planters, hoped to gain independence for Saint-Domingue and take over the plantations. The slaves were also eager to be rid of the French, but not so that *afranchi* landowners could simply take the place of the French planters. Some slaves sided with the French government, believing that the recent French Revolution with its promise of "liberty, equality, and fraternity" would extend to them. Other slaves believed that their only hope of freedom lay in a complete break from France.

Slave resistance to the French took several forms. During the seventeenth and eighteenth centuries, many slaves ran away to inaccessible mountainous areas. These slaves were called *mawon* (from the French word *marron* and the Spanish word *cimmarón,* both meaning "runaway slave"). The *mawon* formed communities and practiced small-scale agriculture and hunting. Many *mawon* went on covert trips back to their plantations in attempts to free friends and family members. On some occasions, *mawon* joined forces with Taino settlements that escaped the extermination campaigns of the Spanish in the seventeenth century. Other slave resistance efforts attacked the French plantation system directly. In the 1750s, a *mawon* leader named Makandal led an unsuccessful campaign to poison the drinking water of several plantation owners. Later, in 1791, another *mawon* called Boukman officiated at a ceremony at Bois Caïman, effectively declaring war on the French plantation owners.

The Haitian Revolution, which lasted from 1791 to 1804, brought the colonial period to an end but left political power in the hands of the *afranchi* elite. While French planters were either exiled or executed, the former *afranchi* class, now split into *milat* (mulatto, light-skinned) and *nwa* (*noir*, dark-skinned) factions, assumed control of much of the business of the new country. The vast majority of the former slaves were located in the rural areas and continued to work the land but enjoyed few benefits from their newly won freedom.

Today, the vestiges of the plantation system endure in the form of social-class and color stratification. Elites, still divided into *milat* and *nwa* groups, vie for control of the country, while the predominantly dark-skinned rural population provides the tax base for the economy. While color prejudice is still felt in modern Haiti, class discrimination is the more pervasive and persistent impediment to social change.

CREOLIZATION IN HAITI: LANGUAGE

The different cultural heritages of Haiti have shaped not only the history of the country but also its language and religions. Unlike the Spanish-speaking Caribbean nations, Haiti has its own language, which is not intelligible to speakers of French. Haitian creole (as it is known in English), or *Kreyòl ayisyen*, as Haitians call it, is a mixture of several different languages, including French, which makes up most of the language's vocabulary; various African languages; Spanish; some Portuguese; and, more recently, English. The term *creole* refers to a linguistic phenomenon that emerges when two groups speaking different languages come into contact and must find a way to communicate. The language formed as a result of this contact is called "pidgin." Normally, pidgin languages are used by people in contact situations: pidgins tend to exist when different groups trade with each other but return home to speak a different language. When a pidgin language becomes a native language for a group, it is said to be a "creole" language.

Kreyòl was originally a contact language between the French slaveholders and their African captives. It eventually became the native language for the majority of the Haitian population; all Haitians, with the exception of some of those who have grown up outside Haiti, speak and understand *Kreyòl*.

Despite *Kreyòl*'s widespread use in Haiti, elite Haitians, most of whom speak both French and *Kreyòl*, look down on *Kreyòl* as an "ungrammatical" use of French. As a result, *Kreyòl* was first recognized as the "national" language of Haiti only in the 1980s—French is still the "official" language of government and business. Haitian education, which had previously been conducted almost exclusively in French, then began to use *Kreyòl* as a language of instruction, but only for the first few elementary school grades.

Elite prejudice toward *Kreyòl* and its rural speakers has political consequences as well. Since non-elites have access neither to a good education nor to a French-speaking environment, they are effectively shut out of the official domains of government and business. Elites have successfully blocked efforts to reform language instruction in Haiti, fearing that an educated, literate populace will organize itself and present a threat to the status quo. Jean-Bertrand Aristide's election to the presidency of Haiti in 1990 was interpreted by many Haitians as an indication that the masses of poor, monolingual Haitian *Kreyòl* speakers were finally going to be recognized by the Haitian government. Aristide's ouster in a coup d'état in October 1991 demonstrated how the needs of Haiti's poor may continue to be frustrated by the desires of the elite classes.

Kreyòl's continued existence as the principal language of Haitians is due in part to its ability to change to meet the needs of Haitian speakers. Like most spoken languages, *Kreyòl* is in a constant state of transformation, incorporating new vocabulary and revitalizing older words and phrases to meet new demands. *Kreyòl* is famous for incorporating words that not only express new ideas but also comment subtly on changes in a modern society. For example, Haitians call the used clothing shipped from the United States *kènèdi*, after John F. Kennedy, the U.S. President who established the Peace Corps. Other examples of American commercial influence on Haitian markets include laundry detergent, known as *fab* (after the popular American brand of soap), and cameras, called *kodak*.

CREOLIZATION IN HAITI: RELIGION

Vodou, the Haitian religion that blends several West African spiritual traditions with Roman Catholicism, is similar in many respects to other African-derived religious traditions in the Caribbean. Like the *Shango* religion of

Trinidad, Jamaican *kumina*, and Cuban *santería*, *vodou* uses music, dance, and spirit possession as part of its religious rituals. *Vodou* synthesizes African spirits, called *lwa (loa)*, with the Catholic saints, resulting in multiple identities for popular religious figures. The Virgin Mary of Roman Catholicism is frequently associated with the *lwa* of love and beauty, Ezili Freda, while Saint Patrick, who is most often associated with driving the snakes from Ireland, is interpreted as a corollary of Danbala, a *lwa* symbolized by a serpent. Initiates in the *vodou* community, called *ounsi*, dance to the music provided by drums, a small iron gong, and a rattle; their goal is to have the *lwa*, who are said to reside in Ginen (Guinea, or Africa), travel to Haiti and possess the bodies of their Haitian devotees. The *lwa* are said to "mount their horse" during a spirit possession; the worshiper becomes the vehicle of expression for the *lwa*. In a ceremony, persons who achieve a spirit possession exhibit gestures that enable others to recognize that a possession is taking place. Often the worshiper appears to be in a physical struggle, making sudden and vigorous gestures that differ in character from the usual movements of the dance.

Once the *lwa* has mounted his or her "horse," the worshiper takes on the personality traits of the *lwa*. A worshiper possessed by Ogou, the *lwa* associated with iron smithing, war, and the military, often calls for his machete and some rum, while an individual possessed by Ezili Freda might demand gifts of perfume, fine clothes, and jewelry. Other worshipers, recognizing the presence of a *lwa*, may stop and pay their respects to the visiting spirit; some may ask the *lwa* for advice or a favor.

Vodou ceremonies can be held anywhere, from an *ounfò* (temple) in rural Haiti to the basement of an apartment building in Flatbush, Brooklyn. What is necessary for a successful ceremony is the creation of a sacred space where the *lwa* will feel welcome. The proper spiritual atmosphere is created in part by the ritual drawings of the *lwa* in cornmeal or flour, called *vèvè*. *Vèvè* act as signs to the *lwa* that a ceremony is taking place and that they are invited to attend. Each *lwa* has characteristic *vèvè* symbolizing different aspects of his or her personality. Ezili Freda, associated with love and beauty, has a *vèvè* with a heart design, while Ogou, associated with iron and war, often has a machete as part of his *vèvè*.

Lwa also have their own music, in the form of ritual songs. Ceremonies usually feature a series of songs intended to invite the *lwa* to participate in the ceremony. The first song is always sung to Legba, the *lwa* who guards the crossroads. His songs usually feature the phrase "Papa Legba, ouvri bayè pou nou" (Father Legba, open the gate for us), a plea for Legba to give the worshiper access to the world of the spirits. Other songs follow in a prescribed order, each devoted to a particular *lwa*. Songs are in a combination of *Kreyòl* and *langaj*, a ceremonial language derived in part from ritual language used in some West and Central African religions. *Langaj* is a "deep" form of ritual language that defies direct, singular translations.

Lwa yo are organized according to *nanchon*, or "nations," which take their names from geographic locations or ethnic groups in West and Central Africa. Ethnomusicologist Lois Wilcken has called *vodou nanchon* "confederations," recognizing the coalescence of different African spiritual practices into a single worship service. Ceremonies often salute the *lwa* of Rada, Petwo, Nago, Ibo, and Congo with their songs and dances. Each *nanchon* probably had its own musical ensemble at one time, but today, the major *nanchon* use either Rada or Petwo instruments.

The Rada *nanchon* uses an ensemble of three *tanbou* (drums), called *manman* (mother), *segon* (second or middle), and *boula*. The ensemble is similar in function to the *tumba francesa* and *batá* ensembles of Cuba, since in each of these it is the largest, lowest-pitched drums that lead the group. The *manman* is the largest drum and is played with a single stick and one hand. The master drummer plays the *manman;* he (most drummers are male) directs the ensemble and determines when the musicians will move to another rhythm or song. The *segon*, slightly smaller than the *manman*, plays rhythmic patterns and can vary the patterns slightly, but not to the extent permitted by the lead drummer. The *boula* plays a steady rhythmic pattern and helps keep the other drummers coordinated. The drums used in the Rada ensemble are made from hard woods and are covered with cowhide and tuned with pegs that are driven into the body of the instrument. The Petwo *nanchon* uses two drums made of softer wood than that of the Rada drums; the heads are covered in goatskin, are fastened to the body of the instrument with cords rather than pegs, and are always played with the hands.

Lwa have a reciprocal relationship with their devotees. Spirits provide good harvests, plentiful rain, and good mental and physical health in exchange for their followers' sacrifices. These sacrifices can be either a live sacrifice of an animal or *manje sèk* (dry food, i.e., not consecrated with the blood of a live sacrifice). Often sacrifices accompany an important celebration such as an initiation or yearly feast. When such animals as chickens, pigs, bulls, and goats are sacrificed, their meat is consumed by the religious community. For large celebrations, such as the annual festival at Souvenance, Haiti, during Easter week, many animals are sacrificed, ritually offered to the *lwa*, then prepared for the attenders to eat.

Ask anyone from the United States what comes to mind when they hear the word "voodoo" and the responses will range from the creepy to the

Souvenance, Haiti, 1988. A set of Rada drums: *segon* on the left; *manman*, or mother drum, played by master drummer in center; and *boula* on the right (photo by Michael Largey)

Souvenance, Haiti, 1988. A *vodou* altar festooned for the annual Souvenance ceremony, with pictures of saints on top, and *govi* pots, believed to hold the spiritual power of initiates, on left (photo by Michael Largey)

Souvenance, Haiti, 1988. An *ounsi* (*vodou* initiate) achieves a possession trance (photo by Michael Largey)

comical: voodoo dolls, zombies, black magic, superstition, cannibalism, and devil worship are but a few of the popular ideas associated with Haitians and their religion. Movies such as the James Bond adventure *Dr. No* or the more recent *Angel Heart* and *The Serpent and the Rainbow* satisfy a taste in the United States for lurid depictions of black Haitians practicing so-called primitive orgiastic rites. These attitudes about Haitians are founded on racism and perpetuated by ignorance about Haiti's people and culture.

While it is tempting to think that such images of Haitians are a relatively recent phenomenon, U.S. discomfort with its Haitian neighbors dates back to the early days of the Haitian Republic. In the decades after 1804, when Haiti became the first independent black republic, southern whites in the United States were concerned that the example of a successful slave insurrection would inspire a similar revolt on their plantations. Since the early nineteenth century, then, white U.S. fiction about Haiti has been concerned with the depiction of Haitians as savages, consumed by a thirst for white blood. Negative stereotyping of Haitians by white writers has persisted through the twentieth century in movies and books that transform the religion of Haitians from a healing ceremony into a satanic ritual. Readers should be aware that despite the pervasiveness of pejorative images about *vodou,* the fictionalized version of Haitian religious practices has little to do with Haiti, *vodou,* or reality in general.

CARNIVAL AND *RARA*

During the week before Ash Wednesday, several Caribbean nations celebrate what is collectively known as Carnival. Trinidad is perhaps most famous for its celebrations, complete with resplendent floats, fantastic costumery, and festive dancing and music making. The celebration can last up to a week before Ash Wednesday, but the preparation for the event often takes months. Some participants in the festivities, especially those involved in the construction of costumes, begin their work the previous year.

In Haiti, the celebration of Carnival is also accompanied by parades featuring floats called *cha madigra,* popular music provided by Haitian dance bands mounted on the backs of flatbed trucks, and masses of dancing revelers moving through the streets. The *cha madigra* are usually sponsored by local businesses, which hire young women to sit atop the floats and wave to the crowd. Haitian companies such as Freska (a popular toothpaste firm), Maggi (a bouillon-cube manufacturer), and Royal (a margarine producer) use the opportunity to plug their products and to associate themselves with their Haitian audiences. Since Haiti is predominantly an import market, local producers have to compete with less-expensive American and French brands of merchandise. Carnival and its association with Haitian traditions give local manufacturers a forum for promoting their goods as "authentically Haitian."

Foreign products also sponsor floats and masqueraders; the aspirin manufacturer Bufferin hired a group of masqueraders to ride papier-mâché horses emblazoned with the Bufferin logo back in the late 1970s. Non-Haitian products can also be the target of ridicule by Carnival participants. In the film *Divine Horsemen,* filmmaker Maya Deren included a group of masqueraders carrying signs for Ex-Lax, a product that is the butt of many jokes in the United States as well.

The association of Carnival with commercialization dates back to the 1920s, when the Haitian government became active in the promotion of the celebration. During the American occupation of Haiti (1915–1934), the government of Louis Borno was sensitive to the criticism that it had sold out to American interests. Because Carnival is also a time for voicing social criticism, the Haitian government is frequently the target of Carnival songs and jokes. By making Carnival more of a commercial venture and downplaying the critical nature of Carnival song lyrics, the government, with the tacit support of the elite members of Haitian society, hoped to keep Carnival under official control. By involving Haitian manufacturing in the celebration, attention could be focused away from the criticism of the political regime.

Carnival is also a time for competition between rival groups of masqueraders, dancers, and musical organizations. Since the advent of electronic sound amplification, popular music bands have ridden through the streets of Port-au-Prince, playing for enthusiastic crowds. Bands congregate near the customs office and engage in a mock battle; each aims to capture the attention of the crowd and, in so doing, push their competition out of the limelight.

Public behavior during Carnival is very different from everyday life. In Port-au-Prince, masses of people crowd the main streets, pressing up against one another in an effort to see the masquerades and musicians pass by on the *cha madigra*. During the Carnival celebration of 1982, I had the opportunity to witness Carnival crowd dynamics firsthand when I was having a drink at a bar in Port-au-Prince called the Rond Point. Located at a crossroads near the French Institute of Haiti and the American embassy, the bar was at one of the meeting places for competing bands. The management of the Rond Point had already removed the plate-glass windows from their frames so that exuberant dancers would not fall through the sheets of glass.

As the crowd swelled, my friends and I decided to go outside and experience the Carnival atmosphere up close. As we reached the street, the press of people made it impossible to move; people were so tightly packed together that individuals moved involuntarily with the motion of the crowd. At one point, I was lifted off the ground and carried for several feet.

In most Caribbean countries with a Carnival tradition, Mardi Gras, the "Fat Tuesday" before Ash Wednesday, is the final day of festivities. On Wednesday morning the Lenten season begins, and the Carnival paraphernalia are burned, the musical instruments are "put to sleep" until the following Carnival season, and people return to their routines. In Haiti, Carnival is immediately followed by a festival that lasts until Easter Sunday and which is known as *rara*.

Rara refers to the street celebrations held in Haiti from the beginning of the Lenten season until Easter Sunday. While the most intense *rara* activity is usually during the week before Easter, each Sunday during Lent, masqueraders roam the streets of Port-au-Prince and Pétionville (a wealthy suburb in the mountains above the capital) and other towns around the country in search of an audience. Music is provided by the *bann rara* (rara band) on homemade instruments such as the *kònè* (a pressed-zinc trumpet that can measure over three feet), the *vaksin* (a large, single-note bamboo trumpet, played in groups of three or more), the *tanbou* (a single-headed, animal-skin-covered drum), the *graj* (a metal scraper similar to those used in Dominican merengue bands), the *big* (bugle), and *tcha-tcha* (maracas), as well as any struck object carried by dancing participants. Usually, members of the *bann rara* who are not playing the instruments listed above provide rhythmic ostinatos on soft-drink or beer bottles (the local brand, Prestige, is popular, but its stubby neck makes it difficult to handle; many participants go for the longer-necked Dutch import, Heineken).

Like their counterparts in Carnival celebrations, *rara* members also engage in boisterous behavior during their sojourns into the streets. Song texts often refer to political topics or events in recent history; many texts are downright obscene. Often the ribald nature of the texts masks a deeper meaning, sometimes in the form of political satire directed at the regime in power. I have heard that one *rara* song about a woman who decided to straighten her pubic hair with a hot comb was directed at Michèle Bennett, the wife of the former Haitian dictator Jean-Claude "Baby Doc" Duvalier.

One of the goals of the mobile *bann rara* is to confront as many passersby as possible and, ideally, to make pedestrian and automobile traffic come to a complete stop. Once the normal flow of people has been interrupted, the dancers are better able to engage audience members directly, asking for donations for the *bann rara* and presenting onlookers with the option of what might be called "pay or play." Passersby caught in the roadblock caused by a large *bann rara* can choose to join in the festivities or to pay a toll for the privilege of passing through.

At first encounter, a large group of people dancing and singing their way through the streets may seem like an undifferentiated mob. While the informal membership of the group can and should swell dramatically during the *rara* celebration, the principal members of the *bann rara* constitute an organized, hierarchically structured group. The patron of the *rara* is the *prezidan*. He usually purchases the more-expensive instruments, costumes, flags, and celebratory paraphernalia for the members. The *kòwònel* leads the band in their street marches and can be recognized by his whip and whistle, which he uses to move the dancers along their route. Male dancers and baton twirlers, known as *majò jonk*, dress in multicolored scarves, somewhat reminiscent of the Jamaican "pitchy-patchy" character of *jonkonoo*. They work with the female dancers, known as *renn* (queens), to bring as many spectators into the procession as possible. *Renn* frequently work in pairs, engaging male audience members with friendly, mocking, and vaguely suggestive dancing.

Renn are also responsible for collecting tolls from participants. One Sunday afternoon during Lent in 1981, I was enjoying a pizza with a friend in a street-level café. We didn't pay much attention to the growing volume of a nearby *bann rara*, so before we knew what happened, we were surrounded by a group of thirty or more. The two principal *renn* danced at the front of the group, asking us to join in the procession. We answered that we would love to participate, but unfortunately, our pizza had just arrived and we were going to have to eat it before it became cold. One of the *renn*, sitting in my lap, acknowledged that cold pizza would be a terrible waste, so she and her compatriots took our slices and continued down the street. We couldn't help but laugh at our situation; we had paid the price for refusing to participate in the *rara* celebration.

MISIK TWOUBADOU

First-time travelers to Haiti might have their initial encounter with Haitian music on the tarmac of the Port-au-Prince airport. Often, the airport authorities hire musicians to perform Haitian folk songs, other popular songs from elsewhere in the Caribbean, or an occasional arrangement of some current American song hit for the entertainment of the arriving passengers. These musicians, called *twoubadou*, can also be found in larger restaurants, playing requests for patrons for small donations, or outdoors performing for celebrations. Troubadours perform in small ensembles, usually featuring a guitar or two, a pair of maracas or a *graj*, a *tanbou*, and a large lamellaphone with three to five keys, called either *manibula, maniba*, or *malimba*, depending on the geographic region.

As ethnomusicologist Gage Averill points out, despite the relatively recent development of *misik twoubadou* in Haiti, most Haitians assume that the genre is an indigenous Haitian music, presumably because of its association with rural (and poor) musicians. Derived from the *guajiro* traditions of Cuba and related to the *jíbaro* musical tradition of Puerto Rico, *twoubadou* music was brought by itinerant Haitian sugarcane cutters who traveled back and forth to Cuba to harvest the seasonal crop. The instruments in the ensemble are portable, since most *twoubadou* had to carry all of their possessions back and forth between Haiti and the sugarcane fields abroad.

Migrant labor has played an important role in Caribbean history since the era of colonial domination. Cash crops such as sugarcane and coffee require labor-intensive processes to get goods from the fields to the market. Haitians have been part of a network of migrant labor since the late eighteenth century, when Haitian workers routinely traveled to Cuba to help with the sugarcane harvest. Haitian migrants have also shaped the musical styles in the areas they work. *Tumba francesa* is the Cuban phrase for Haitian recreational drumming; the style is still practiced among expatriate Haitian cane cutters. In the Dominican Republic, Haitian sugarcane cutters, who live in cane-harvesting camps, celebrate *rara*, albeit in a slightly altered form. Called *gaga*, the Dominican version of *rara* features the same emphasis on colorful costumes, revelry in the streets, and political satire in the form of street theater. *Gaga*, like *rara*, has ties to the *vodou* religious system, except the *lwa* associated with the *gaga* festival have identifiably Dominican attributes.

In Haiti, the *twoubadou* style has come to be associated with the small combo featuring guitars, maracas, and single-headed drum. Perhaps the most famous contemporary exponent of the *twoubadou* style among popular entertainers is Jean-Gesner Henry, better known as 'Coupé Cloué. Nicknamed for the soccer moves *coupé* (cut) and *cloué* (nail), Coupé Cloué is renowned for his sexually suggestive lyrics.

HAITIAN DANCE MUSIC

Dancing is an important part of Haitian life.[1] As we have seen in the case of *vodou*, the religious experience of spirit possession is usually accompanied by dancing, singing, and drumming. Carnival and *rara* celebrations feature exuberant dancing and movement in the streets. Dancing is also a social activity, used for celebrations such as church socials and informal parties, as well as evenings out with friends. In small restaurants, social dance music is provided by the relatively small *twoubadou* groups, while larger clubs with big dance floors often feature dance bands reminiscent of the American big bands in size.

Social dance music has been one of the most heavily creolized music forms in Haiti. European dance forms such as the *contredanse*, quadrille, waltz, and polka were introduced to white planter audiences during the colonial period. Musicians, either slaves or freedpersons of color, learned the European dance forms and adapted them for their own use.[2] One of the most popular African-influenced dance styles was the Haitian *mereng* (*méringue*), related to the Dominican merengue. Along with the *carabinier*, the *mereng* was a favorite dance style of the Haitian elite and was a regular feature at elite dances. The Haitian expression "Mereng ouvri bal, mereng fème bal" (the *mereng* opens the ball, the *mereng* closes the ball) alludes to the popularity and ubiquitousness of the *mereng* as an elite entertainment. In nineteenth-century Haiti, the ability to dance the *mereng*, as well as a host of other dances, was considered a sign of good breeding.

Like other creolized dance styles, the *mereng* was claimed by both elite and proletarian Haitian audiences as a representative expression of Haitian cultural values. Elite Haitian composers, many of whom were trained in Europe and wrote in a European-influenced style, used the *mereng* as a vehicle for their creative talents. Composers such as Occide Jeanty; his father, Occilius; Ludovic Lamothe; Justin Elie; Franck Lassègue; and Fernand Frangeul wrote *mereng* for solo piano and sometimes for small groups of wind instruments. Often these elite *mereng* were named for people, such as Occide Jeanty's "Maria," or events in the composer's life, for example, François Manigat's "Eight Days While Staying in Cap (Haïtien)."

The *mereng* is based on a five-note rhythm, or quintuplet, known in French as a *quintolet* and in Spanish as a *cinquillo* (see Chapter 2). The *quintolet* is unevenly subdivided, giving an approximate feeling of "long–short–long–short–long." While the concert *mereng* tended to use the syncopated version, Haitian piano soloists such as Ludovic Lamothe tended to play the *quintolet* more like five even pulses, giving the *mereng* a smoother, subtler feel.

Occide Jeanty's "Maria" was written for the Musique du Palais, the official presidential band for the Haitian Republic. Jeanty was chief director and composer for the group and wrote most of the band's performance repertoire. The *quintolet* in "Maria" is the syncopated version, appearing first in the saxophones and horns, then answered by the flutes, clarinets, and trumpets. Most *mereng* for concert band followed this pattern, keeping the *quintolet* figure moving from low to high register, thus allowing the melody to alternate the *mereng* rhythm with sustained, heavily vibrated notes. The percussion parts also alternate the musical pulse and the *quintolet* rhythm, giving the *mereng* an additional lilt.

Mereng were also used by proletarian audiences during Carnival time, especially in the nineteenth century. Unlike the elite *mereng,* intended for use on the dance floor, the Carnival *mereng* were directed at the elite members of Haitian society, either criticizing unpopular persons in power or ridiculing their idiosyncracies. The formulaic insults of the Haitian Carnival *mereng* bore some similarity to the early calypso *picong* or "stinging" style.

While the *mereng* remained a popular dance form for Haitians well into the twentieth century, other musical forces have made their influence felt in Haitian dance music. American big bands gained popularity in Haiti in the early twentieth century, due to the presence of U.S. Marines in the country from 1915 to 1934, the presence of radio, and the back-and-forth travel of elite Haitians to France. Haitian bands incorporated American jazz into their repertoires, performing popular tunes for American as well as Haitian audiences. One Haitian president, Nord Alexis, was so fond of the "new American" style that he hired Ford Dabney, the popular American jazz-band leader, in 1904 for a three-year stint as an official musical adviser to the Haitian presidential band.

After the American invasion of Haiti in 1915, some Haitians viewed the popularity of music from the United States as a threat to the vitality of Haitian music, specifically the *mereng.* While Haitians in the countryside formed resistance militias to repel the American Marines, elite Haitians, located mostly in urban areas, chose to show their displeasure with the American occupation with forms of "cultural resistance," including music, dance, literature, and visual arts. Rejecting the culture of the invading Americans as vulgar and uncouth, some Haitian intellectuals recommended turning to the rural roots of Haitian culture, specifically the *vodou* religious ritual. Haitian physician, ethnographer, and politician Jean Price-Mars wrote his book *Ainsi parla l'oncle* (Thus spoke the uncle) in 1927, exhorting Haitians to explore the folktales, music, and religion of the rural working masses. Price-Mars believed that research into the folklore of the Haitian countryside could inspire a national artistic movement that would challenge European domination of aesthetic judgment.

There were several musical responses to Price-Mars's call for a national Haitian music. Classical composers like Justin Elie, Ludovic Lamothe, and Werner Jaegerhuber wrote orchestral and chamber music utilizing either *vodou* melodies or tunes inspired by Haitian religious ritual. Others, like the leaders of popular dance bands, introduced the drum, scraper, and melodies from the *vodou* ceremony into a big-band format. Perhaps the most famous of these "*vodou*-jazz" groups was Jazz des Jeunes ("Youth Jazz"), which used *vodou* rhythms such as the *kongo*, *ibo*, and *yanvalou* in musical arrangements that were based on dance-band formats. Teamed up with singer Lumane Casimir, the Jazz des Jeunes cultivated a sound and look that appealed to the Haitian public; band members dressed in "folkloric" garb of colorful cloth, while dancers moved to the *vodou*-influenced rhythms.

Latin music, especially from Cuba, was also a shaping influence on the development of Haitian dance music. *Twoubadou* music, mentioned above, was an important Latin-influenced genre that found a ready audience among Haitian dance bands in the early twentieth century. With the advent of the phonograph and radio in Haiti during the 1920s, more Haitian audiences were listening to the sounds of Cuban *son* bands such as Sexteto Habanero, Septeto Nacional, and Trio Matamoros. Haitian bands adapted the sounds of the Cuban trios, using the two-guitar, maracas, and single-headed-drum ensemble. In the 1940s and 1950s, larger Latin bands grew in popularity throughout the Caribbean. Arsenio Rodriguez, the blind Cuban *tres* player, toured several Caribbean islands during the 1950s with his band, featuring an expanded brass section.

Haiti's closest neighbor, the Dominican Republic, exerted its musical influence over Haitian music through its exportation of the Dominican merengue dance. While the Dominican Republic had several different styles loosely referred to as merengue, the Dominican merengue of the 1950s was predominantly the *merengue típico cibaeño*, promoted by the Rafael Trujillo regime as a symbol of Dominican national culture (see Chapter 5). Dominican radio stations, playing the Trujillo-praising *merengues* in a big-band format, reached the radios of Haitian middle- and upper-class audiences. Orchestras under the directorship of Luis Alberti and Antonio Morel were staples on the Dominican radio stations received in Haiti.

The influence of the Dominican merengue on Haitian popular music did not, however, mean Haitians were eager to embrace the politics of the *merengue cibaeño*. Dominicans and Haitians have had a rocky relationship since the invasion of the Dominican Republic by Haitian military forces in 1822. While the political tension between the two countries has been expressed by overt military action, such as Trujillo's massacre of tens of thousands of Haitian cane cutters in 1937, Haitians and Dominicans also fight for their national dignity using the provenance of the merengue as a weapon. Intellectuals from both countries have written extensively on how the merengue originated in their homeland. Haitian historian Jean Fouchard's book titled *The Méringue, the National Dance of Haiti* was written in part to counter Dominican claims that the present popularity of the merengue was due to the Dominican interpretation of the rhythm; Fouchard thought the Haitian *mereng*'s influence on the more recent Dominican version was the reason for the dance's success. To Fouchard's ears, only the reinstatement of the original Haitian *mereng* could save Haitian orchestras from adopting the "foreign-sounding" Dominican merengue.

Despite intellectuals' bickering over the origins of the merengue, Haitian musicians were eagerly adopting the Dominican style to their bands. Nemours Jean-Baptiste and his group, the Ensemble aux Calebasses, altered the merengue beat slightly and, in 1955, named their invention *konpa dirèk* (French, *compas direct*), or "direct rhythm." Weber Sicot, a former saxophonist in Nemours's band, formed his own group called Cadans Rampa de Weber Sicot and introduced a variation on the *konpa dirèk* beat that he called *kadans ranpa*, or "rampart rhythm"—a reference to the "ramparts" from which Sicot would challenge his new rival for Haitian musical supremacy. The musical rivalry of the two orchestras worked as a promotional device. Fans for both bands formed clubs, which adopted official colors and flags for their respective musical "teams."

In the early 1960s, the British musical invasion that swept the United States came to Haiti in the form of rock music. Children in upper-class Haitian families, with access to radio and phonographs, formed small combos that they called *yeye*, a not-too-subtle reference to the "yeah, yeah, yeah" lyrics of the Beatles that took audiences in the United States by storm in the early 1960s. When these *yeye* bands added the *konpa dirèk* repertoire to their playlists, the resultant sound was called *mini-djaz: mini* referring to the latest American craze of miniskirts, and *djaz* being the *Kreyòl* spelling of "jazz." *Konpa dirèk* bands—or simply, *konpa* bands—began to scale down their numbers to compete with the smaller, more flexible *mini-djaz*. Tabou Combo, one of the most popular *mini-djaz* bands today, started as a small, neighborhood group in Pétionville, the elite suburb of Port-au-Prince. Other groups coming from Pétionville include D. P. Express (the "D. P." coming from the band's former name, Les Difficiles de Pétionville) and Les Frères Dejean.

Lyrics for *konpa dirèk* tended to focus attention on either the rivalry between bands or relationship troubles. Often the words would have double entendres either in a suggestive, sexual manner or in a more veiled social critique. Tabou Combo's "Mario, Mario" derides class prejudice against musicians, calling for the sympathies of the audience to favor Mario, a musician *san fanmi* ("without family," or "without connections"), in his pursuit of Miss Entel (Miss So-and-So). Another Tabou Combo hit, "Konpa ce pam," praises *konpa* as an important vehicle of communication between black people in the African diaspora:

Kolonizasyon fe tout moun depandan
Sa pale franse, angle, panyol.
Men yon gwo fason pou nou kominike
Lè misik frape, tout moun vibre.

Colonization makes all people dependent,
it makes them speak French, English, and Spanish.
We have a way for all to communicate:
when the music sounds, everyone starts moving.[3]

POLITICS AND THE HAITIAN DIASPORA

In 1957, François Duvalier was elected to the Haitian presidency by a narrow margin. Although Duvalier was not a seasoned politician, he was a trained physician and was well known among Haitian voters as one of the people responsible for the eradication of the tropical disease yaws in Haiti, thus earning him the sobriquet "Papa Doc." Duvalier campaigned on a "noirist" platform, calling for an end to the political control of the country by the Haitian mulatto elite. After the election, however, it became clear that Duvalier had no intention of reforming Haitian government. After a series of bloody purges designed to eradicate his political opposition, François Duvalier declared himself president for life in 1964.

Duvalier's rule was characterized by violent repression of dissent, torture of political rivals, and the establishment of a secret police force called the V.S.N. (Volunteers of National Security), more commonly known as the Tonton Makout. Duvalier feared the power of the regular Haitian army and started the Tonton Makout to protect himself from a coup d'état. The Makout secret police were an unpaid militia with presidential authorization to extort money from local citizens. Often the local magistrate, called *chef de section*, was also a Makout who routinely demanded bribes in exchange for protection.

The V.S.N. were given the nickname "Tonton Makout" to evoke a sinister image intended to intimidate the Haitian populace. Tonton Makout, or "Uncle Strawbag," was the bogeyman of Haitian folklore, who would stalk small children and sweep them up in his bag. Blue denim uniforms and dark sunglasses were the trademark of the Tonton Makout, images borrowed from *vodou* religious imagery: blue denim is the cloth of Kouzin Azaka, a *vodou* spirit associated with agriculture, while dark sunglasses belong to the Gede spirits who guard the cemetery and who preside over the dead. Duvalier associated himself with the *vodou* image of Baron Samedi, the chief guardian of the cemetery and most sinister of the Gede spirits.

A popular joke from the early 1980s captures the feelings of dread most Haitians had of Duvalier. A woman had a sick child, so she took him to the *oungan* (*vodou* priest) and asked the priest to cure the child. The *oungan* told the woman, "Place a picture of Satan on the child's forehead at midnight tonight, and when the child wakes up, your son will be cured." The woman went home and looked for a picture of Satan to no avail. Since all Haitian homes at the time had a photograph of François Duvalier on the wall, the woman placed Duvalier's picture on her son's head at midnight. When she awoke the next morning, she found, much to her horror, that her son was dead! Distraught, the woman went back to the *oungan* and told him what happened. The *oungan* asked, "Did you put a picture of Satan on the boy's forehead, just as I told you?" She responded, "Well, not exactly. I put a picture of Papa Doc on him instead." "Oh my God," the *oungan* gasped. "The medicine you used was too strong!"

François ruled Haiti as a dictator from 1964 until his death in 1971. Before his death, Duvalier altered the Haitian Constitution, allowing him to pass on the presidency for life to his nineteen-year-old son, Jean-Claude Duvalier. Known as "Baby Doc," Jean-Claude's rule of Haiti was characterized by a continuation of the exploitative practices of his father. In 1980, Jean-Claude married Michèle Bennett, a wealthy socialite and daughter of a corrupt light-skinned businessman. The marriage alienated Jean-Claude from his power base and set the stage for an even more repressive period in Haitian politics.

Upper- and middle-class Haitians began leaving Haiti in large numbers in the early 1960s, settling in the United States, Canada, France, and Zaire. Most of these Haitian emigrants settled in urban areas such as New York City (especially Brooklyn, Queens, and Manhattan), Boston, Montreal, and, more recently, Miami. Expatriate Haitian communities continued to grow throughout the Duvalier reign, creating a large and culturally active Haitian network outside of the country. Haitians living in the United States have become an important source of revenue for families still living in Haiti; workers in New York, Miami, and Boston send millions of dollars home to family members annually. Haitians abroad became known as the "tenth department," an addition to the nine departments, or states, in Haiti proper.

Songs of protest against the Duvalier regime first developed in the Haitian diaspora, especially in New York. Farah Juste is perhaps the best-known patriotic singer from the period just after François Duvalier's death. Her early work with Soley Leve (Rising Sun) firmly established her as an outspoken critic of the Duvalier regime. When she started her solo career in the early 1970s, her credibility and popularity kept her a regular feature of musical presentations sponsored by Haitian organizations in the diaspora.

Within Haiti, other politically motivated singers were starting to speak out against the excesses of the Duvaliers. Manno Charlemagne and Marco Jeanty were perhaps the earliest protest singers to actually record in Haiti in 1978–1979. After Baby Doc's marriage to Michèle Bennett, several *mini-djaz* performers joined the growing numbers of critical musicians willing to voice their dissatisfaction with the Duvaliers. One such song was "Libète" (Mini Records MRS 1140), by Magnum Band, which lamented the deaths of Haitian *bòt pipèl* (boat people) who took to the seas in their small boats in hopes of reaching the United States.

As the political pressure against the Duvaliers mounted, the dictatorship showed signs of weakening in the early 1980s. Jean-Claude, Michèle, and a retinue of Haitian military leaders left Haiti on February 7, 1986, aboard a plane furnished by the U.S. government. The ouster of the Duvaliers was followed by a period known as *deshoukay* (or *deshoukaj*), the "uprooting" of the dictatorship. The word *deshoukay* refers to pulling out a plant by the roots to ensure it will not grow back later. The homes of exiled supporters of Duvalier were stripped of their contents; even door frames, plumbing, and roof joists were taken, to wipe away the traces of the former regime. Members of the Tonton Makout were captured and subjected to vigilante justice by irate local crowds.

Songs provided another, albeit less violent, outlet for the collective frustrations of the Haitian people. Immediately after the fall of the Duvalier regime, the Frères Parent released their 1986 album *Operation deshoukaj* (Mishga Records 002), which featured the full side of a twelve-inch LP for their title track. Their denunciation of the Tonton Makout included a "score of Makout—zero, the Haitian people—double score!" as well as a forecast that departed dictator Jean-Claude Duvalier would not be welcomed in hell by the devil. Other artists used familiar Haitian images to urge their expatriate listeners to return to Haiti and help restructure the society. Carole Démesmin, a *vodou manbo* (female priest) and popular singer, released a song called "Tounen lakay" ("Come home," or "Return to the house") on her *Lawouzé* album, urging Haitians to return home for the rebuilding of the country. She sings, "N'ap bat tanbou jiska soley leve" (We'll hit the drum until the sun rises), referring to the anti-Duvalier movement Soley Leve of the early 1970s. The group Sakad's "Rebati kay-la" (Rebuild the house) also likens the Haitian state to a house badly in need of repair.

The *mini-djaz* and *konpa dirèk* styles of the 1960s and 1970s were augmented in the 1980s with the emergence of the music of the *nouvel jenerasyon* (new generation). Actually, the *nouvel jenerasyon* style was part of a long association between Haitian musicians and the more avant-garde sounds from American jazz. Gérald Merceron, a lawyer and self-taught musician, organized his own record company and produced several albums with the help of the musical director of Radio Métropole, Herby Widmaier. Calling their musical creations "la nouvelle musique haitienne" (the new Haitian music), Merceron and his friends Lionel Benjamin, Carole Démesmin, and Widmaier mixed several genres on their *Bokassa grotraka* album, including an arrangement of the Haitian folksong "L'Artibonite" for full orchestra. Merceron's experimentation with Brazilian, Central African, and American jazz and avant-garde styles set the stage for others to incorporate new sounds into the *mini-djaz*, dance-band format.

The *nouvel jenerasyon* sound is difficult to summarize, since it is more of an attitude toward music than a strict genre. Ralph Boncy, a Haitian poet and amateur musicologist, characterized the *nouvel jenerasyon* as a cultural movement and identified such attributes as the importance of *Kreyòl* names for Haitian musical groups, a return to the music of the countryside for inspiration, increased emphasis on the text as a literary product, and standardized song lengths. A good example of the *nouvel jenerasyon* sound is "Tout moun ale nan kanaval" (Everyone has gone to Carnival), a love duet in which Emeline Michel and her singing partner, Sidon, lament the loss of their relationship. The relaxed tempo and sparse instrumentation of this song is in marked contrast to the sometimes frenetic guitar and constant percussion drive of the *mini-djaz* sound:

Everyone has gone to Carnival.
I stay by myself, it's not too bad.
I don't want to go dance.
You know what I'm thinking about.[4]

VODOU-JAZZ TODAY

Although the word "*vodou*-jazz" was coined to describe the music of early bands such as Jazz des Jeunes, later bands used the formula of folkloric themes, *vodou*-influenced rhythms, and dancers to revitalize the *vodou*-jazz idiom. In the middle of the 1980s, the band Foula, under the direction of lead drummer Aboudja, fused American-influenced jazz and a battery of *vodou* drummers to create a new sound in *vodou*-jazz. After the fall of the Duvalier regime in 1986, several other groups joined the *vodou*-jazz scene, including Sanba Yo, Sakad, and, most recently, Boukman Eksperyans.

As we saw in the introduction to this chapter, the group Boukman Eksperyans is named for the slave leader who incited the slave insurrection in the late 1700s. The group, and especially its leader, Théodore "Lolo" Beaubrun, have been outspoken critics of the military regime, especially since the ouster in 1991 of President Jean-Bertrand Aristide, the first popularly elected Haitian president. Fusing *vodou* rhythms with politically critical lyrics, Boukman has been the target of government reprisals. The song "Jou nou revolte" (The day we revolt), from Boukman Eksperyans's 1992 album *Kalfou danjere* (Dangerous crossroads), both recalls the day Haitians revolted against oppression in the revolution against the French and foretells the revolution that is to come when the military is overthrown and Haiti's elected government is restored. Boukman's earlier album *Vodou adjae* contained fewer references to direct political action but emphasized the importance of maintaining the *vodou* heritage of Haiti; songs such as "Se kreyòl nou ye" (We're creole) ridiculed the Haitian elite's disdain for the country's national language, saying that "some Haitians would rather speak French, English, or Spanish than *Kreyòl*."

While *konpa, nouvel jenerasyon*, and *vodou*-jazz appeal to many Haitians young and old, there are several genres, particularly black American rap and Jamaican *raggamuffin* (or *ragga*), that have been adopted by younger Haitian singers. George "Master Dji" Lys Hérard, a Haitian *rapè* (rap artist), released his hit "Sispann" ("Stop," or "Suspend") as a call to end the political violence after the aborted election of 1987, in which Haitian voters were massacred at the polls on Rue Valliant in Port-au-Prince. Hérard's collaboration with other Haitian *rapè* on the album *Haiti: Rap and Ragga (Match la Rèd)* (The game is worse) intersperses the lover's style of rap, as in "Manmzèl" (Mademoiselle), with more politically charged music by other artists, such as "Conscience noire" (Black conscience) by Supa Denot and T-Bird.

The political lyrics of many new Haitian groups created some antagonism between the Haitian military junta and Haitian musical artists. While the official reason for his death has yet to be released, Master Dji was killed in Haiti in May 1994. Other artists, like Boukman Eksperyans, have been harassed by the Haitian military and put under constant scrutiny when they perform in their homeland. Given the importance of musical expression in a country where political freedoms have been so regularly denied to the people, Haitian music continues to be a vital outlet in the continued political struggle of Haitians.

MUSIC IN THE LESSER ANTILLES: MARTINIQUE, GUADELOUPE, DOMINICA, ST. LUCIA

The musical soundscape in the Lesser Antilles is similar to Haiti's, since both areas rely heavily on radio for the dissemination of local music.[5] All of the countries of the Lesser Antilles, including Martinique, Guadeloupe, Dominica, and St. Lucia, have Carnival traditions in which masked revelers take to the streets during the week before Mardi Gras. While foreign music like calypso and soca enjoy a brief popularity during the Carnival season, the islands of the Lesser Antilles have their own musical traditions that are enjoyed during the rest of the year. Local musical traditions include the *bélè* and *gwo ka* song-dances, which include drum accompaniment. These musical styles feature dancing and group singing, often led in a call-and-response format with a song leader. The quadrille, a ballroom dance similar to the Haitian *mereng*, is related to dances popular during the early colonial period. Despite the constrained dance movements and relatively static rhythmic patterns, the quadrille is valued as an important historical cultural artifact.

Unlike Haiti, which has been independent since 1804, two of the islands of the Lesser Antilles, Martinique and Guadeloupe, are *départements*, or states, of France. These islands, along with St. Lucia and Dominica, have predominantly black populations, descended from African slaves. St. Lucia and Dominica are independent and have a greater legacy of English colonialism; English is the language of state for both countries, but people on both islands speak French-based creole languages with a high degree of mutual intelligibility.

The musical styles of the four Antillian islands under consideration here are also mutually intelligible, due to the long process of musical cross-fertilization in the area. *Zouk*, the most recent product of Guadeloupe and Martinique, is popular throughout the region. According to ethnomusicologist Jocelyne Guilbault, *zouk* is a synthesis of several popular Caribbean musical styles including *biguine, cadence-lypso*, Haitian *konpa dirèk* and *kadans ranpa*, and several popular music styles from the United States.

A significant antecedent for *zouk* is *biguine*, a musical style from Guadeloupe and Martinique and a favorite among dance orchestras from the 1930s to the 1950s. The basic *biguine* rhythm, played on the maracas, is a variant of the *cinquillo* rhythm found in Haitian *mereng* and in the cymbal part of *konpa dirèk*. During the 1930s, *biguine* orchestras played for dances held in a variety of locations, including dance halls, church parties, birthday parties, and private affairs. During the 1940s and 1950s, as radio connected the islands of the Caribbean and touring musicians from other islands visited the Lesser Antilles, Guadeloupean dance bands absorbed aspects of Cuban *guaguancó*, Haitian *konpa dirèk* and *kadans ranpa*, and jazz from the United States.

Zouk also traces its ancestry to *cadence-lypso*, or *cadence*, the local dance music from Dominica. *Cadence* is popularly believed to be a fusion of the Haitian *kadans ranpa* and calypso from neighboring Trinidad and Tobago. Exile One, a Guadeloupe-based group that experimented with calypso fusion in the early 1970s, created a *cadence* calypso-influenced dance music that used *kwéyòl* lyrics. Like the politically inclined calypso, *cadence* lyrics often included social commentary on local events.

Zouk is still the most current popular music genre of the Lesser Antilles. Claiming its fundamental rhythmic organization from the *cinquillo*-based genres of *konpa dirèk*, *kadans ranpa*, and *biguine*, zouk has moved away from the big-band ensembles once popular in Guadeloupe and Martinique in favor of a sparer, more electronically influenced sound. Most successful *zouk* bands feature synthesizers, drum machines programmed to imitate such popular local percussion instruments as the *tibwa* (long sticks played on the rim of a drum or on a piece of bamboo), and digital samplers.

The first major *zouk* group to emerge was the Guadeloupe-based ensemble Kassav'. Deriving its name from cassava, the starchy root that is a part of the Antillean diet, Kassav' released its first album in 1979 and has continued to be a powerful force in the popular music scene in the Lesser Antilles. Kassav's lyrics are in *kwéyòl*, emphasizing the group's connection with their Antillean audience. The band also regularly features dancing as part of its live act to promote audience involvement.

In its 1985 hit "An-ba-chen'n la" (Under the chain), Kassav' sings of the importance of bringing its musical message to others and increasing outsiders' awareness of the Antilles and its people:

We must often leave our country
in order to bring our music to others.
I want everyone to know that the Antilles exists
and that it is love that commands us.[6]

Other popular *zouk* artists include Eric Virgal, known for his renditions of "*zouk* love" or the more romantic, slow-tempo ballad; Edith Lefel; and

Joelle Ursull, the first Antillean representative for France in the 1990 Eurovision contest. The group Malavoi performs *zouk* in addition to the older genres of *biguine* and quadrille and the foreign styles of merengue and rumba. While Malavoi shares its producer George Debs with Kassav', the group maintains an eclectic repertoire with an unusual array of acoustic instruments, including cello and violins.

With its increased visibility on the world-music market, *zouk* will likely evolve in different directions, selectively retaining aspects of Antillean identity while incorporating new sounds and technology. Maintaining a balance between its need for international and local appeal, *zouk* joins the long list of Caribbean musical genres that seek to keep their audiences dancing.

BIBLIOGRAPHY

Literature on *vodou* and its music includes Lois Wilcken (with Frisner Augustin), *Drums of Vodou* (Tempe, Ariz.: White Cliffs Media Company, 1992); Jean Price-Mars, *So Spoke the Uncle* (*Ainsi parla l'oncle* [1928]), trans. Magdaline Shannon (Washington, D.C.: Three Continents Press, 1983); Karen McCarthy Brown, *Mama Lola: A Vodou Priestess in Brooklyn* (Berkeley: University of California Press, 1991). For French Caribbean popular music, see Jocelyne Guilbaut, Gage Averill, Édouard Benoit, and Gregory Rabess, *Zouk: World Music in the West Indies* (Chicago: University of Chicago Press, 1993); Gage Averill, "Haitian Dance Bands, 1915–1970: Class, Race, and Authenticity," *Latin American Music Review* 10, 2 (1989); and "Haitian Dance Band Music: The Political Economy of Exuberance" (Ph.D. diss., University of Washington, Seattle, 1989). Other interesting publications include Jean Fouchard, *La Méringue: Danse nationale d'Haïti* (1955; reprint, Port-au-Prince: Éditions Henri Deschamps, 1988); and Ernst Mirville, *Considérations ethno-psychanalytiques sur le carnaval haitien* (Port-au-Prince: Collection Coucouille, 1978).

RECORDS

Boukman Eksperyans, *Vodou adjae* (Mango 162-539 889-2) and *Kalfou danjere* (Mango 162-539 972-2); Verna Gillis and Gage Averill eds., *Caribbean Revels*, (Smithsonian Folkways C-SF 40402); Carole Démesmin, *Lawouzé* (Shap 1003); Frères Parent, *Operation deshoukaj* (Mishga 002); various artists, *Konbit: Burning Rhythms of Haiti* (A & M CD 5281); various artists, *Haiti: Rap and Ragga (Match la rèd)* (Déclic Communication 319-2).

7

Jamaica

Jamaica is a land of many distinctions. Of all its remarkable contributions to our planet's cultural repertoire, none can compare with its music. In the space of a few short decades, this postcolonial island nation of some 2.5 million people, with all its economic woes, has accomplished a feat that few other countries (and then only major economic powers such as the United States and Great Britain) have been able to swing. Jamaica has conquered the world with its popular music.

Ask a college student almost anywhere in the world today, and he or she is likely to have some idea—even if only a superficial or distorted one—of what ska, reggae, dancehall, and *ragga* are. Jamaican popular music has gained the stature of a global musical currency, alongside jazz, blues, funk, and rock. In its rise to international fame and acceptance, reggae has traveled farther down the road of mass-market commodification than any other Caribbean music. As if to chastise rock fans and critics who once dismissed reggae as a monotonous, ethnic, ghetto music with limited appeal or the music industry analysts who time and again have forecast its demise, the familiar chugging Jamaican sound regularly issues from radios and television sets across the once reggae-resistant United States.

These days, high-powered advertising agencies use "the reggae beat," with or without references to its land of origin, to move products ranging from automobiles to toothpaste. Practically every bargain-basement Casio keyboard now comes factory-programmed with generic quasi-reggae rhythms. Music mega-stores like Tower Records devote entire sections to reggae, now recognized as an autonomous marketing "category" (whereas other Caribbean popular styles, such as *soca, zouk,* or merengue, are still generally relegated to the "international" or "world music" bins, alongside

---

Chapter 7 was written by Kenneth Bilby.

Finnish, Bulgarian, Indonesian, and other musical exotica). In the latest concession to the substantial inroads made by Jamaican popular music in the international pop marketplace, *Billboard* magazine began publishing a separate reggae chart in early 1994.

The international impact of Jamaican popular music has certainly not been limited to the sort of shallow commercial exploitation one has come to expect from the hype-drenched multinational music business. In complex and varying ways, reggae has been adopted by a wide range of local communities around the world—Hopi and Havasupai Indians in Arizona, Palenquero Maroons in Colombia, urban youths in Nigeria and South Africa, working-class skinheads in Britain, Maoris in New Zealand, and aboriginal Australians, to name a few—as an expression of something deeper than mere "entertainment." Some are moved by its spiritual values, others by its emphasis on pan-African identity or its expressions of class consciousness, and yet others by its message of universal liberation.[1]

Whatever its significance to those who listen to it outside of Jamaica, reggae's elevation to what *Billboard* magazine has called "one of the world's top pop music forms" has meant that there is no shortage of writing about it.[2] However, much of the available commentary on the subject comes filtered through a distant music consumer's lens. As one writer put it, "When you read books or articles about reggae . . . most of what you read is about what has become popular outside of Jamaica and generally ignores the Jamaican experience."[3] With notable exceptions, relatively little attention has been paid to that which makes the music uniquely Jamaican. Now that it has found a secure place in mainstream markets, reggae is often treated by the pop-music media as if the details of its emergence within a specific cultural context mattered little—as if this quintessentially Jamaican form of musical expression could be understood and fully appreciated with no more than passing reference to its specifically Jamaican background. Music critics who would not dream of paying attention to any of the huge variety of foreign musical styles still deemed "obscure" in the United States or Europe readily pass judgment on reggae recordings (whose lyrics they may not even understand), as if these were in the same category as the latest rock releases. The recent induction of Bob Marley into the Rock and Roll Hall of Fame— as if Jamaican popular music were just another fabrication of the modern North American entertainment mill—is perhaps symptomatic of the larger tendency to ignore the cultural specificity of reggae, now viewed matter-of-factly as an international pop music that can be defined, like any other, in terms of externally imposed marketing categories. (If Bob Marley were alive today, he might well ask why Stevie Wonder, Eric Clapton, or Tina Turner, all of whom have scored reggae-inflected hits, have not been "honored" with induction into the Reggae Hall of Fame. And how many exponents of other Caribbean styles are likely to end up anytime soon alongside Brother Bob in the "rock 'n' roll" pantheon?)

This is not to deny a long and close association between American pop music and reggae. The role of southern U.S. rhythm and blues in the development of modern Jamaican music is well known, and a good portion of Jamaica's prodigious musical output bears clear marks of North American influence. The influence of Jamaican music itself has been felt on U.S. shores as well for a long time now. By the mid-1980s, it was becoming hard to find major rock acts who had not delved at one time or another into reggae. Indeed, many observers agree that it was the early (if limited) success of reggae in "crossing over" that paved the way for the recent growth of a substantial world-music market in Europe and the United States. (Some readers will recall that more than a decade before heading for South Africa to record *Graceland*, Paul Simon had some success experimenting with reggae in Jamaican studios, where he recorded "Mother and Child Reunion.")

Clearly, the history of reggae is closely linked with that of recent North American and British pop and the manufactured marketing categories that have grown up alongside them. Nonetheless, the convention of treating reggae as a slightly exotic version of some dominant U.S. form, a kind of "upside-down rock 'n' roll" (as it has sometimes been characterized), obscures a great deal. Jamaican popular music is not simply an appendage of American (or American-derived British) popular music. Underneath the carefully crafted pop sheen of much of the island's exported music—not to mention the less-polished music produced for purely local consumption—lie deep and distinctive cultural wellsprings.

As reggae and its contemporary successor, dancehall music, expand their markets and become increasingly commodified, they also risk becoming further decontextualized and dispossessed of their unique Jamaican identity. It is partly for this reason that I have consciously chosen here to pay more attention than usual to the local traditional sources of Jamaican popular music—the "roots" so often invoked symbolically yet seldom actually discussed in writings on reggae. While acknowledging the importance of the continuing give-and-take between Jamaican and Euro-American pop, the perspective I advocate here gives greater weight to that side of the musical equation that has usually been glossed over: the vital indigenous component of what remains a living and evolving local Jamaican musical idiom. Despite the phenomenal spread of reggae beyond its birthplace and the growth of a global audience, most of the music produced in Jamaica today continues to speak primarily to local concerns and to draw on the rich fund of ancestral cultural resources that Jamaicans can claim as uniquely their own.

1976: TRAVELING THROUGH REGGAE'S "GOLDEN ERA"

Sitting at the dinner table across from me was an eminent patron of the arts, a grande dame known for her creative work in the local theater movement, which had been gaining ground since Jamaica's independence in 1962.

"I am a baan-ya," she told me in stilted patois, explaining that this was the Jamaican way of saying that she was a "born-here" person, a true native of the island. I could tell that she wanted to dispel any doubts that might have been raised by her European features and rather British-sounding accent; after all, she was about to assert her authority on matters Jamaican. I had started a polite conversation about the *Kumina* drumming one might hear on any given night in certain neighborhoods of Kingston but quickly found myself being corrected. *Kumina,* she informed me, was the last vestige of true African culture in Jamaica and was certainly not a feature of urban life. In fact, she said, it had nearly disappeared even in the remote country districts. Besides, *Kumina* was a ritual involving animal sacrifice, and such things were not permitted in town.

One reason this conversation has stuck in my memory is that it provided me with a striking lesson in the width of the gulf that separates "uptown" (the social and literal space inhabited by the economically privileged minority) and "downtown" (the realm of the huge majority of disenfranchised ghetto-dwellers) in Kingston and, by extension, in other parts of Jamaica. It is a social division that is fundamental to life in urban Jamaica, and nowhere is it more clearly reflected than in the history of Jamaican popular music.

The uptown cultural expert sitting across from me did not know that I had spent most of the night before at a *Kumina* ceremony in Hunts Bay, one of many impoverished, ramshackle neighborhoods in West Kingston—a downtown area that children of "respectable" Kingstonians are taught to avoid like the plague. There had been nothing unusual about the occasion; a member of the community who had died was being commemorated and was being asked for spiritual aid. What was out of the ordinary was that I, a foreigner, was present. The reason I was there was that the organizers of the *Kumina* ceremony had needed to find a way to transport a goat from the village of Freetown in distant Clarendon parish to Hunts Bay on sudden notice. Some *Kumina* drummers from Spanish Town, with whom I had

Kumina drummers, Spanish Town, Jamaica, 1975 (photo by Ken Bilby)

been studying, knew that I had a rented car and had tracked me down to ask for help.

I remember the drive well. We arrived in Freetown to find that another *Kumina* dance was already in progress there. As we approached, flecks of light came rippling through the slats of the bamboo dancing booth, and shadows played across the ground. Someone came and guided us into the booth, where we were served Red Stripe beers while one of my companions was invited to sit in on the drums. The music reminded me of a popular Ghanaian style called *kpanlogo,* but with a deeper, more resonant bass pattern, a rhythm like the beating of an excited heart, which I had been told was the spiritual root of *Kumina,* the "heart-string" connecting the living and the dead. The drummers were doing their work well; a man with a piece of red cloth tied around his head spun around with a few jerking steps and fell into a graceful dance between the drums. After a few moments, he approached me and took my hand, staring me in the eye and saying something totally unintelligible to me. "African language," some bystanders told me. "He's thanking you." Later, as we lowered the goat into the trunk, its hooves bound with rope, one of the drummers explained that the spirit of an "old African" had used the dancer's body to speak to me and offer thanks for the use of the car.

All the way to Spanish Town, the bleating of the goat in back made me uncomfortable. Someone suggested that we stop on the edge of the town for a drink before continuing on to Kingston, so we pulled up to a zinc fence with a small crowd of young men in front. Inside, the small makeshift bar was dwarfed by a massive bank of speaker boxes. The vibrations blasting out of them seemed to penetrate every fiber of my body. It was the loudest music I had ever heard—louder even than the overdriven Marshall amplifiers of a hard-rock concert, but with one main difference: the loudness was concentrated in the all-enveloping rumble of the bass rather than in the searing treble of live guitar-driven rock. The naked speaker cones jumped right out of the boxes at us, along with the words: "Jah live, children, yeah." Bob Marley's defiant answer to those who were ridiculing the Rastafarians by pointing to the death of their divinity, Ethiopian emperor Haile Selassie, had just been released, and the streets were buzzing with Rasta reaction. After all, how could God die?

Back in the car, the *Kumina* drummers rolled a couple of cone-shaped marijuana cigarettes, or "spliffs." While lighting up, one of them, Bongo Jack, told me, "Some people call the herb 'ganja,' but in the African Congo language we call it *diamba*. The Rastas have learned the truth that the old Africans always teach us, you know; it's the wisdom weed." The younger drummer sitting in back nodded his head in agreement. Emblazoned on his T-shirt was the silk-screened image of a wild-haired Bob Dylan in dark sunglasses.

My passengers warned me to stay alert and keep an eye out for Babylon; a police blockade might appear at any moment. Once again, Marley's trenchant lyrics captured the moment: his famous refrain "three o'clock roadblock" kept circling in my head. As we zoomed through Central Village, Jack pointed out the Spanish Town Cask and Drum Company on the left, where Rasta *kete* drums were made to order. We had just heard the sound of one of these drums, called the repeater, in Marley's "Jah Live." Jack explained that the Rasta repeater was "coming off the same root" as his own *Kumina* drum but was designed a little differently. In fact, he knew some other "Bongo men"—*Kumina* players—living in the Spanish Town area who liked the unique sound of the repeater drum and used it sometimes when playing for *Kumina* dances.

As we approached the outskirts of the capital, the smell of burning sugarcane came wafting into the car. The night sky ahead glowed an ominous red. It was January, and national elections were around the corner. The political violence was escalating, and everyone and everything seemed to be on edge, especially in war-torn West Kingston. My guides made sure that I made no wrong turns, for our destination was only a few blocks away from a section of the city that had been reduced to cinders a couple of days before, the latest casualty to the wave of political terror sweeping over West Kingston. Here we were, only a few miles from uptown Kingston, yet we were worlds apart.

We turned a corner and pulled into a yard. There we were met by a couple of "gatekeepers," who guided us into a partially hidden recess where the car would be safe. Once the goat was out of the trunk and in the right hands, we were led through an opening in a zinc fence into the yard where the *Kumina* was being held. At least two hundred people were present, all of them strangers to me. Several did not remain strangers for long, though. Every few minutes a new person would come up and introduce himself or herself, telling me to feel welcome and not to be afraid; for although these were "dread" times in West Kingston, I had nothing to worry about—I was fully "protected" here at the *Kumina*. It was, I realized, a major ceremony. Friends and relatives from all over the eastern part of the island had come together to do their part. One man introduced himself to me as a Maroon from a community in the Blue Mountains, where descendants of escaped slaves had maintained their own culture and identity. Maroons and *Kumina* people, he said, were from "different nations." He told me to enjoy the *Kumina,* and suggested that I visit his village in the hills if I wanted to hear Maroon music, which, he said, was even "deeper" than *Kumina*.[4]

The feeling of harmony within the *Kumina* yard was underscored by the music. Early in the evening, a large group, mostly women, congregated over on the side to sing "Sankeys" (a term applied by Jamaicans to a large variety of hymns, some of which were learned from the popular nineteenth-century hymnal published by the evangelist Ira David Sankey). The performance was loosely organized, with people coming and going as they pleased. Yet it held together nicely. Everybody seemed to know the words by heart, and many showed an uncanny ability to improvise individual melodic parts that somehow managed always to become woven together into a rich harmonic fabric. The sound was clearly derived from Protestant hymnody, but the performance style was wholly unlike the hymn singing found in most European or North American churches. People sang at the tops of their voices, swayed their bodies to the mellifluous rhythm, gesticulated, leaned on one another's shoulders. Several of the singers stopped from time to time to take a swig of *kulu-kulu,* the raw, overproof white rum that was being passed around.

Before long, the impromptu choir was singing psalms. A woman had worked her way out front, Holy Bible in hand, and the gathering was now "tracking" along with her. As the song leader read out the text, one line at a time, the others repeated after her in a complex, polyphonic chorus. The improvised melodic parts snaked over and under one another, creating surprising harmonies and dissonances. The anthropologist in me told me that this particular kind of call-and-response singing, though clearly traceable to the tradition of "lining out" psalms that first became established in seventeenth-century rural Britain, was also fully compatible with the antiphonal style of music making brought by enslaved Africans to Jamaica. This was not just an idle thought, for I was well aware that Rastafarians sometimes performed hymns and psalms in the exact same way as this at their own ceremonies, which they called *nyabinghi*, viewing them as an expression of their African identity. I was also aware that the Afro-Protestant musical heritage of which this tradition was a part had made a major contribution to Jamaican popular music through Rastafarian reggae and other channels.

There was no doubt whatsoever about the African origins of the drumming that was now picking up momentum in the center of the yard. The three drummers were seated on their instruments, which were turned on their sides. Two of them played rock steadily, keeping to a single, unvarying heartbeat pattern. On top of this, the lead drummer created excitement with skillful improvisations. All of the drummers used their heels against the skins to vary the pitch.

Next to them was a "center pole," through which certain spirits, summoned by the drums, could travel on their way to the bodies of the dancers they chose to possess. Around this center, a ring of dancers slowly rotated with a gentle counterclockwise motion. Throughout the night, this circle continued revolving in time, contracting or expanding as dancers left and were replaced by others. The combination of sound and motion was subtle and beautiful. Even when the drumming became especially hot, lifting the excitement to a new peak, the dancing remained cool, graceful, disciplined, with only an occasional disruption whenever one of the dancers' bodies, suddenly seized by a visiting spirit, was thrown temporarily into convulsions.

As daybreak neared, the goat made its final appearance, borne on the shoulders of one of the drummers who had accompanied me on the journey from Clarendon. Moving into the ring, the man danced the goat several revolutions around the center pole, waving a machete in his hand. The air was filled with one of the "African country" songs of *Kumina:*

> tangalanga mama gyal yu kalunga
>   tangalanga besi-oo kalunga
> tangalanga besi mama kalunga
>   tangalanga besi-oo kalunga

With no warning, the man stepped inside the ring and placed the goat on the ground. For a minute or two, the animal lay still on its side, while the man rejoined the moving circle. And then, as the ring came around one more time, it happened in a split second: the goat suddenly stretched out its neck. Without missing a beat, the dancer spun around and brought the blade down, severing the head with a single blow.

To the east, the angry hue of the Kingston night was giving way to a blood-red dawn. Within a few hours, the sleepless maids and construction workers would be back on the job, while their unemployed friends and relatives, as usual, would be wandering the streets and gutters in search of a meal; and uptown Kingston would be none the wiser.

MUSIC INA DOWNTOWN STYLE:
RECORDING THE UNRECORDED

The Rastafarian brethren have a saying: "The half has never been told." This seems particularly true of Jamaica's musical history. Indeed, there is reason to believe that the story of Jamaican popular music will never be told in its entirety. This is not only because of the difficulty of teasing out the diverse strands that contributed to the music's early development but because of the unusual fluidity and complexity of the social milieu in which it emerged. During the decades leading up to the 1960s, when the seeds of Jamaica's indigenous popular music were being planted, West Kingston was a new and rapidly expanding urban fringe made up of migrants from various parts of the island. Recently arrived from "country," these sons and daughters of peasants—among them, the poorest of the poor and the least schooled of Jamaica's unlettered masses—were seen as scarcely worthy of the attention of those in a position to record in print the latest trends in Jamaica's social and cultural life. Yet it was they who laid the foundations of what was to become a thriving urban musical culture.

Located at the interface of the rural and the urban, the "traditional" and the "modern," many of those who made important contributions to Jamaica's emerging popular music did so anonymously, in the course of their daily lives. The paths of musical influence were often convoluted and indirect, products of the innumerable musical encounters, both planned and spontaneous, that formed part of everyday social life in Jamaica's new urban spaces. Whether at church, in dance halls, at *buru* gatherings, in *Kumina* yards, or in any number of other musical contexts, these ordinary Jamaicans, possessing little or no formal musical training, regularly made music that fulfilled a variety of social functions. For them, the act of making music was enmeshed in community life. As humble practitioners of rural folk musical traditions transplanted to the city, most of these individuals went unheralded, and most of them are probably destined to remain unknown. Nonetheless, their voices echo down to us in the present.

As ethnomusicologist Robert Witmer wrote, "Without hypothesizing the existence in Jamaica of a rich and vibrant—but almost entirely undocumented—Afro-Jamaican folk or traditional music culture running parallel to the [pre-1960] mainstream urban popular music culture whose history is documented . . . the rise of distinctive indigenous Jamaican popular music in the 1960s remains inexplicable."[5] The older musical languages that were available in West Kingston during the formative period of Jamaica's urban musical culture were many. Neo-African drumming traditions, some of them going back to the ceremonial and social dances held on slave plantations during the eighteenth and nineteenth centuries, had survived in several parts of the island. Among these were the *etu, tambu,* and *gumbe* traditions, concentrated in the western part of the island, and the *buru* tradition, found primarily in the central parishes of Clarendon and St. Catherine. Like *Kumina* drumming, some of these neo-African styles were tied to African-derived forms of religious worship. Most of them employed an ensemble of two or three drums, one of which led with improvisations while the others provided supporting rhythms, and an assortment of percussion instruments such as rattles and scrapers. European influence was almost absent from these styles.

Much more widespread than these surviving neo-African forms were the musical expressions of Jamaica's hundreds of rural Afro-Protestant churches and sects, most of them variants of the general form of worship known in Jamaica as *Pocomania* (sometimes spelled *Pukkumina*), or "Revival." These indigenous religions were forged out of the nineteenth-century encounter between the religious concepts brought to Jamaica by enslaved Africans and the teachings of European missionaries. Like their religious practices, which included possession by both ancestral and biblical spirits, the music of these groups blended African and European influences. Many Revivalists used a combination of two or three drums—one or more "side drums" played with sticks (often equipped with a homemade snare) and a bass drum played with a padded beater—to accompany their singing. Sometimes other percussion instruments and hand clapping were employed as well. While the melodic style of many Revivalist hymns, such as the ubiquitous "Sankeys," was European-derived, some songs were of more mixed derivation, and certain other features of the music, such as the drumming and the form of rhythmic breathing known as "groaning" or "sounding," betrayed a clear African influence.

These *Poco* or Revival churches were scattered across the island. Over time, they spread to the larger towns and cities, and today they remain a force to be reckoned with not only in the Jamaican countryside but in poorer urban neighborhoods.

Not all of the older musical traditions available to Jamaicans during this period were religious. Before the 1950s, the closest thing to an indigenous popular music in Jamaica was the mento. Though its exact origins are obscure, it is clear that the mento was born of a creolizing process that blended elements of a variety of European social-dance musics with African-derived stylistic features. Varieties of European-derived ballroom dances such as the quadrille, the lancer, and the mazurka were popular in Jamaica both during and after the era of slavery, and the instrumentation, harmonic structures, and melodic contours that typified them contributed much to the music played by village bands across the island until recent times. To the fiddles, flutes, and guitars of these rural bands were added banjos, rhumba boxes (bass instruments with plucked metal lamellae), drums, rattles, scrapers, and other instruments wholly or partly of African origin. This creole social-dance music, originally more European-sounding, eventually acquired a new rhythmic feel, due to the African-derived aesthetic preferences of the musicians who played it.

It is not clear exactly how and when the mento emerged from this background, but its linkage with these older, creolized European dance styles can still be heard in the common practice of replacing the fifth (or sometimes sixth) figure at quadrille dances with a *mento* (sometimes called a "round dance"). By the 1940s, the term mento had already come to embrace a fair amount of variation. Mento could be performed by ensembles consisting of little more than a harmonica and a few percussion instruments, by rural string bands featuring banjo and guitar, or even by larger orchestras that included piano, trap drums, and a brass section. The musical style called mento had also long been associated with a genre of topical songs reminiscent of other Caribbean styles, such as calypso. Indeed, by the 1940s, mento was already being influenced by Trinidadian calypso (and was itself exerting an influence on the music of the other islands). Cuban influence is also suggested by the frequent use in mento of what is called a "rhumba box" in Jamaica, as well as the fact that in some rural parts of the island, the words "mento" and "rhumba" are used interchangeably to refer to the same musical style. (The Cuban style known as the *son* was often mistakenly called "rumba" in English-speaking countries; in its original rural form, played in the eastern part of Cuba, the *son* sounds rather similar to mento as played by Jamaican string bands, making use of similar instrumentation, including what Cubans call *marimbula*—the same bass *mbira*, or so-called thumb piano, known as rhumba box by Jamaicans.)

Add to these musical forms several kinds of work songs used to accompany a wide variety of chores in rural Jamaica, and the list of potential musical resources expands. Nor does the list end there; we must not forget the fife-and-drum music, of mixed African and European parentage, associated with the masked dance known as *jonkonnu* (or "john canoe") in most parts of the island. And the list goes on; a host of other, lesser-known musical traditions could be cited. Some of these, such as the "digging songs" used in cultivating and planting crops or the "ring-game" songs used for rural entertainment, have long been leaving their mark on mento. In fact, certain songs commonly performed as mentos today actually originated as digging songs or ring-game tunes.

This ongoing tendency to absorb songs, melodies, and other stylistic elements from a variety of sources helped to make mento a sort of generic Jamaican folk music—a kind of synthesis of Jamaica's varied traditional musics. Over time, it became the closest thing to a Jamaican "national" music, known and appreciated across the island. Unlike many of the other forms mentioned here, mento had no special association with any particular community, region, religion, or social group within Jamaica (though it continued to be identified with its rural Jamaican roots). As a musical form capable of speaking to those who were flowing into the capital city from all over the island, mento was well positioned to serve as the basis of Jamaica's first wave of indigenous popular musical expression.

Following the Second World War, the nightclubs of downtown Kingston were driven by the music of dance orchestras, or "road bands," modeled in part on the African-American big bands of the United States. Jamaican bandleaders and musicians such as Val Bennett, Sonny Bradshaw, Roy Coburn, Redver Cook, Eric Deans, Wilton Gaynair, Bertie King, Milt McPherson, Baba Motta, George Moxey, and Luther Williams presided over a steady diet of North American jazz and "swing" standards, supplemented by an occasional Cuban number. Other Caribbean styles, such as merengue and calypso, were also popular on the dance floors. Jamaica's own mento, however, was viewed with a certain ambivalence by these pioneering urban dance bands. Some looked down on it as "coming from country" and dismissed it as "unsophisticated"; others performed it with relish. Regardless of how they viewed the style, almost all bands featured at least an occasional mento to satisfy audience demand.

In contrast to these new dance bands, the older guitar-and-banjo mento bands that could also be found in the environs of Kingston at the time seemed to be on the wane. Some of them, however, found new life performing in tourist venues, where they often presented themselves as "calypsonians" in an attempt to benefit from the popularity then enjoyed by the somewhat similar Trinidadian calypso. Despite this misleading use of language, most Jamaican "calypsonians" were really mento singers who continued to perform in the indigenous Jamaican style.

When a businessman named Stanley Motta opened the first commercial recording venture in Kingston in the late 1940s, mento was the kind of music that caught his attention. Thus it was that the first local popular music that began to circulate on record was a form of mento that, though somewhat urbanized and occasionally featuring new instruments such as piano and traps, remained for the most part very close to its rural roots. Among the mento bands and singers who made records and received some radio play during this era were Laurel Aitken (later to achieve fame as a ska singer), Baba Motta, Bedasse Calypso Quintet, Count Lasher, Lord Composer, Lord Flea, Lord Fly, Lord La Rue, Lord Messam, Lord Tanamo, Lord Power, Hubert Porter, Reynolds Calypso Clippers, and Harold Richardson and the Ticklers. Like the rural mento tradition from which their music was derived, these artists' recordings sometimes contained social commentary, but more often they consisted of reworkings of older digging songs or ring-play tunes. A portion of their output also reflected the increased emphasis on bawdy or suggestive lyrics acquired by mento in the context of urban clubs, where the pelvic-centered dance movements associated with the style had become more pronounced and had taken on a more erotic cast.

These early efforts at recording mento were soon overshadowed, in the later 1950s, by a new phenomenon, the "sound system," which would play a crucial role in Jamaican popular music over the next few decades; indeed, it continues to play a vital role even today.

In neighborhoods with limited financial resources, live dance bands were seldom affordable. The advent of increasingly powerful audio systems provided a solution: the owner of a set consisting of little more than a turntable, a few heavy-duty speaker cabinets, and a souped-up amplifier or two could now produce sufficient volume to draw large crowds to yard parties and "blues dances" and keep them dancing through the night. By the late

1950s, such sound systems were proliferating in downtown Kingston. Two of the early operators most often mentioned in accounts of this period are Clement "Coxsone" Dodd (whose system was known as Sir Coxsone's Downbeat) and Duke Reid (known as The Trojan). Although these two stand out for the tremendous influence they had and for their longevity, literally dozens of lesser-known sound systems—sporting evocative names such as Admiral Cosmic, Count John the Lion, and Count Piah the Bluesblaster—operated in the metropolitan area in the early days. These systems played what their urban patrons wanted to hear: the hot African-American rhythm and blues then reigning in the United States, with special preference shown for the New Orleans sound. But most of them made room for a certain amount of variety, spinning an occasional Cuban dance number, perhaps, or a calypso, and almost all of them played at least some mento records. The many competing sound systems at this time also included a number of mobile sets that toured rural areas and catered to more traditional tastes, and these tended to play a larger proportion of mento tunes.

A major impetus for the development of a local recording industry came when North American rhythm and blues began to take a new direction toward the end of the decade, so that it became increasingly difficult for sound-system operators to import U.S. recordings in the styles favored by Jamaicans. In this fiercely competitive world of small entrepreneurs, the ability to obtain exclusive copies of "hot" records and to keep them out of the hands of other operators could make or break a sound system. To offset the dwindling supply of records from the United States in the preferred style, some sound-system operators invested in basic recording equipment and began pressing records of local artists performing rhythm and blues. Two of the most important recording studios in the history of Jamaican popular music, Clement Dodd's Studio One and Duke Reid's Treasure Isle, got their start in this way, as did a number of others.

Before long, these local recordings were displaying subtle evidence of stylistic change; Jamaican rhythm and blues music was beginning to differ, though only slightly, from its North American counterpart. All of these circumstances—increasing rural–urban migration, the growing popularity of sound systems, the birth of a local recording industry, and the growth of a Jamaican style of rhythm and blues, increasingly taking on a sound of its own—coincided with a unique and critical period in Jamaican history. The Federation of the West Indies, to which Jamaica had belonged since 1958, was disintegrating, and Jamaica was on the verge of political independence, which was finally achieved in 1962. The prevailing mood of nationalistic pride had the effect of encouraging—at least, in the arts—an increasing openness toward indigenous cultural expressions and stimulated a certain amount of conscious musical experimentation with rural folk forms. It was in this general climate that Jamaica's first truly new and distinctive form of urban popular music, known as ska, emerged.

Most observers agree that the style that came to be known as "ska" developed gradually, as Jamaican studio musicians began to alter the basic rhythmic structure of the U.S. rhythm and blues music that they were accustomed to playing. This process of modification continued imperceptibly for some time, until eventually it could be said that a new, distinctively Jamaican style had come into being. But here the consensus ends. Precisely because this emergent popular music was a product primarily of downtown musicians, producers, and audiences, beyond the pale of "respectable" uptown society, the circumstances of its genesis were not carefully documented by the local media; in fact, they were hardly documented at all, and today we are left with little more than the recordings themselves and the testimonies of those who participated in their making. As a result, there is a good deal of controversy and sometimes even acrimonious debate over the question of origins.

Every so often, musicians or producers "who were there at the time" come forward with claims regarding some pivotal change in the music that they or other individuals are supposed to have instigated. Sometimes these claims carry the implication that the birth of an entire new style, such as ska or reggae, must be credited to a single innovation or musical contribution. At the same time, music critics and scholars, faced with sketchy and ambiguous sources, often argue solely on the basis of formal resemblances to preexisting styles for the primacy of one or another influence in the development of Jamaican popular music. Thus some have taken the position that reggae, apart from the rhythm and blues contribution, is derived essentially from mento; others that it owes most to Revival or other Afro-Jamaican cult rhythms; and yet others that it can be traced to *jonkonnu* music, or even to the military drumming to which some of the key studio musicians had earlier been exposed while attending school or serving in the Anglo-Jamaican army.

The problem with such competing claims, aside from the fact that it is virtually impossible to prove or disprove them, is that they presume a simple, linear path of development from a single, original Jamaican source, with each new "stage" of the music (such as rock steady, reggae, or dancehall) representing a stylistically uniform extension or outgrowth of the one that preceded it; throughout all the stages, the influence of the main, original source is supposed to have remained predominant. But Jamaican popular music has evolved in a considerably more disorderly manner than this and has always been stylistically more heterogeneous and complex than such a view would suggest. In fact, if one allows for the possibility of constant, multiple influences from a variety of traditional Jamaican sources, varying in importance over time, then all of the arguments for different origins could be said to have some validity. Indeed, I would argue—as a number of others have—that the urban popular music of Jamaica, like mento before it, represents nothing less than a synthesis of many diverse stylistic influences, both Jamaican and foreign, the balance of which has continued to shift over time.

From this perspective, it is pointless to debate, for instance, whether the characteristic driving rhythm played by horns and other instruments in ska (and apparently carried over to the guitar and piano in much reggae) is derived from the hand clapping of Revival churches, the beat of the time-keeping Rastafarian *funde* drum (in one particular early style of *nyabinghi* drumming), or the strumming of the banjo in mento, all of which display a similar emphasis on the offbeat. Even if the first appearance of this feature in recorded Jamaican popular music could be pinpointed to a particular session and the musicians who participated could explicate its actual origin, the fact would remain that studio musicians in the years ahead, with varied personal exposure to traditional musical contexts and styles, might recognize in this same feature the echo of a Revival clap, a *nyabinghi* beat, or a mento strum and might be moved by an intuitive sense of connection to modify their playing in the direction of one or another of these styles or to introduce other traditional features that they felt to be compatible with what they were hearing. In this way, the music would remain open to stylistic influences from traditional sources, some of which might result more from a kind of organic "osmosis" than from conscious intent.

There is no doubt that local studio musicians have brought to Jamaican recording sessions a wealth of varied musical experience. Consider, for example, the Skatalites, a seminal dance band during the ska era, whose members doubled as studio musicians and can be heard playing on some of the most influential Jamaican recordings released during the early 1960s (as well as earlier recordings, made when many of them were part of the legendary band Clue J and the Blues Blasters). Most of these superb musicians received formal training at the Alpha Boys School, an orphanage and home for the underprivileged in depressed West Kingston, where they and many other prominent local artists learned the rudiments of European classical music, jazz, and marching music and discovered the joys of brass-ensemble playing. All of these influential players were also well versed in U.S. rhythm and blues, as they had to be to survive as session musicians during the period leading up to the birth of ska.

But their exposure to traditional or folk music varied considerably. Trumpeter Johnny "Dizzy" Moore, for instance, claims that rather than any of the traditional Jamaican styles, it was the European "martial" drumming he encountered during his time at Alpha and later in the army that had the strongest influence on his playing and that it was this that led to the development of the ska "beat."[6] In contrast, tenor saxophonist and fellow Alpha alumnus Tommy McCook recalls making regular visits to the camp of Rastafarian master drummer Count Ossie (Oswald Williams), beginning in the late 1940s, where he would often sing along with the Rasta chants and would sometimes jam on saxophone with the drummers. This experience made a profound impression on him, and he cites it as an important influence on the new music that he and his fellow band members created together.[7] Other Skatalites, such as trombonists Don Drummond and Rico Rodriguez and saxophonist Roland Alphonso, also came under the influence of Count Ossie. In contrast, one of the Skatalites' vocalists, Lord Tanamo, was a well-known mento singer, whose recordings in that style circulated around Kingston long before the advent of ska. Clearly, if one were to poll a larger number of early Jamaican studio musicians or to probe in greater depth, a yet broader range of experience would come to light, and a number of other opinions regarding sources would doubtless emerge.

What seems certain is that much of the background of Jamaica's first great burst of popular musical activity remains partially hidden, and this has helped to obscure the extent to which "country"—as Kingstonians somewhat condescendingly call rural Jamaica—contributed to the mix. It is equally certain that the lack of interest on the part of local writers and critics during the early period can be explained by the fact that urban popular music in Jamaica represented, as it still does, the voice of "downtown," that is, the impoverished masses of shantytown dwellers recently transplanted from country to town. In recording the unrecorded, Jamaica's early record producers did much to amplify this previously unheard voice but left the documentation and analysis of the various musical idioms on which it drew to others. Thus much of "the half that has never been told" remains untold to this day.

KUMINA INA TRENCH TOWN STYLE: ONE THREAD OUT OF MANY

The thread we are about to trace actually extends back at least to the 1930s, when Leonard Percival Howell, the original and most influential prophet of Rastafari, while preaching in rural St. Thomas Parish decided to incorporate the Congo-based drumming, songs, and ritual language of the local *Kumina* religion into his vision of Ethiopian divinity.[8] By the time we pick up the thread in the 1950s, more than a decade has passed since Howell and his followers adopted *Kumina* and transformed it into the liturgical music of their Rastafarian faith. The date is December 7, 1953, and it is only a matter of months before Howell's notorious Rasta commune, Pinnacle, nestled in the hills above Spanish Town, will be broken up once and for all by Jamaican police, forcing the displaced Howellite Rastas to take shelter in the Kingston ghettos and other parts unknown.

We find ourselves in a dusty compound, tucked away in the bowels of Trench Town, one of West Kingston's worst slums; only a few blocks away is the tenement yard that will become the home of a twelve-year-old boy from "country" named Robert Nesta Marley some four years from now. This is the neighborhood in which the future "King of Reggae" will spend his adolescence and early adulthood, later to be immortalized in his 1971 song "Trench Town Rock" and again in his more recent tribute "Trench Town":

> We come from Trench Town.
> They say can anything good come out of Trench Town? . . .
> [They] say we're the underprivileged people so they keep us in chains.
> Pay tribute to Trench Town.[9]

An impromptu musical gathering is taking place. Two young men sit facing each other, each grasping a small drum between his knees. The two instruments are similar: both are made from small kegs held together by staves, and each has a single head attached by metal rods. Sitting to the side is another young man, whose face is almost eclipsed by the large, double-headed bass drum resting on his lap. Dreadlocks are nowhere to be seen in the yard, and there is nothing else to suggest that any of these musicians might be Rastafarian.

A small crowd of men, women, and children surrounds the ensemble. The sounds the musicians coax from the skins have the audience transfixed. The two drummers in front play with their hands. One plays a simple, unvarying pattern on the offbeat—a muffled double pulse reminiscent of a heartbeat (see also Example 15):

$$|: .. X X | .. X X :|$$

The bass drummer brings his padded stick down on the first beat of each of these double pulses, varying the timbre by alternating between closed and open strokes. The remaining drummer takes the lead, punctuating and embellishing the steady rhythm laid down by the other two with a rapid-fire barrage of rim pops and heavily accented slaps. Every once in a while the bass drummer departs from his fixed pattern, unleashing a brief but thunderous torrent of complex counterrhythms before settling back into his place in the background. Two other men standing on the sidelines play a scraper and a pair of rattles, adding to the rhythmic complexity.

MUSICAL EXAMPLE 15

A woman and one or two men from the surrounding crowd join the drummers in a song:

When my pilot come I'll take an aeroplane ride,
I will be so happy with the King right by my side.
A house is not a home without the Lord inside.
When my pilot come I'll take an aeroplane ride.

Everyone knows this as a Revival song. It is sung in *Poco* churches all over West Kingston. But it is no longer the exclusive property of Revivalists. Indeed, later in the evening, right around the corner from here, young Rastafarians belonging to the United Afro–West Indian Federation will sing their own version of the same song when holding their own meeting.

The drummers pick up the pace a bit and launch into another song. It is hard to make out the words, but we can pick up a few lines:

I am a warrior, out in the field.
I can say, I can show,
I can tell it all about . . .
when I get over yonder in that happy paradise,
when I get over yonder in that field.

After a few more songs, followed by some hot improvisation on the drums, it is time to wind down. Before packing up, the drummers explain that the music they play is called *kumina*. Unlike the *Kumina* played in rural areas, however, it has no connection with death ceremonies. Rather, it is played in a variety of nonreligious contexts, such as major gambling games, Emancipation Day observances, or celebrations marking the release of fellow ghetto dwellers from prison. An even more striking difference, to one who is familiar with the *Kumina* religion in rural areas, is that the drums used by this group are not the kind that one would expect to see at a *Kumina* ceremony but, rather, a modified version of the ensemble used in the secular drumming style called *buru* in St. Catherine and Clarendon. Although they are held in the same position as the *buru* drums, the rhythms are not those of *buru;* nor are they quite the same as those of rural *Kumina* drummers, although the rhythmic foundation of this urban *kumina* music— the repeating double pulse played on one of the drums—is essentially the standard "heartbeat" pattern of the traditional *Kumina bandu,* or bass drum, shifted to the offbeat, or "afterbeat," while the "rolling" and "cutting" of the lead drum clearly resembles that of the *Kumina* lead drum, called the *playing kyas.*

What we have encountered here is a newly invented neo-African music born on the urban fringe. Recognizable neither as pure *Kumina* (the older style from which it took its name) nor *buru* (the style from which it took its instruments), it is a blend of the two, to which yet other elements, such as Revival songs and melodies, have freely been added.

With hindsight, we can say that this originally non-Rastafarian urban musical blend, called *kumina* back in 1953, lives on in the Rasta drumming of Count Ossie—one of the creators of Rastafarian *nyabinghi* music as we know it today—and in the playing of those drummers whom he influenced or personally trained before his death in 1976. As can be heard on several of his classic 1970s recordings with the Mystic Revelation of Rastafari, Count Ossie and his drummers frequently played an offbeat variant of *nyabinghi*

Urban *kumina* musicians in Trench Town, West Kingston, Jamaica, 1953 (George Eaton Simpson)

drumming that is almost identical in sound to the *kumina* drumming that could be heard in Trench Town in 1953. There can be little doubt that this highly influential master drummer, responsible for introducing so many of Jamaica's top studio musicians to traditional Rastafarian drumming, picked up the basic elements of this new, urban *kumina* style while roaming the alleyways of West Kingston in search of musical inspiration during the late 1940s and early 1950s and then elaborated and made them his own. Among those whom Count Ossie encountered during his early quest for African musical roots were the *Kumina*-playing Howellites who began flowing into the shantytowns of the capital in increasing numbers after the closing of their rural commune in 1954. These old-line Rastas doubtless reinforced the rural *Kumina* influence in the new, urban musical stew then simmering in West Kingston, which would eventually be carried back to Rasta camps in the hills and become known as *nyabinghi* music.

It was this same urban style of *kumina* drumming that, after having been claimed by Rastas, made a major impact on the Jamaican popular music scene while the local recording industry was still in its infancy. By the late 1950s, Count Ossie and his drummers were already making public appearances at a number of venues in Kingston. In 1959, a young resident of Trench Town named John Folkes invited Ossie and his group to contribute to a historic recording session. Produced by Prince Buster, the session yielded a stunning recording of a rhythm-and-blues composition by Folkes titled "Oh Carolina." One of the first songs ever recorded in the studios of the Jamaica Broadcasting Corporation, "Oh Carolina" turned out to be a smash hit, partly because of the novelty of hearing Rasta drums and percussion grafted onto a proto-ska rhythm-and-blues beat. Most Jamaicans did not know it, but what they were hearing was an urban *kumina* rhythm. More than three decades later, the offbeat double pulse of Count Ossie's *funde* drum in "Oh Carolina"—an unmistakable echo of the sound that enlivened Trench Town gatherings in the early 1950s—still jumps out at the listener, presaging what Jamaican musicians call the *skengay* (the rhythm guitar "afterbeat" that was soon to become a defining feature of reggae).

Today, it is generally acknowledged that "Oh Carolina" is one of the most influential recordings in the history of Jamaican popular music. It would be easy to overlook the submerged thread that connects it to the musical event of 1953 reconstructed above. Yet there is no reason to believe that events like this were unusual in Trench Town and the surrounding areas, even if we lack records of their occurrence. The only reason we know of this particular *kumina* session is that a lone anthropologist named George Eaton Simpson, who was in West Kingston making a study of Revival churches at the time, happened to be present when it was taking place. Had Simpson not brought along a tape recorder and camera, this musical event, like others of its kind, would have remained entirely undocumented.[10] It is a sobering thought for those of us who would like to know more about the origins of a music whose makers lived their lives largely beyond the view of the "polite," uptown society that controlled the media and almost everything else of value in this colonial setting.

ROOTS AND CULTURE:
DOWNTOWN TRIUMPHANT

One mass medium that the privileged classes in Jamaica did not control was the 45 rpm record. Emerging from the downtown sound-system culture, the local recording industry quickly took on a life of its own. Not surprisingly, local producers aimed for the largest record-buying market, and in Jamaica, this meant the struggling masses of ordinary citizens. For once, Jamaica found itself with a major means of cultural production and dissemination over which the local elite could exercise only limited control.

It was not long after the appearance of ska that popular music in Jamaica began to reflect the social tensions caused by the glaring divisions between downtown and uptown. These were a product of both economic and cultural disparities: uptown society, which constituted but a tiny percentage of the total population, possessed a huge proportion of Jamaica's material wealth; at the same time, its members were oriented culturally toward the outside, particularly England and the United States, and tended to regard anything of local origin as inferior, especially anything produced by black, lower-class urbanites.

The first major expression of proletarian consciousness in Jamaican popular song centered on the theme of the "rude boy," the rebellious urban youth whose response to squalid living conditions was petty crime, violence, and a boastful, aggressive stance. This era spanned the late ska, rocksteady, and early reggae periods (roughly 1965–1969). These musical phases were themselves a manifestation of major changes taking place in Jamaican society, which popular music was both reflecting and helping to foster.

Along with the postindependence search for a national identity came the growing feeling that Jamaicans should return to their roots for inspiration. Although recordings in the transitional rock-steady style (circa 1966–1968) continued to draw heavily on North American soul music, the underlying rhythm had become more distinctively Jamaican, less clearly related to rhythm and blues. By 1968, when reggae proper became established on the scene, indigenous influences were becoming yet stronger, partly as a result of social currents in the larger society. Class consciousness was converging with increasing cultural assertiveness. The popular expression "roots" came to refer as much to the downtown ghetto experience of suffering and struggle as to the African sources of Jamaican culture. Linked to this trend was the rapid growth of the Rastafarian movement, especially among poor urban youth. By the 1970s, the Rasta emphasis on African roots, black redemption, and social awareness had become the dominant force in Jamaican popular culture.

The voice of the downtown "sufferer" now came to the fore. Reggae recordings regularly and openly protested the gap between rich and poor. In 1976, Max Romeo epitomized this class tension in a reggae song that told of how "uptown babies don't cry, they don't know what suffering is like."[11] His was but one of hundreds of songs treating the theme of social injustice during this era, many of them from a Rastafarian perspective. When Bob Marley, on the brink of international fame, sang, "Dem belly full, but we hungry,"[12] those living uptown had no choice but to listen.

The merging of Rastafarian consciousness with reggae led to one of the most fertile periods of Jamaican popular music. This was the era that saw Bob Marley and the Wailers rise to international stardom. Rasta-oriented artists Big Youth, Burning Spear, Peter Tosh, Bunny Wailer, Culture, and a host of others created some of their best work and began to be heard abroad. This new surge of musical creativity helped to spur a Rasta "cultural revolution" that affected the entire society. Even many sons and daughters of the upper and middle classes began to take on the trappings of the Rasta faith. The international success of Bob Marley and the growing interest in the Rastafarian movement in other countries also helped enlarge the market for reggae in other parts of the world, which in turn gave a boost to the local music industry.

As we have seen, the Rastafarian musical influence dates back to the very earliest days of Jamaican popular music, when Count Ossie participated in several important recording sessions and key musicians such as the Skatalites began to identify with the expanding Rasta movement. But it was not until the full-fledged cultural reawakening of the 1970s that Rasta themes and imagery—and especially, the emphasis on Africa—came to occupy a central place in popular culture and music. These, in turn, helped inspire a new round of musical exchanges and reopened a channel through which traditional Afro-Jamaican forms such as *Kumina* and Revival would continue, by way of Rasta *nyabinghi* drumming and chanting, to have an indirect influence on reggae.

Bob Marley's handful of *nyabinghi*-based songs, such as "Rastaman

Chant," "Babylon System," and "Time Will Tell," are only the most obvious examples of influence from traditional Rasta music during this period. Beginning in the early part of the decade, the basic rhythms of the *nyabinghi* drums were used as the foundation for many other, lesser-known reggae recordings—cuts such as "Love Again" and "Meditation" by Jackie Mitoo and the Invaders with Count Ossie—which would never be widely heard outside of Jamaica. And by the mid-1970s, a distinctive genre of Rasta reggae had emerged, characterized by a more even balance of rhythmic elements from *nyabinghi* and reggae. A few good examples of recordings in this style are "Jah Give Us Life," by Wailing Souls; "Jah Gift to Man," by Horace Andy; "Rasta Man" and "Free Jah Children," by Bunny Wailer; and "A Jah Jah," by Rita Marley. Dozens of other records in this genre flowed out of Kingston studios during the latter half of the decade. A few even showed strong hints of *Kumina* influence, such as "Congoman," by the Congos.

In fact, a large proportion of the reggae produced during this period, including local covers of North American hit songs, displayed influences from Rasta music. The *nyabinghi* lead drum, the repeater, was now regularly featured on pop records—sometimes even those that made no reference to Rastafarian themes, such as love songs. Studio musicians sometimes transferred *nyabinghi*-derived rhythms, originally played on drums, to other instruments such as organ, piano, and guitar. This Rasta influence helped to promote rhythmic experimentation and led to an expansion of musical space; individual instruments were now free to play a greater variety of rhythmic patterns and began to function more like the interlocking parts of an African drum ensemble. One example is the rhythm track backing the song "Innocent Blood," by Culture (Musical Example 16). Reggae melodies, harmonies, and song texts during this period were also heavily influenced by the Afro-Protestant heritage of traditional *nyabinghi* music, which drew many of its songs from Revival hymns.

Influences moved in the other direction, too, from reggae to *nyabinghi*. Artists specializing in more traditional Rastafarian music, such as the Mystic Revelation of Rastafari, Ras Michael and the Sons of Negus, and Light of Saba, began to incorporate *nyabinghi*-reggae fusions into their repertoires.

Because the Rasta renaissance coincided with the first major breakthrough of reggae music on the international pop market, many foreign listeners were led to assume that Rastafarian culture and reggae were inseparable. Even during the 1970s, however, not all reggae was Rasta-oriented, and influences from other traditional sources continued to creep into the mix. Jamaican popular music has always been more varied than the one-

MUSICAL EXAMPLE 16
"Innocent Blood" (Culture)
Rhythmic patterns:

sided Rasta image that the music industry promoted for many years in its attempts to capitalize on the popularity of outstanding Rasta reggae artists Bob Marley, Peter Tosh, Bunny Wailer, Burning Spear, and others working in the same vein. Indeed, every phase the music has gone through, from ska to reggae, is replete with examples of continued borrowing from folk or traditional sources, of which Rastafarian *nyabinghi* music is but one. It is not an exaggeration to say that Jamaican music has been fundamentally shaped by this ongoing interchange between new and old. As dub poet Oku Onuora says, "Because of the richness of reggae, because of the heritage of reggae . . . like African-derived rhythms like mento, poco, kumina, which gave rise to Rastafarian chants, drummin', which gave rise to ska and then to rock steady . . . because of this rich cultural heritage of the music, it is able to shift—the colorin', we are able to vary the color."[13]

The influence of mento, in particular, has been underrated. Not only would some argue that the characteristic ska afterbeat actually stems in part from the strumming patterns of the banjo or guitar in mento, but ska versions of traditional *mento* tunes were common during the early 1960s. One thinks of popular recordings such as "Penny Reel," by Eric Morris; "Rukumbine," by Shenley Duffus; "Sauce and Tea (Helena)," by the Monarchs; "Old Fowl Ska," by Roland Alphonso; and "Wheel and Turn," by Frank Anderson and Tommy McCook. There were also quite a few original ska compositions done in a mento-inspired style, such as "Sugar Bag" and "Tackoo," by Lee Perry. To some extent, this early infusion of mento was a sign of pride in the times, as the independence celebrations of 1962 were still fresh in Kingstonians' minds.

If anything, the influence of mento increased during the reggae era. The subtle weave of rhythm guitar and keyboards that distinguishes the afterbeat of mature reggae (at first, played on guitar alone) from its rock-steady equivalent has a definite mento feel (Musical Example 17).

MUSICAL EXAMPLE 17

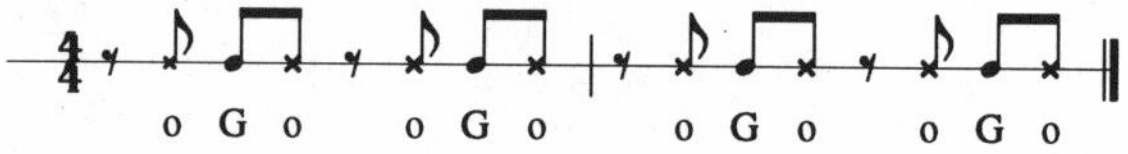

o G o   o G o   o G o   o G o

o = organ   g = guitar

The slower tempo of rock steady and reggae also brought them closer to mento. In fact, the historic 1967 recording that many argue to be the very first reggae song—"Nanny Goat," by Larry Marshall and Alvin Leslie—was unmistakably mento-based, as were other songs by Marshall, such as "Throw Me Corn" and "Son Son." Both "Throw Me Corn" and "Nanny Goat" were tremendously popular in Jamaica as dance numbers, and what is today called the "Nanny Goat riddim"—the drum-and-bass tracks from this recording—continues to be recycled in an endless series of new permutations.

Few listeners outside of Jamaica know that there was a whole substyle or genre of mento-reggae (sometimes called "country music") that enjoyed tremendous popularity in the island during the 1970s. Its most prolific exponent was Stanley Beckford, lead singer of the Starlights (also known as Stanley and the Turbynes), who released hit after hit, beginning in 1973 and continuing through the decade. Some of his better-known songs, such as "Healing in the Balm Yard," were reggae versions of older mento songs, while others, such as the huge hits "Soldering" and "Leave Mi Kisiloo," were his own mento-reggae compositions. Other singers working in this style of "country music" also had big hits, such as the Prince Brothers with "Open the Door (A Fe Mi Something)" and Calypso Williams (King Bed Bug) with "Screw the Cock (Cork) Tight." In 1977, a Trinidadian calypsonian based in Jamaica, Lord Laro, scored another smash hit in this vein called "Reggae Mento Rockers" (also released under the title "Disco Mento Rockers"), showing that interaction between Trinidadian calypso and Jamaican mento could cut both ways. Yet other locally prominent reggae artists have made contributions to this genre, such as Eric Donaldson (author of the famous song "Cherry Oh Baby," covered by the Rolling Stones and

Bob Marley brings together political rivals Michael Manley and Edward Seaga on-stage, 1978 (*Everybody's Magazine*)

UB40), Bobby Ellis, the Fabulous Five, Orlando Folks and the Ideal, Lloyd Lovindeer, the Moonlights, Roy Rayon, Sugar Belly, and the Tellers; nor should it be forgotten that some of the mento singers of the 1950s, such as Count Lasher and Lord Tanamo, continued to compose and record into the 1970s, now backed by the current mento-reggae style (while others, such as Count Zebra, continued to record and have minor hits in the old acoustic style of mento). Despite the popularity of mento-reggae in its homeland, most foreign reggae fans heard little or none of it and thus remained oblivious to one of the sweetest and most thoroughly Jamaican sounds of that era.

The Afro-Protestant musical contribution to reggae has been given somewhat more recognition than that of mento. The 1972 film *The Harder They Come,* which did so much to popularize reggae abroad, includes an extended scene of Jimmy Cliff's character, an aspiring reggae star named Ivan, working up a sweat in the Revival-influenced choir of a Pentecostal "clap-hand" church. In another scene, Ivan persuades one of the church musicians to back him on electric guitar while trying out a new reggae composition. Despite the fact that Ivan's love of "temporal" reggae music leads to a confrontation with the preacher, the existence of a connection between church music and secular reggae in downtown Kingston is made apparent by their juxtaposition in the film. Another reggae film that was popular with foreign audiences, *Rockers,* includes a scene with traditional Revivalist dancing and drumming, hinting at the possibility of a connection between old-time religion and reggae. Such fleeting images aside, few non-Jamaicans have the opportunity or the inclination to learn anything about Jamaican Revivalism, and thus most foreign reggae listeners remain unaware of the extent to which the influence of this indigenous Afro-Jamaican religion permeates Jamaican popular culture, including music.

The Revivalist influence on popular music goes back to the early days of ska, when Revival-tinged recordings such as "Six and Seven Books of Moses" and "Hallelujah," by the Maytals; "River Jordan" and "Freedom," by Clancy Eccles; and "River to the Bank," by Baba Brooks, were among the mix of styles then to be heard on downtown sound systems. Even the Wailers, before fully embracing the Rastafarian faith, recorded a number of Revival-influenced spiritual songs during the ska period. With the ascendance of Rasta-oriented reggae, those elements of traditional Rastafarian music derived from Revivalist sources were transferred to urban popular music along with the rest, lending much of the reggae of the 1970s a hymn-like quality that would be familiar to the ears of churchgoers all over rural Jamaica. The melodies and chord progressions of many Rasta reggae songs, as well as the biblical language and prophetic messages that typify the genre, owe much to Revivalism.

Not all of the Afro-Protestant influences in reggae, however, came by way of the medium of Rastafarian songs; some occurred more directly. This is particularly clear in the case of the Maytals, whose gospel-tinged sound sometimes reminds North American listeners of the black gospel tradition in the United States. Whatever resemblance the Maytals' style may bear to black religious music in the United States, it cannot be considered derivative. Although lead singer Toots Hibbert, like many of his contemporaries, listened to and admired U.S. gospel music sung by the likes of the young Sam Cooke (with the Soul Stirrers), he and the other Maytals were also steeped in local Revivalism. When they were making their ska records, they were simultaneously singing in a church choir. Not only is there a strong Jamaican Revivalist feeling in the Maytals' many religious reggae songs after the ska era—for example, "Loving Spirit," "In the Dark," and "Got to Be There"—but some songs even directly quote traditional Revival melodies. The appropriately named "Revival Reggae," for instance, sets the meaning-

Dub poet Mutabaruka

less syllables of an old Revival chorus—a type of chanting often associated, in the traditional context, with the onset of spiritual possession—to a driving reggae rhythm.

Few reggae fans in other countries are aware that there exists in Jamaica a type of local gospel music, usually called "Christian music," that has close ties to the reggae industry. Often associated with Pentecostal congregations, this genre of recorded music—represented by singers and preachers like Gloria Bailey, Claudelle Clarke, the Gospel Blenders, the Grace Thrillers, Evangelist Higgins, the Don Sam Group, and Otis Wright—has assimilated both black and rural white gospel styles from the United States and blended them with various other foreign and local influences. Stylistically speaking,

Lloyd Lovindeer
(Richard A. Williams)

much of this music is quite close to reggae, but with certain distinguishing features, such as differently accented drum patterns, a busy tambourine, and sometimes prominent clapping; some of it, in fact, is reggae in all but name. This is not surprising, since these gospel singers share studios and producers with reggae artists. Many top studio musicians whose names are normally associated with reggae can also be heard on these Revivalist-influenced Christian recordings, among them Radcliffe "Dougie" Bryan (guitar), Harold Butler (keyboard), Ansel Collins (keyboard), Grub Cooper (drums and keyboard), Carlton "Santa" Davis (drums), and the internationally acclaimed Lowell "Sly" Dunbar (drums). Even some well-known reggae vocalists, such as Larry Marshall (Bro. Marshall), the Tamlins, and Carlene Davis, have had parallel careers as "Christian singers."

Like blues and gospel music in the United States, secular reggae and local gospel music have never really been entirely separate, and influences have gone both ways. This is but one more way in which the Afro-Protestant Revivalist heritage has continued to feed into popular culture and music in this intensely spiritual country.

TECHNO-ROOTS: FROM REGGAE TO *RAGGA*

As the 1980s got underway, yet another thread going back to the early days of Jamaican popular music rose to a position of preeminence. "Dancehall deejay music," as the new rage became known, was actually traceable to the sound-system dances of the late 1950s and early 1960s, when in-house disc-spinners would take over the mike and introduce the latest records with a flourish of verbal theatrics intended to whip up crowd excitement. Eventually, this developed into an art form called "toasting"—a kind of stylized rapping, rhyming, and vocal "percussing" over specially cut "dub plates" (acetate discs). Deejays soon became recording artists in their own right, releasing records and scoring hits of their own by toasting over the prerecorded rhythm tracks of songs that had already chalked up substantial sales. Although the musical style of the underlying tracks changed over the years, the thread connecting the early toasters and the latter-day dancehall deejays was unbroken; the pioneering deejays of the late 1950s and early 1960s, such as Count Machouki and Sir Lord Comic, were followed in the later 1960s by King Stitt and U Roy and in the 1970s by Big Youth, Dennis Alcapone, I Roy, and a host of others. But it was only in the 1980s, with the rise of big deejaying stars such as Yellowman, that this genre came to dominate the Jamaican music scene. The numbers of young deejays putting out records multiplied rapidly.

Dancehall reggae during this period was known for its spare instrumentation and less-complex rhythms, the musical accompaniment taking a backseat to the deejay's vocals. At the same time, producers and studio engineers began to play a larger role in shaping the final product. In fact, they had made important creative contributions before this, particularly during the late 1960s and the 1970s, when they had experimented with new devices such as electronic delays and had helped create a new, largely instrumental genre of reggae called "dub."[14] Dub music had always had a close association with the deejaying tradition and had also helped spawn a related verbal art form known as dub poetry.[15] The increasingly prominent role played by producers and engineers during the 1980s was a logical extension of this earlier experimentation with studio technology, as well as of the rising popularity of deejaying. Because deejays usually recorded over preexisting "riddims" or backing tracks rather than composing entirely new pieces, producers could recycle and remix old materials from their vaults to provide backing for new deejay releases, thus reducing their dependence on session musicians and arrangers.

The year 1985 is generally regarded as a turning point in reggae. In that year, producer Prince Jammy (now known as King Jammy) released a song by Wayne Smith called "Under Me Sleng Teng," the backing tracks of which were manufactured almost entirely on a Casio electronic keyboard. The song was a huge hit, its underlying tracks turning up in more than four hundred other recordings in the following months. This "Sleng Teng riddim" helped launch a new variety of digital or computerized dancehall music that remains dominant today.

The new music found many detractors, both locally and abroad. Many deplored the decreasing attention given by younger deejays to the socially conscious or "cultural" themes so prominent in Rasta reggae and decried the growing popularity of "slack" lyrics, dominated by sexual boasting, drug references, and macho challenges. Indeed, with its increasingly violent posturing, its "lickshots" (simulated gunfire), and its sparse rhythm tracks, generated entirely on electronic equipment, the dancehall music of the late 1980s and early 1990s was seen by many reggae fans as a creative low point for Jamaican popular music—a slump from which many feel it has yet to recover. But whatever its merits or shortcomings, it was the music of a new generation of downtown "sufferers," and like the music of a previous generation of "rude boys," it spoke resolutely to their own experience and did so in the contemporary language of the still-growing Kingston underclass.

The new name given to the genre, *ragga*, or *raggamuffin*, confirmed that youth-oriented class consciousness had returned to the forefront of Jamai-

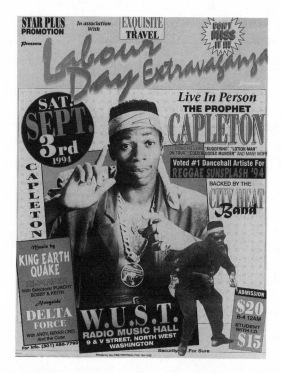

Ragga ina Washington, D.C., dance poster

can popular music with a vengeance. (Though its name is derived from the word "ragamuffin," the Jamaican musical style is usually spelled *ragga-muffin*). Like the Rasta term *dread* before it, this originally derogatory word was claimed by dispossessed youth and redefined as a defiant and aggressive self-identifying label. In the words of the *ragga* singer Half Pint, "Ragga-muffin [is] a youth who grow up outside where him can stand the weather and no havin' no flu, him can stand hunger, him can stand a pain, him can endure. A lot a people," he adds, "interpret raggamuffin as if it a criminal morality."[16]

Like earlier forms of reggae, *ragga* music is stylistically more diverse than is generally recognized, partly because it has also drawn on deeply rooted older forms. By the early 1990s, even as foreign reggae fans and critics were complaining about what they saw as a desertion of the music's local roots for an artificial and "soulless" sound shaped by an imported digital technology, local musicians were remarking on its increasing debt to older, rural Jamaican musical forms. Asked in what direction Jamaican popular music was currently moving, Wayne Armond of the Kingston-based reggae band Chalice had this to say: "What it's encompassin' is very old Jamaican music—mento, poco, you know, all the ethnic music from early Jamaica, only

Dance poster

this is now being played on a drum machine, but the influences are valued. . . . You hear them in dancehall music. Not the old Studio One beats, further back than that. Before reggae, before even the advent of ska or rock steady, I'm talking about the things they call burru, way, way back from my great-grandfather in slavery days, that's what we're talking about."[17] Clearly, something more has been going on in recent Jamaican music than the foreign press is equipped to tell us about.

We can get a glimpse of what most foreign observers have missed by going back to 1984—just before "Under Me Sleng Teng" ushered in the "digital revolution"—to take a look at a lesser-known series of developments that would eventually bring the new music of Jamaica closer than ever to its rural roots, even as it was entering the present digital era. In that year, a dancehall deejay named Lord Sassa Frass had a local hit with a record called "Pocomania Jump." Musically speaking, it was in the typical dancehall style of that era and owed little to traditional Revival music. Yet its fanciful lyrics, which brought together dancehall "posses" and "the parson, the deacon, and son" in Sassa Frass's imaginary "Revival tent," were full of references to the paraphernalia and spiritual workings of traditional *Poco* churches. "Poco jump, poco jump, mek we do de poco jump," went the chorus, and the piece ended with the heavy rhythmic breathing, or "trumping," associated with dancing and spiritual possession in the Revival religion.[18] (Sassa Frass's later-released LP also included a cut called "Kumina to Kumina," which, despite the title, bore little or no evidence of musical influence from *Kumina*.) Virtually unnoticed outside of Jamaica, this locally popular record—despite its offhand, somewhat whimsical treatment of the subject—brought *Pocomania* and Revival once again into the public spotlight and helped set the stage for the creation of a new style of dancehall music actually based on traditional Revival rhythms, though this would take several years to surface in full force.

Not long after the "Sleng Teng riddim" took hold, two studio musicians who had been instrumental in the popularization of the digital sound, Steely (Wycliffe Johnson) and Clevie (Cleveland Browne), began looking for a new sound. Their search led them to traditional sources. Taking a chance, they made a conscious decision to incorporate the drum rhythms of the Revival religion into their digital dancehall mix. What they came up with was a stripped-down version of a Revival beat played on a simulated snare drum. With its faster tempo and relatively busy drum rhythms, the new sound represented a dramatic departure from previous styles of dancehall reggae. While Steely and Clevie were experimenting, others were also looking to Revivalist sources for inspiration.

In 1989, a very popular dancehall deejay named Lloyd Lovindeer—yet another local Jamaican star who remains largely unknown outside the Caribbean—released an influential album called *One Day Christian*. Though the title cut satirized the hypocrisy of corrupt preachers (and was aimed especially at wealthy North American televangelists), the rest of the album simply reveled in the infectious new Revivalist-dancehall beat that it showcased. Saturated with Revivalist themes and musical influences—including the prominent snare drum that Steely and Clevie had been experimenting with—it was nevertheless primarily a party record, and it included two big local hits, "Pocomania Day" and "Poco Party." Lovindeer followed this with another *Poco* dancehall album called *Find Your Way*.

The success of *One Day Christian*, on which Steely and Clevie had played drums, keyboards, and bass, led the duo to produce an album called *Poco in the East*, released in 1990. One whole side was devoted to deejays toasting over electronic *Poco* dancehall rhythms. They followed this up later in the year with an entire album in the new genre, called *More Poco*. *Poco* dancehall had now become a bona fide trend, and even young deejays known for their gun lyrics and "bad boy" posturing began to come up with their own contributions, such as Cobra (a.k.a. Mad Cobra), who recorded a cut called "Poco Jump."

Although this explicitly Revivalist-based style of *Poco* dancehall music seems to have faded recently, its influence has been inestimable, owing to the enormous popularity of Steely and Clevie as producers. A large portion of what is called *ragga* today developed from this sound. Other producers have jumped on the bandwagon and are now manufacturing their own up-tempo digital tracks with similarly driving imitation drum rhythms. Much experimentation is going on in the studios, resulting in greater variety. One can hear an increasing emphasis on simulated bass-drum patterns, some of which are uncannily reminiscent of the rhythmic feel of the *bandu* drum of *Kumina*, though rarely duplicating its rhythms precisely. Some variants of this new percussion-centered digital sound still feature the high snare of *Poco* dancehall, while others combine various timbres and rhythms into new syntheses whose origins cannot be located in a particular traditional source but which sound thoroughly Jamaican, with occasional suggestions of *Kumina*, *Poco*, *nyabinghi*, and other Afro-Jamaican forms.

The result of all this experimentation is a new genre that must be considered the most original trend in dancehall: a substyle of *ragga* music that has changed so much that, if one is to go by strictly musical criteria, it can no longer be considered reggae at all, since its stylistic connections with the music known by that name during the 1960s and 1970s are no longer clear. Though created with computer technology, it is closer in sound to the surviving neo-African music of rural Jamaica than any popular music before it. (It should be noted that because rhythm tracks in this style have no equivalent to a lead drum, this music usually lacks the rhythmic complexity produced by the improvisations of that instrument in a traditional ensemble; however, it could be argued that the more rhythmically innovative deejays function much like the missing lead drum). In the words of dub poet Linton Kwesi Johnson, "With the discovery of digital recording, an extreme minimalism has emerged. . . . On the one hand, this music is totally technological; on the other the rhythms are far more Jamaican: they're drawn from Etu, Pocomania, Kumina—African-based religious cults who provide the rhythms used by Shabba Ranks or Buju Banton. So despite the extent of the technology being used, the music is becoming even rootsier, with a resonance even for quite old listeners, because it evokes back to what they first heard in rural Jamaica."[19]

There is considerable irony in the situation. North American devotees of what is now called the "classic" reggae sound of the 1970s may praise the music played by an old-style, U.S.-based Rastafarian band, with no following in Jamaica, as "roots reggae" while dismissing the new *ragga* sound as a homogenized, commercial form of techno-pop that has strayed from the "roots." But part of what makes this *ragga* style less palatable to such listeners is the decreasing prominence of those elements of reggae that actually owe more to European and North American sources (and thus sound more familiar to foreign ears)—vocal and instrumental melodies and harmonies that stem largely from the Western tradition, for instance—in favor of an aesthetic that leans more toward the African side of Jamaica's musical heritage. The fact is that much of the new *ragga* music is more firmly rooted in local soil than ever. With its heavily percussive Afro-Jamaican sound, its debt to Jamaica's rich oral culture, and its lyrics that are almost exclusively in "deep" Jamaican Creole (or *patwa*—a language intelligible only to Jamaicans or foreigners who make the effort to learn it), it is, as reggae once was, definitely an acquired taste for those brought up on "mainstream" Euro-American pop.

Those foreign listeners who have learned enough of the Jamaican language to have access to texts may be disturbed by the sexual content, violent imagery, or vehemently antihomosexual rhetoric of many contemporary *ragga* recordings. Like recent stylistic changes in the music, this choice of subject matter reveals a tenaciously local orientation and says much about the degree to which the music continues to be rooted in the lived experience of its performers. The sexual "slackness" of many lyrics, overblown and sexist as it may have become, is nonetheless part of a tradition of sexual banter and double entendre in Jamaican popular music that goes back to mento and before. The violence of "gun lyrics" mirrors the harsh reality of life in a desperately poor part of Kingston that continues to be ravaged by political warfare, drugs, and crime. And the strident vilification of homosexuality is rooted in local values that have been shaped by a fundamentalist reading of biblical scripture. As young, downtown deejays have reclaimed Jamaica's indigenous popular music from the pretensions of international marketers aiming to please cosmopolitan audiences, it has become harder for foreign consumers of that music to romanticize the experience from which it springs or to see in it an entirely "progressive" response to social injustice.

However, the variety of themes treated in *ragga* lyrics should not be underestimated. Alternative emphases, including Rastafarian perspectives, have actually been present in dancehall music since it took over in the 1980s, and current releases indicate that social-protest and Rasta-oriented lyrics may once again be on the rise. Nor should dominant trends, such as the new *ragga* style discussed above, be allowed to conceal the variation that keeps Jamaican popular music alive. In an interview a few years back, veteran Jamaican singer Bob Andy described how established marketing categories have a tendency to create a false sense of stylistic homogeneity. "In Jamaica what we have long been doing is capsuling everything and calling it Reggae," he said. "Reggae is but one aspect of Jamaican music," he added, pointing out that "Peter Tosh, Bunny Wailer and myself have done songs that emphasize all of the beats—ranging from *ska, mento,* and *rock steady* to *Reggae* and *Dance Hall.*"[20] The dancehall music of today—often called "dancehall reggae," thereby ensuring some continuity with a previously established international marketing category—also draws from all these older sources (including many perennial "riddims" sampled directly from old Studio One recordings).

But it would be wrong to give the impression that *ragga* has looked only to the past or to local sources for musical ideas. Despite the current popularity of resurgent Afro-Jamaican rhythms, one can detect strains of hip-hop, contemporary R & B, rock, and other foreign genres in much of the recent music coming out of Jamaica. Stylistic experimentation continues, and novelty is as valued as ever. A rapid succession of new dances with such names as "cool and deadly," *buttafly,* "Santa Barbara," and *bogle* and of new rhythms and riffs with equally original names—for example, *bangara, cordiroy* (i.e., "corduroy"), "Indian beat," and "talking drums"—keeps the music in a constant state of flux. Internationally prominent studio musicians such as Sly Dunbar travel across the world, listening to all kinds of music, and return with new ideas that eventually make their way onto the local music scene. Jamaica is, after all, hardly isolated from musical trends in the United States and Europe.

Indeed, the most obvious foreign influence on Jamaican music in recent years has been from hip-hop. The latest series of exchanges between urban African-American and Jamaican musics arose spontaneously out of contacts between black American and Jamaican communities in New York and other U.S. cities during the 1980s. More recently, following the success of crossover artists such as Shabba Ranks, collaborations between U.S. singers and Jamaican deejays have been promoted by record companies in a calculated manner. As of this writing, more than two dozen Jamaican deejays—crossover stars such as Buju Banton, Patra, and Tiger—have been signed by major labels. So far, those on the Jamaican side of the equation have managed to maintain their distinctive musical identity, using their own Jamaican Creole language even when toasting over an entirely hip-hop rhythm. (Shabba Ranks has even had some success introducing U.S. audiences to *Poco*-derived dancehall rhythms, not to mention the Rasta *nyabinghi* drumming featured on a video he did with comedian Eddie Murphy.) Not only this, but dancehall/*ragga* has had a remarkable impact on African-American hip-hop artists as well, and the Jamaican presence is now firmly established—for the time being, at least—on black-oriented radio in cities like New York and Washington, D.C. Back in Jamaica, however, there is much talk of the potential threat that fusions such as *ragga*-hip-hop might pose to the integrity of Jamaica's local popular music should the process go too far.

The tension between local identity and globalizing trends is likely to remain a fundamental theme in the future of Jamaican popular music. Reggae and dancehall varieties are now played by musicians on every continent, and non-Jamaican recording artists working in these genres have had major successes in several African countries, Europe, the United States, and Japan. Fusions based primarily on Jamaican styles, such as Asian-influenced *bhangramuffin*, have also led to gigantic record sales. Even ska continues to be marketable outside of Jamaica, and in the United States, the recent emergence of a new generation of "third-wave" ska bands (as well as a new hardcore, punk-influenced fusion dubbed "ska-core") has attracted the attention of major labels.

Meanwhile, hundreds of hopeful young *raggamuffins* congregate day after day in front of Kingston's dozens of recording studios, patiently waiting for auditions. One need not be as big as a Bob Marley or a Shabba Ranks to escape from poverty. Jamaica, after all, is reputed to have the highest per capita output of records of any country in the world. An estimated two hundred new singles are released in Kingston every week, most of which will never leave the island.[21] No wonder Jamaica continues dancing to its own beat, hoping that the world will follow. So far, the producers searching for new sounds have known where to look. Here, in the place that gave the world reggae, uptown with its international connections may call the shots, but the greatest hope still lies with downtown.

CODA: RASTA *KUMINA* INA *RAGGAMUFFIN* STYLE

In May 1989, a small group of Howellite Rastafarians gathered in a yard in the parish of Clarendon for a bit of *Kumina* drumming. They were followers of Leonard Howell, the first prophet to declare the divinity of Rastafari, and had remained faithful to their leader even after his death in 1981. Unlike other Rastas, who had adopted *nyabinghi* drumming, they continued to worship Rastafari to the related but older rhythms of the *Kumina* drums, which Howell himself had always used in his services.

Suddenly, a young man appeared on the scene, apparently without invitation. Standing over the seated drummers, he demanded everyone's attention, beginning with a dramatic salutation. "Well, now, me bredren, nuff respect," he intoned. "Give thanks and praises to the Almighty God who give I strength and guidance!" After a pause, he glanced at the drummers and said, "Well, now, come now, me bredren!"

The drummers took the cue and started playing the sacred *bandu* and *kyas* in typical *Kumina* style. The young deejay came in right on top of the beat, toasting in perfect time with the *Kumina* rhythms, making as if he were holding a mike. To everyone's delight, the yard was momentarily transformed into a sound system driven by its own ancient power, with no need of amplifiers, speakers, or microphones, as the young *raggamuffin* pulled words out of the air:

Lord have mercy
yes yes yes
diplomat ina de party
hear me now, star
hear me now, star
me seh me born a Kingston
and me no born a country
yes, born a Kingston
and me no born a country
now me settle pon de micro
me's a mike MC
come ram dancehall
then mek we cork party
whether you a fifty
whether you a twenty
now me settle pon de mike
it's intelligently
what a tribulation
what a tribulation
poor people ina Africa
dem deh a suffer
de people dem down deh
dem a dead by hunger
why, de wicked boy down deh
why, dem call him Botha
now me settle pon de mike
and me have fi chat like preacher
'cause Jah Jah, don't forget
Jah Jah a de teacher
so no wicked cannot come
no wicked cannot enter
a Jah Jah up a heaven
Jah Jah a de father . . .

well massive, man! . . .
Lord have mercy![22]

In a mere two minutes, this spontaneous encounter had bridged a good part of the history of Jamaican popular music, showing how close, in 1989, the old and the new had remained.

For many Jamaicans, music is not only a source of pleasure but a healing balm and an aid in the struggle for survival, as it has been for centuries.

Scenes such as this one, played out in back corners far from the eyes and ears of the world's millions of music consumers, remind us that long after the powerful record executives of today are gone and forgotten, Jamaica will go on singing with a voice all its own.

BIBLIOGRAPHY

Sebastian Clarke, *Jah Music: The Evolution of the Popular Jamaican Song* (London: Heinemann, 1980); Howard Johnson and Jim Pines, *Reggae: Deep Roots Music* (London: Proteus Books, 1982); Stephen Davis and Peter Simon, *Reggae International* (New York: R & B, 1982); Kenneth Bilby and Fu-Kiau kia Bunseki, *Kumina: A Kongo-Based Tradition in the New World* (Brussels: Centre d'Etude et de Documentation Africaines, 1983); Hilary S. Carty, *Folk Dances of Jamaica: An Insight* (London: Dance Books Ltd., 1988); Yoshiko S. Nagashima, *Rastafarian Music in Contemporary Jamaica* (Tokyo: Institute for the Study of Languages and Cultures of Asia and Africa, 1984); Rebekah Michele Mulvaney, *Rastafari and Reggae: A Dictionary and Sourcebook* (New York: Greenwood, 1990); Brian Jahn and Tom Weber, *Reggae Island: Jamaican Music in the Digital Age* (Kingston: Kingston Publishers Limited, 1992); Colin Larkin, ed., *The Guinness Who's Who of Reggae* (Enfield, U.K.: Guinness Publishing, 1994).

RECORDS

TRADITIONAL GENRES: *Jamaican Cult Music* (Folkways FE 4461); *Folk Music of Jamaica* (Folkways FE 4453); *From the Grass Roots of Jamaica* (Dynamic 3305); *Grounation: The Mystic Revelation of Rastafari* (MRR Records); *John Crow Say: Jamaican Music of Faith, Work and Play* (Folkways FE 4228); *From Kongo to Zion: Black Music Traditions of Jamaica* (Heartbeat HB 17); *Churchical Chants of the Nyabingi* (Heartbeat HB 20); *Jamaican Ritual Music from the Mountains and the Coast* (Lyrichord LLST 7394); *Drums of Defiance: Jamaican Maroon Music* (Smithsonian/Folkways SF 40412); *The Jolly Boys* (Lyrichord LLST 7314); *Beer Joint and Tailoring: The Jolly Boys* (First Warning 75707-2); *Lititz Mento Band* (Haus der Kulturen der Welt SM 1512-2).

MODERN POPULAR MUSIC: *Ska Bonanza: The Studio One Ska Years* (Heartbeat HB 86/87); *Explosive Rock Steady* (Heartbeat HB 72); *One Love: Bob Marley and the Wailers* (Heartbeat HB 111/112); *Bob Marley: Songs of Freedom* (Tuff Gong/Island TGCBX1–4); *The Harder They Come* (Island ILPS 9202); *The Starlights: Featuring Stanley Beckford* (Heartbeat HB 102); *From the Roots: The Maytals* (Trojan TRLS 65); *Wiser Dread* (Nighthawk 301); *This Is Reggae Music* (Island 300329 + 30); *One Day Christian: Lovindeer* (TSOJ); *Poco in the East* (Dynamic); *More Poco* (V.P. VPCD1142); *As Raw as Ever: Shabba Ranks* (Sony/Epic EK 47310); *Jah Screw Presents: Dancehall Glamity* (RAS CD 3117); *Tougher than Tough: The Story of Jamaican Music* (Mango CD1–4, 518 400-3). A large number of recordings by artists working in both "classic" reggae and dancehall/*ragga* genres are widely available in the United States on Heartbeat, RAS, Mango, and many other labels.

8

Trinidad, Calypso, and Carnival

Christopher Columbus's first sight of land on his third voyage was a row of three hills on the southeastern tip of a large island, which he consequently dubbed Trinidad, or "trinity." Approaching shore, the famed navigator, still in search of the Orient, was disappointed, as before, to be greeted by a delegation not of Chinese mandarins but of near-naked albeit friendly-seeming Carib Indians in canoes. Columbus tried to welcome them by having his men dance and play fife-and-drum music, but the Caribs, either feeling threatened or simply finding the music disagreeable, showered the ship with arrows and paddled off. It was an inauspicious start for musical syncretism in Trinidad and perhaps foreshadowed the fact that neither Spaniards nor Indians would play major roles in the island's subsequent musical culture.

The Spanish, indeed, took little interest in the island, and by the mid-1700s, there were still few settlers on Trinidad. King Charles III extended an invitation to Catholic French Caribbeans to resettle on the island, thereby attracting several thousand Frenchmen and their slaves from the Windward Islands, which had recently been conquered by the British. The French immigrated to Trinidad and Tobago (henceforth referred to here as Trinidad) largely to escape British Protestant rule. Subsequently, in 1797, the British took Trinidad, imposing an English colonial administration over what continued for a century to be a largely French and Afro-French creole population.

When the black former slaves deserted the plantations after emancipation in 1834–38, the British imported some 143,000 peasants from India to work the fields. Along with them came handfuls of Portuguese, Chinese, Syrians, and others. All of these gave Trinidad a rather cosmopolitan racial mixture, as is reflected in its place-names, which are variously Amerindian (e.g., Chaguanas), Spanish (San Fernando), French (Laventille), British (Belmont), East Indian (Fyzabad), and however you choose to classify "Port of Spain."

Trinidadian national character, insofar as one can generalize, acquired a rather different hue from that of the other British colonies. The French creole cultural base, the relative prosperity, the brevity of the slave era, and the comparative mildness of British colonial rule in Trinidad seem to have favored the development of an easygoing national culture that prizes humor and fun over puritanism or pathos. If Jamaican "roots reggae" inclined toward expressions of suffering, underclass anger, and visions of messianic redemption, Trinidad's cultural heart lies more in irreverent and ribald calypsoes and, above all, in Carnival, a two-month celebration of music, dance, partying, and various sorts of mass, bureaucratically managed fun.

Most of Trinidad's musical vitality and cultural dynamism has developed in spite of rather than because of British rule. Until well into the twentieth century, the colonial government, as elsewhere in the British West Indies, took little or no interest in education, preferring to spend its money on prisons; a 1797 law in Barbados explicitly forbade teaching slaves to read or write. The British, in their racism and Anglicizing zeal, tried further to stamp out everything they found distasteful or excessively foreign, from Chinese *whe-whe* games to neo-African religion and music.

In spite of such efforts, Trinidad remains host to a number of distinctly non-English music traditions. The music of the East Indians, who are now coming to outnumber blacks and constitute the largest demographic group, is considered Chapter 9. Spanish musical influence, deriving more from immigrants from neighboring Venezuela than from early colonial rule, persists in the form of a Christmastime music called *parang*. *Parang* is traditionally performed by troupes of amateurs (Spanish, *parranda*) who, like their counterparts in Puerto Rico and elsewhere, go from house to house partying, singing, and playing guitar- and mandolin-type instruments (here, *bandolin* and the Venezuelan *cuatro*). This music, which closely resembles the Venezuelan *joropo* (a Hispanic-derived folk-song genre), is still widely popular in areas of Trinidad. Even though neither the singers nor the listeners speak Spanish, Trinidadians throng to Yuletide functions to socialize, drink ginger beer, and dance ballroom-style to *parang*'s syncopated rhythms, dulcet strings, and exotic-sounding Spanish texts. Indeed, far from dying out, *parang* has been flourishing more than ever since the 1960s, invigorated by amateur competition networks. (As we will see, there are competitions for just about every kind of music in Trinidad, making for a very lively musical culture.)

Another distinctive musical tradition is that associated with the syncretic *orisha* religion or *Shango*, evidently brought mostly by the nine thousand indentured Yorubans who immigrated in the mid-1800s. Like its counterparts in Cuba and elsewhere, *Shango* centers in ceremonies in which Yoruba deities (*orishas*) are honored through dance and music, the latter consisting primarily of chants in Yoruba or archaic patois, accompanied by a drum trio. The British did their best to ban *orisha* worship, and the threads of tradition—including, for example, knowledgeable singers and drummers— had grown weak by the 1970s. Hindu deities and East Indian worshipers had also found places in *orisha* religion. Nevertheless, the religion has undergone something of a revival in recent years, although it remains a rather private phenomenon, with little presence in public culture. Elements of *orisha* worship, including possession trance, are also found in the music and religious practices of Spiritual Baptists (Shouters), which resemble in some respects Afro-Protestant faiths like Jamaican Revival Zion.

Bongo dancing constituted another African-influenced tradition, in which participants would take turns dancing in the center of a ring while others sang or played drums (as in Puerto Rican *bomba* and Cuban *rumba*). Although once common at wakes, the genre has been rare for decades.

THE DEVELOPMENT
OF CALYPSO AND CARNIVAL

Interesting as such traditions are, by far the most characteristic, prominent, and popular musical culture of the country is that of calypso and Carnival, as developed primarily by lower-class Afro-Trinidadians since the 1700s.

Shango drums at a *palais* near Port of Spain, Trinidad, playing (from left to right) *oméle, iya* (or "cutter"), *bo,* and shaker (Jocelyn Guilbault)

Calypso has always had its counterparts, audiences, and performers elsewhere in the West Indies, but it is in Trinidad and Tobago that calypso and Carnival have flourished the most.

While many of the early roots of calypso—including the origin of the word—remain unclear, Trinidadian scholars have reconstructed much of the genre's history. By the 1780s, the word *cariso* had appeared, denoting some sort of satirical, extemporized creole song, but modern calypso emerged somewhat later as the product of a set of diverse musical influences. These included, in varying manners and degrees, the *belair* (a kind of French creole song), the *lavway* (a masquerade procession song), neo-African genres like *juba* and *bamboula*, British ballads, Venezuelan string-band music, other West Indian creole song types, and the *calinda* (*kalinda*), which was associated with stick fighting. Stick fighting was a popular pastime among lower-class blacks, in which two opponents, backed by supporters and musicians from rival plantations or neighborhoods, would fight with light, yard-long canes until blood was drawn. Each gang featured a lead singer called the "chantwell," who would preface the fight with songs boasting of his team's skill and lewdly insulting the adversaries. The fight then proceeded with drum accompaniment (in a manner similar to Cuban *maní* and Brazilian *capoeira*).

By the latter half of the nineteenth century, the diverse genres described above—along with *camboulay* (French, *cannes brulees*), a re-creation of a fire drill accompanied by drumming—came to be centered in pre-Lenten Carnival. Carnival had started as a dainty festival in which the French aristocrats would don frivolous masks and pay social calls. The planters allowed their slaves to celebrate in their own fashion, and by the mid-1800s, lower-class (*jamette;* from French, *diamètre*) blacks had come to dominate the event. *Jamette* Carnival soon took on its own character, with its rowdy street dancing, *camboulay* processions, stick fights, and masquerade troupes featuring phony military regiments and folkloric characters like ghoulish Jab-Jabs and stilt-walking Moko Jumbies.

The British authorities, ever fearful of a Haitian-type rebellion and dismayed by the brawls often provoked by the stick fights, banned *camboulay* in the early 1880s; in the process, they provoked bloody riots in which skilled stick fighters more than once put the lightly armed, fumble-footed policemen to run. Nevertheless, the ban on drumming was enforced, as is related in one early calypso: "Can't beat me drum in me own native land." From that time until the present, Carnival evolved as a site of contention between its lower-class Afro-Trinidadian celebrants and the bourgeois and administrative reformers who have sought somehow to control, co-opt, or

"Ole' Mas"—Carnival in 1888 (*Illustrated London News*)

cleanse it. In this vein, a local journal in 1884 denounced the "bawdy language and gestures" of dancing women in Carnival, just as do newspapers over a century later.

CALYPSO IN COLONIALISM

By 1900, Carnival music had coalesced into two main types. One was that of the *mas* (masquerade) processions, in which some two or three dozen costumed revelers, led by a chantwell, would sing rowdy call-and-response chants. Drums being strictly forbidden, until the late 1930s such processions often came to be accompanied by a "tamboo-bamboo" (tambor-bamboo) ensemble of bamboo tubes struck with sticks. While the biggest processions took place in Port of Spain, smaller groups cultivated Carnival contests, plays, and songs throughout the island.

Meanwhile, calypso developed as a more elaborate, text-oriented song performed for seated audiences in large tents erected for the occasion. The period from 1900 to 1930 saw the rapid refinement, institutionalization, and commercialization of this new form of entertainment. By the 1920s, local merchants, liquor companies, civic committees, and enterprising singers were setting up tents throughout Trinidad as commercial enterprises;

audiences paid a small admissions fee to cheer or mercilessly heckle the amateur calypsonians competing for cash prizes in contests judged by local aficionados. Particularly influential in the music's development were the innovations of singer and entrepreneur Chieftain Walter Douglas, who from 1921 would set up a fancy tent in a bourgeois neighborhood and, using a genteel-sounding Venezuelan-style string band, promoted sophisticated "oratorical" calypsoes, rather than lewd, *calinda*-type ditties. (These calypsoes were often called *sans humanité*—loosely, "without mercy"—for the stock, semi-nonsense derivative phrase *santimanitey* that often punctuated verses.)

Calypso evolved rapidly under such conditions. String and brass instruments replaced the noisy street-band ones, and solo singing with refrain replaced the *calinda*-style call-and-response format. Early calypsonians (many of whom were also stick-fight chantwells) continued to use snippets from responsorial *calindas, Shango* songs, and assorted creole folk songs, but most came to rely on a set of familiar, major-key stock tunes that were essentially English in character. (Many Trinidadians prefer to ascribe an African origin to calypso, as suggested by the West African term *kaiso*.) Singers adopted bombastic sobriquets and transferred the *calinda* boasting tradition to the calypso stage, specializing in improvised verbal *picong* duels (from French, *piquant*). Patois, which had predominated until 1900, quickly died out as calypsonians like Lord Executor tried to outdo one another in their displays of pompous rhetoric. While schoolteachers fulminated against their students' fondness for "long-winded words and high-flown phrases," calypsonians matched their wits and vocabularies, as later parodied by Mighty Sparrow in his "Well-Spoken Moppers":

> Pompomloomically speaking you're a pussyistic man,
> most elaquitably full of shitification.

The subject matter of calypsoes broadened accordingly, encompassing commentary on current events, picaresque tales, and lewd double entendres, as well as boasts and insults. Ribaldry and sarcasm remained the genre's mainstay, and the lyrics continued to show delight in mocking pretensions, exposing elite scandals, and ridiculing upper-class women.

For their part, calypsonians (or *kaisonians*) came to enjoy considerable notoriety, being alternately denounced and celebrated for their irreverent music and indolent, hedonistic lifestyle. While the quintessential calypsonian shunned work and managed to be gainfully shacked up with a supporting mistress, most found mere survival to be a challenge, since they could perform professionally only two months a year. To this day, few calypsonians have been able to support themselves solely through their art; hence

Lord Executor, when not singing, was a petty clerk; Poser is a bus conductor; and Short Pants and Chalkdust teach school. Many calypsonians, including the Mighty Sparrow himself, have emigrated, returning only for Carnival season.

In the 1930s (what some call the "golden age" of calypso), Decca and RCA Victor started producing records of artists like Atilla the Hun and Roaring Lion, recorded mostly in New York. Although the records sold well in the Caribbean, the United States, and even Africa, the artists received more fame than money, since most of the profits stayed with the record companies or with entrepreneurs like bandleader-impresario Lionel Belasco. The most celebrated case involved the Andrews Sisters' early 1940s recording of Lord Invader's "Rum and Coca Cola," which sold some five million copies in the United States. Decca and the Andrews Sisters made the song famous, and they also made the money. Lord Invader and the enterprising Belasco successfully sued the American publishers of the song, although Invader, in true calypsonian style, frittered away his settlement and died broke.

As Carnival and calypso's prominence as a vehicle for the vox populi grew, so did the controversies surrounding the music. Should the colonial authorities try vigorously to control and limit it, or should they accept it as a boost to tourism and business and a way for the lower classes to let off steam? Should ribald and politically oppositional calypsoes be tolerated or repressed? Which *mas* processions should be supported—the unruly downtown ones or the bureaucratically controlled ones of Port of Spain's Savannah Park? How should factors of originality, poetry, melody, and presentation be weighed in judging calypso competitions? And how should the judges be selected?

Behind such administrative controversies lay the more profound struggle of Trinidadians to survive. Carnival merriment notwithstanding, many Trinidadians continued to live in abject poverty, and the colonial government remained committed more to the masses' exploitation than to their welfare. As Patrick Jones (Lord Protector) sang in 1920:

> We are ruled with the iron hand;
> Britain boasts of democracy, brotherly love, and fraternity,
> but British colonists have been ruled in perpetual misery.

Indeed, the pious British praises of human rights and freedom of speech did not apply in the colonies, where any sort of oppositional discourse, such as Marxist or black-nationalist Garveyite literature, was rigorously banned. Attempts by mine and farm workers to organize were brutally crushed, and while the British maintained a facade of parliamentary government, labor leaders like Uriah Butler were kept out of power.

Censorship of calypsoes reached a peak during the 1930s. Any song criticizing the state or dealing with Afro-Trinidadian culture or religion was subject, however unpredictably, to banning. Calypsonians were required to submit their lyrics to censorship offices before singing them, and policemen were posted in tents to monitor performances. Tents hosting objectionable songs could be shut down and singers' licenses revoked. Shipments of allegedly subversive records pressed in New York were dumped in the sea, and in general, calypso's role as a mouthpiece of popular sentiment was severely curbed.

Such restraints, along with the prevailing hegemony of imperial ideology, partially explain what may seem by modern standards to be the rather low sociopolitical consciousness of most calypso before the 1970s. Many calypsoes were obsequiously loyalist, especially during World War II. Some praised the British for the emancipation of slaves, forgetting England's own active role in the slave trade. Several singers righteously endorsed Britain's stated opposition to the 1936 Italian invasion of Abyssinia, not knowing that the British had secretly sanctioned the act. Few songs displayed any sense of positive racial consciousness, instead ridiculing people as "black and ugly," reinforcing negative stereotypes about *orisha* worship, and presenting the ideal woman as rich, white, and stupid. As is discussed below, representations of women were especially reactionary.

Only a handful of singers had the integrity, vision, and temerity to challenge the norm and voice genuinely progressive sentiments. Particularly prominent among these was Raymond Quevedo (Atilla the Hun, 1892–1962), who, aside from being a leading calypsonian for nearly half a century, was an indefatigable labor leader and legislator. While Atilla failed to transcend the sexism of his era, many of his songs presented the common man's point of view and, from the 1950s, explicitly called for independence.

The World War II years and the establishment of two large U.S. military bases brought an unprecedented prosperity to many Trinidadians, including calypsonians. While hundreds of locals earned their first decent wages working at the bases, enthusiastic and relatively affluent GI's filled the calypso tents at Carnival time. Meanwhile, however, calypsonians watched with dismay as local women forsook their company for that of the free-spending GI's. Lord Invader's 1943 classic "Rum and Coca Cola" relates how his girlfriend, along with her mother and sisters, drove off with some soldiers:

They bought rum and Coca Cola, way down Point Cumana,
both mother and daughter working for the Yankee dollar.

With the end of the war and the departure of the GI's, many women had no option but to return to the sweet-talking, unemployed calypsonians. The Mighty Sparrow's immortal "Jean and Dinah" captured the mood:

Well the girls in town are feelin' bad
No more Yankees in Trinidad
They gonna close down the base for good
The girls'll have to make out how they could. . . .
It's the glamor boys again
We are going to rule Port of Spain
No more Yankees to spoil the fete
Dorothy have to take what she get
All of them who used to make style
Takin' their two shillings with a smile
No more hotel and Simmons bed
By the sweat of thy brow shalt thou eat bread
Jean and Dinah, Rosita and Clementina,
On the corner posing, bet your life it's something exciting
And if you catch them broke you can get 'em all for nothing
Yankee's gone and Sparrow take over from now.[1]

This song also illustrates the primary rule of scansion for calypso, which is that you can put as many or as few syllables in a line as you want.

The 1950s were a fertile decade for calypso. The "Young Brigade" of Kitchener and Lord Melody (Melo now deceased, Kitch far from young) was in full swing. The Jamaican-American Harry Belafonte was popularizing calypso in the United States (much to the resentment of genuine Trinidadian calypsonians). With greater freedom of expression and impending independence, some calypsoes both reflected and promoted a greater sociopolitical awareness. In 1955, Atilla, for example, denounced the racism of the *Trinidad Guardian* newspaper's beauty-queen contest:

For this *Guardian* competition
is nothing but real discrimination.
One thing in this world will never be seen
is a dark-skinned girl as Carnival Queen.

More significantly, the decade—and particularly, the year 1956—saw the emergence of perhaps the two most important figures in modern Trinidadian culture. One was Eric Williams, "the Doctor," the brilliant scholar, charismatic orator, and much-loved prime minister who dominated his party (the People's National Movement, or PNM) and the nation's politics in general until his death in 1981. The other was Francisco Slinger, better known as Mighty Sparrow, who won the Calypso Monarch contest in 1956 at the age of twenty-one and continues to be the genre's most unfailingly excellent performer. The two figures are further linked in that Williams owed more than a little of his popularity to Sparrow's eloquent support.

Mighty Sparrow has long been the measure of the ideal calypsonian. Possessed of a strong, sure voice, he sings and performs well. He is prolific, managing to release an LP every year when many singers can barely muster two songs. His melodies are simple and effective, while adhering to the typical sing-songy calypso style. Most important, his lyrics (some of which he acknowledges to have been written by a collaborator) are consistently clever, pithy, and catchy; many have become so familiar as to constitute a body of modern West Indian folklore in themselves. He is a master of the art of being ribald without being vulgar.

Although he is not a profound sociopolitical thinker, Sparrow's topical commentaries often seem to capture the mood of the nation, and he has not hesitated to criticize Eric Williams on occasion. In 1957, fresh from his first Monarch victory, he successfully organized a boycott of the Savannah Dimanche Gras competition to demand better pay for contest winners. He went on to win the Road March (the most frequently played song, chosen each year at Carnival) six times and the Monarch competition seven times before retiring from the contests in 1974. In 1992, when Carnival was first broadcast internationally via satellite, he reentered the Monarch competition and again won the prize—cash and a car. (The next year, however, he lost to Calypsonian Chalkdust, who almost missed the finals when his own car broke down in central Trinidad.)

Sparrow's running *picong* duels with the older Lord Melody delighted audiences throughout the fifties and sixties. A typical exchange went:

Sparrow:
Well, Melody, come close to me.
I will tell you plain and candidly,
don't stop and turn around and smile
because you have a face like a crocodile.

Melody:
Sparrow, you shouldn't tell me that at all,
I used to mind you when you were small.
Many nights I used to mash your head
in crossing to go to your mother's---![2]

As of the mid-1990s, Sparrow is still going strong. When, in 1993, Calypsonian Ras Shorty I's moralizing song "That Eh Enough" criticized

Sparrow's still-libidinous image as inappropriate to a man his age, Sparrow retorted wittily with "The More [Girlfriends] the Merrier," recalling Shorty's celebrated hedonistic days (as Lord Shorty) before his conversion to Rastafarianism.

MODERN CALYPSO AND CARNIVAL

With independence in 1962, calypso and Trinidadian history entered a new chapter. Inspired by the civil rights movement in the United States, a vigorous local Black Power movement arose, nearly toppling the PNM government in 1970. At the same time, the increasing prominence of East Indians in the country's economic and cultural life has obliged all Trinidadians to recognize the profoundly multicultural nature of their national identity— "All o' we is one," as the saying goes. The biggest development was the unprecedented prosperity brought by the formation of OPEC (Organization of Petroleum Exporting Countries) in 1973, which exponentially increased the profits from local oil reserves, and by a concurrent rise in sugar prices. Under Williams's guidance, in the course of the ten-year boom much money was wasted, and long-term planning was bungled, but most Trinidadians, whether through hard work, trickle-down economics, or civil service sinecures, came to enjoy an essentially bourgeois standard of living. Throughout the island, the old "trash-house" shanties were replaced by modern concrete houses, often complete with TV and carport.

The era has been eventful for calypso as well. By 1970, calypso was on the defensive against rock and reggae, but at the same time it was revitalized by the new social and musical movements. Stylistically, the main calypso-related development has been the advent of soca. In 1977, Lord Shorty (who stands six feet, four inches tall) set out to improve on calypso's customary bouncy, slightly ragged, but basically bland and generically Caribbean accompaniment patterns. With arranger Ed Watson, he came up with a composite pattern they called "soca" (or "sokah," to reflect the East Indian influence), which, in a loosely standardized form, has been the norm in most calypso since. The chorus of soca artist Arrow's 1983 "Hot Hot Hot" (later covered by Buster Poindexter and, in Hindi, by Babla-Kanchan) typifies the soca beat, as schematically represented in Musical Example 18.

The term "soca" is often used to refer to modern calypso in general, although it is also used more specifically to distinguish dance music, as opposed to calypso proper, whose essence remains the text. Soca lyrics are usually short and inconsequential (unless one considers repeated calls to "wine on a bumsie" to be of literary significance). The usual theme of soca

MUSICAL EXAMPLE 18

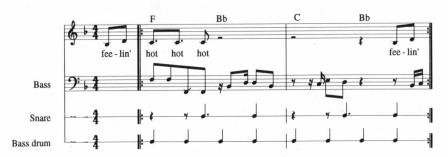

songs is "jam and wine," which denotes not an aperitif but "party and dance." In particular, "wining" is the now-predominant West Indian up-tempo dance style, whose essence is a pneumatic pelvic rotation, ideally executed in synchronicity with another adjacent "winer," whether front-to-back, front-to-front, or back-to-back. It is fun, and good exercise as well. Soca dancing often has a collective character, as dancers respond to singers' exhortations to "jump up" or "get something and wave."

Soca's popularity has sharpened the dichotomy between, on the one hand, dance music—designed for parties, *mas* processions, and the Road March prize—and, on the other hand, lyric-oriented calypso, a somewhat more cerebral genre confined to the tents and aimed at the calypso Monarch trophy. In the 1994 carnival, the dichotomy was institutionalized with the establishment of separate competition categories for soca and calypso. Accordingly, the gamut of calypso controversies now includes the complaints of those who believe that mindless soca, along with imported pop, is drowning out calypso proper. Chalkdust, never one to pull punches or discreetly refrain from naming names, voiced the purist school of thought in his prize-winning 1993 calypso "Kaiso in the Hospital":

> The young ran amuck, they cursed in the worst way,
> drugs and sex they glorified.
> They called themselves Rock, Rap, Zouk, and Reggae,
> And Kaiso's house they occupied.[3]

Such criticisms notwithstanding, most young Trinidadians enjoy soca for what it is, and many have looked to it as the country's hope for a music that will make it onto the world-beat market. After all, reggae's international vogue in the 1970s owed as much to the genre's catchy rhythm as to its messianic fervor. So far, however, neither soca nor calypso proper has attracted much of an audience outside the West Indian market.

Calypso's text orientation is both its strength and its weakness. The tradition of penning verses about current events makes calypso a uniquely dynamic form of grass-roots folklore, closely attuned to people's daily lives, rather than a mere reiteration of sentimental cliches. However, this very specificity limits calypso's appeal to the here and now. A song about a petty corruption trial or a cuckolded minister in Port of Spain can delight local audiences at the time, but it may be forgotten within months and will mean nothing to listeners in neighboring Grenada, not to mention in the United States. Further, calypso verses are too long for pop formats, which demand short, snappy lyrics and danceable refrains.

Accordingly, the calypso recording industry has been a small-time affair, consisting until recently of a few rudimentary studios in Port of Spain and storefront labels like Strakers in Brooklyn. Distribution has been informal at best, and even Mighty Sparrow could be seen selling records out of the trunk of his car on a street corner in Port of Spain. So most records are still slapped together as seasonal throwaway music, produced as tourist souvenirs in batches of a few thousand and often financed by the artist or by merchants whose ads plaster the backs of the LP covers. The small size of the West Indian market and the widespread sale of pirate cassettes have further hampered the development of a soca-calypso record industry. In the early 1990s, however, the situation improved somewhat with the construction of a first-class recording studio in Trinidad by Robert Amar and another in Barbados by Guyanese producer Eddy Grant. Both studios are committed to promoting calypso, and Grant's distribution deals with the U.S.-based RAS Records should afford soca an new international visibility.

Despite such signs of progress, the mass media in most of the West Indies remain dominated by the rap, R & B, and Jamaican dancehall marketed by powerful multinationals. Calypso is mostly heard during Carnival season —after which, it's back to Lionel Ritchie and Buju Banton. Local attitudes perpetuate such compartmentalization: many West Indians feel saturated with calypso by the end of Carnival season, and as one Trinidadian lamented, "If my mother hears me playing a soca record after Ash Wednesday, she shouts, 'Shut that devil's music off—it's Lent now!'" American programming also dominates television, especially since local stations cannot afford to produce the same sorts of slick shows. In the song "Satellite Robber," by Trinidadian calypsonian Commentator (Brian Honoré), the satellite disc boasts:

I'm here to rip out your heart, tear your culture apart,
make you worship the American flag.

The next verse responds:

> I said please, Mr. Robber, I beg you remember
> I am independent since 1962.
> He said "Don't aggravate me,
> when it coming to TV, it is I who control you."

In spite of indifferent media support and the competition from rap, reggae, R&B, and "jam-and-wine" soca, calypso remains vital. Now, as before, calypso is constantly in the news; as the recognized "people's voice," it is forever provoking outrage and delight, eliciting public denunciations by offended politicians, and generating endless newspaper editorials and letters. Recent decades have seen the emergence of talented and dynamic new artists who have brought new levels of lyrical and musical sophistication to the art. Particularly prominent since the 1970s are Chalkdust (Hollis Liverpool), celebrated for his trenchant sociopolitical commentaries, and David Rudder, an eclectic, intelligent, rock-oriented composer and bandleader who appeared on the scene in 1986. Liverpool, who earned a doctorate in ethnomusicology in 1993, is the author of a few books on calypso; both he and Rudder (b. 1953) have won the Monarch prize repeatedly. East Indian singers like Rikki Jai and Drupatee Ramgoonai have also entered the fray, enriching the music with their own idiosyncratic Indianisms. Meanwhile, as Jamaican dancehall becomes the favored music of Trinidadian youth, Carnival season now includes several songs in a *ragga-soca* style, fusing calypso and modern reggae.

Calypso's text topics remain as varied and rich as ever. As always, their forte is light social commentary and satire, rather than, for example, the poignant sentimentality of the bolero or the passionate intensity of "classic" reggae. In customary fashion, many lyrics sing the praises of Carnival, steel drums, and calypso itself, sometimes berating other singers for their slackness and theatrical gimmicks. Some songs take potshots at dancehall, which offends many because of its unmelodiousness, its frequent vulgarity, its foreign origin, and the earsplitting volume at which it was played in public minibuses until banned from them in 1994. As calypsonian Bally sang in his 1989 "Maxi Dub":

> The music live and me head on fire,
> Ah beg the driver play a little softer. . . .
> Ah wanted to cry 'cuz I couldn't hear soca.

Other calypso songs denounce apartheid, call for ethnic harmony, warn against drug abuse (e.g., Sparrow's "Coke Is Not It"), criticize the government, and lament the country's current economic decline. Boasting and ribaldry persist, along with assorted miscellany. Rudder's 1993 "Dus' in deh Face" described the excitement of the pan contests at the Savannah fairgrounds, subtly using steel-band rivalry as a metaphor for the violence and crime besetting the recession-torn island. That year's calypso winner was Chalkdust, whose "Misconceptions" whimsically addressed the international satellite audience, including the verse:

> Michael Jackson, please come down here,
> there is a misconception you is fair.
> Come down and play mas with we and get back your color.

Even if such songs are forgotten by the following year, they perpetuate a unique tradition that itself remains contemporary by virtue of its very topicality.

CALYPSO AND GENDER

Trinidadian writers have commented extensively on the occasionally virulent sexism of traditional calypso.[4] From its inception, calypso has been a man's world, rooted in the macho boasting of the *calinda* chantwell, the ribaldry of the early tent scene, and male views on social norms in general. Among Afro-Trinidadians, sociohistorical conditions have tended to promote temporary male–female liaisons as much as marriage and the accompanying

Cartoon regarding banning of loud dancehall music in Guyana's public mini-vans (*Guyana Chronicle October 3, 1993*)

sentiments of commitment and eternal love. Aside from the socially disruptive legacy of slavery, unemployment endemic in the later colonial period often led both men and women to avoid marital ties, which might burden either with an unproductive spouse. However, men, unlike women, enjoyed a public forum—calypso—where they could present their desires and double standards as a norm and an ideal. Hence colonial-era calypsoes often portrayed women as valuable only as meal tickets or as sexual playthings for the calypsonian stud, as in Mighty Duke's "Woop-Wap Man" ("woop, wap —next one!"). Calypsoes traditionally ridiculed women as ugly, sexually infectious ("Don't Bathe in Elsie's River"), and forever trying to tie men down with obeah (black magic) or false accusations of paternity. Calypsonian Mighty Terror, for instance, sang:

> I black like jet and she just like tarbaby,
> still, Chinese children calling me daddy.

But the quintessential traditional calypsonian, even if so victimized by his faithless mate, would generally shun responsibility for the children he did sire—especially as he was more often than not unemployed and wholly dependent on whatever women he could charm. While glorifying motherhood in the abstract, calypsoes showed little sympathy for the flesh-and-blood mothers struggling to raise fatherless children. (*Sans humanité* indeed!) "Sixteen Commandments," sung by Lord Shorty (before his conversion to Rastafarianism), is particularly explicit in its articulation of the male double standard. Warning his girlfriend to be faithful to him and not ask him for money, Shorty sings:

> If thou see me wid a nex' girl talkin', try and understand.
> Pass me straight like you ain't know me,
> let me have my woman.

Similarly, Atilla's "Women Will Rule the World" (1935) warns of women trying to improve their lot and competing with men for scarce jobs:

> I'm offering a warning to men this year:
> Of modern women beware.
> Even the young girls you cannot trust,
> for they're taking our jobs from us.
> And if you men don't assert control,
> women will rule the world.
> They say that anything that man can do
> they also can achieve too,
> and openly boast to do their part
> in literature and art.
> You'll soon hear of them as candidates

for the President of the United States.
If women ever get the ascendancy,
they will show us no sympathy.
They will make us do strange things, goodness knows,
scrub floors and even wash clothes.
If these tyrants become our masters,
we'll have to push perambulators.

God forbid! Indeed, Atilla would be spinning in his grave to see modern Trinidad with its female politicians, professors, and entrepreneurs—not to mention female prime ministers in Great Britain and nearby Dominica.

To forestall such catastrophes, calypsoes would often advise men how to deal with their women, as in "Turn Them Down," an old calypso revived by Sparrow in the 1970s:

Every now and then, cuff them down.
They'll love you long and they'll love you strong.
Black up dey eye, bruise up dey knee,
and they will love you eternally.

One antidote to such sexist manifestos would be for women to enter the calypso arena and speak for themselves, for example, as to whether they do indeed love being "cuffed down." Although calypso may be inherently male in its emphasis on braggadocio, women have, in fact, established a place in it, now institutionalized in Trinidad's Woman Rising competition. Such singers as Calypso Rose and Denyse Plummer (a white Trinidadian) have earned their own audiences and awards, in many cases expressing support for women in the face of beatings, insults, and exploitation. Thus, Easlyn Orr sings "Woman Respect Yourself," while Singing Francine answers the "treat 'em rough" philosophy with "Run Away" (1979):

Dog does run away, child does run away,
woman does run away when man treating them bad . . .
Woman, put two wheels on your heels.

Similarly, Lady Iere's "Love Me or Leave Me" became a slogan for abused West Indian women:

You gotta love me or leave me, or live with Miss Dorothy.
The time is too hard for me to mind a man that's bad.

In general, since the socio-political awakening of the 1970s, flagrantly sexist calypsoes have gone out of style, and male calypsonians have often expressed more appreciative attitudes toward women. A trendsetter in this regard was Lord Kitchener's classic road march of 1973, "Flag Woman," honoring the banner-waving women who animatedly lead carnival bands:

Chalkdust (Strakers Records)

Without an experienced flag woman,
your band will have no control
your music will have no soul.

Similarly, 1993 found Mighty Terror voicing quaint but timely sentiments in his "Tribute to All Housewives":

Every man should assist his wife
and let the love be lasting for life. . . .
Don't beat you wife, take this tip from me.

Such proclamations aside, calypso continues to delight in erotic puns and
euphemisms, where the emphasis is on whimsical wordplay rather than sexual politics. As in other Caribbean genres, practically any ostensibly trivial
or obscure song lyric can be assumed to be some sort of sexual double
entendre, especially if the actual text appears to be totally innocent. Take,
for example, Crazy's 1990s hit "Paul, Your Mother Come," which was
banned from the airwaves. Why? Because audiences immediately recognized
the refrain as a thinly disguised "Paul, your mother's cunt," and they would
gleefully sing it that way at dance concerts. It would be a mistake to denounce such juvenilia as "sexist objectification" or a degrading insult; it's
just pure whimsy, the latest in a long and hoary Caribbean tradition.

THE CARNIVAL CONTEXT

Since 1900, Trinidad Carnival has evolved into a felicitous balance of state-funded, bureaucratically organized competitions and fetes, on the one hand, and various sorts of informal merrymaking—or, to use a favorite Trinidadian word, "bacchanal"—on the other. The bacchanal comprises ad hoc partying, numerous free, open-air dance concerts, and more intimate amusements often realized nocturnally in parks, fields, and other normally public places. All these events are framed by the rhythm of the Carnival schedule itself, including the various competitions for calypso king and queen (and junior counterparts), *mas* band of the year, costume king and queen, Road March king, and Panorama, the national steel-band competition.

In a tropical country without clearly differentiated winter and summer, it is Carnival that provides the seasonal reference point for the rest of the year. Carnival is like a big ocean roller that gathers momentum and size from the Christmas season on and then breaks, foaming and crashing, over the urban streets for two riotous late-February days. The rest of the year is a period of recovery, reminiscing, and gradual preparation for the next year. For calypsonians, preparation may commence as early as late summer, when singers begin composing and recording their songs. These start to be released in

Calypso Rose (Strakers Records)

Cassette piracy in Trinidad—the bane of the recording industry (photo by Peter Manuel)

December, by which time Trinidadians are eager to hear how calypsonians will sum up the political events, social issues, and scandals of the previous year. Audiences are also geared up for the proverbial bacchanal, and the new "jam-and-wine" soca tunes soon become familiar via airplay, record sales, and dance concerts around the country. As Carnival season gets into full swing, music thrives in the twin venues of the calypso tents and the fetes and parties featuring either live bands or deejayed sound systems.

Meanwhile, the leaders of the *mas* bands have decided on a theme, designed the costumes that participants will wear, and by January, they are mass-producing them out of fabrics, wire, sequins, and other materials. By this time, the "pan" (steel-drum) bands have also reassembled, cleaned off and retuned their instruments, and they are practicing one or more current songs chosen and arranged by their leaders. Almost all of this activity, involving considerable organization, self-discipline, and expense, is undertaken by the people themselves, without any significant state assistance. The government's main role is to organize and finance some of the infrastructure for the final events.

By late January, the calypso and pan competitions are underway. In weekend concerts, competing calypsonians, from rank amateurs to big names, perform two songs apiece in "tents" (often theaters) located around the island, accompanied by the tent's house band. Many, but by no means all, of the singers have records out. Panels of judges visit the tents, confer, and, on the basis of lyric, melody, and presentation, pick twenty-four finalists who compete the weekend before Carnival. From that group, eight finalists are chosen to compete at Port of Spain's Savannah fairgrounds on Dimanche Gras, the ("Big") Sunday before Ash Wednesday, which falls in late February. The finals are witnessed either live or on TV by virtually the entire population. The winner, or Calypso Monarch, is then announced, invariably provoking both exuberant acclaim and outraged complaints of bias and ignorance on the part of the judges.

Serious dance parties and bacchanal take place all weekend, but the formal (if that is the word) uncorking of Carnival itself begins with *j'ouvert* (from French, *jour overt*) at 2:00 A.M. on Monday. In *j'ouvert,* the most overt vestige of the *jamette cambouley,* revelers caked with painted mud or

costumed as ghouls drink and dance their way to dawn, accompanied by steel bands and old-style drumming.

By mid-morning on Monday, Port of Spain's Carnival processions, with participants numbering in the tens of thousands, are starting to "jam and wine" their way toward the Savannah. The processions include numerous steel bands, dance bands, and deejayed sound systems mounted on flatbed trucks, all pumping out the new soca hits at deafening volume and surrounded by throngs of dancers and revelers. As one Trinidadian put it, "What I love about Carnival is to be dancing madly in the street, to see some big minister jamming next to me and give him a big hug or pour beer on his head, whatever. Carnival is when we all really become one."

While this is going on, other officials are taking note of which songs the bandleaders, disc jockeys, and steel bands—in response to audience enthusiasm—have selected as favorites; after tallying their observations, the observers announce the most frequently played song as the Road March of the year, whose composer receives a cash prize. Thus, while the Calypso Monarch is selected by judges, the winning Road March is the choice of the people themselves, although in the slightly different category of "jam-and-wine" dance music. (Kitchener and Sparrow have been the most frequent winners since the late fifties.)

For spectators, the focus of the procession is the immense *mas* groups, each of which is conceived and organized around some fanciful theme. Since the mid-twentieth century, winners have included such themes as "Imperial Rome," "Ye Saga of Merrie England," "Pacific Paradise," and "Bright Africa." Participants, including many tourists, pay a hundred dollars or so for their costumes and then drink and dance their way collectively down the promenade. A *mas* band often contains over a thousand members, most wearing identical costumes; it also includes contestants for the costume-king and queen prizes, who are dwarfed by the elaborate and huge costume that he or she arduously pushes.

Since the mid-seventies, the most distinguished and controversial *mas* bandleader has been Peter Minshall, a Caucasian stage designer who lives and works in England, visiting Trinidad—like many others—only for Carnival. Minshall has a distinctive vision of *mas* as a work of conceptual art, a unique sort of gargantuan street theater rather than merely a festive parade around some whimsical theme. His 1983 *mas*, titled "Mancrab/River," is representative: on the first day his entourage, twenty-five hundred people strong, proceeded clad in spotless white robes, led by a pristine "washerwoman" figure. The next day, a monstrous, thirty-foot-high mechanical crab (that year's winning entry for the costume prize) killed the washerwoman, at which point all the other participants doused their white robes in colorful dyes, dramatizing man's destruction of nature. Such extravaganzas have won Minshall many fans, as well as several annual prizes. They have also sparked yet another controversy, raised by those who believe that his notions of high art and his penchant for the macabre and grotesque are inconsistent with the spirit of Carnival.

On the whole, there is nothing quite like Trinidad Carnival. Its popularity and importance can be gauged by the fact that the Monday and Tuesday events in Port of Spain generally draw around seven hundred thousand participants and revelers, about two-thirds of the entire country's population. For outsiders, it is a unique tourist attraction, while for most locals, it is the focal reference point of the year, celebrating a national character based on fun, humor, and togetherness. As Mighty Sparrow sang in 1957:

> The biggest bacchanal is in Trinidad Carnival.
> Regardless of color, creed, or race,
> jump up and shake your waist.
> So jump as you mad, this is Trinidad;
> we don't care who say we bad.

STEEL BAND

Trinidad is internationally famous not only for calypso and Carnival but also as the home of the steel drum, or pan, as it is called. The invention of the steel drum is testimony to the ingenuity and creative perseverance of Afro-Trinidadians in the face of British cultural repression. As was mentioned above, after the British banned the use of drums in Carnival *mas* processions, revelers fashioned "tamboo-bamboo" ensembles by beating with sticks on bamboo tubes (and often, on the heads of rival band members). In the 1930s, innovators started supplementing the clackety-clack of the bamboo by beating on available pieces of metal, from tin pans to brake drums. As the vogue of "biscuit-tin bands" rapidly spread, Port of Spain residents learned to chain down their garbage-can lids to prevent them from being stolen.

Oral histories differ as to who was responsible for the next step, but around 1939, someone discovered that distinct pitches, rather than a simple, crude bang, could be sounded on an empty oil drum (of which there were plenty lying around) if the concave head was dented in a certain way. By the early 1940s, ingenious enthusiasts in Port of Spain were learning how to dent and burn the heads to get two, three, and eventually twenty-some pitches; different classes of steel drums emerged, including "boom

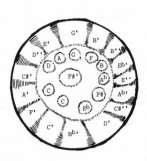

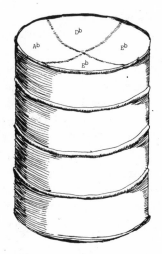

Some standard pan tunings: above, single-so-
prano steel omnivibraphone; right, bass (drawing
by Peter Manuel)

pans" for bass, tenor or "cello pans" for harmony, and sharp-sounding ping-pong drums for melody. Pan fever subsequently took hold of lower-class neighborhoods like East Dry River, Watertown, and Laventille as bands practiced incessantly and jubilantly took their music to the streets at all hours of the day and night.

The British authorities tried to ban the steel bands, partly because of the rowdy fights that often occurred when two bands encountered each other in the streets. A vehement public debate regarding the bands raged in newspapers, Parliament, and other forums. By the mid-forties, a decision was made to try to wean the bands from violence by accommodating and legitimizing them. So they were incorporated into Carnival, and a national ensemble (TASPO) was even sent to tour England. Upright Trinidadians continued to regard panmen as hoodlums, and brawls persisted until the early sixties; as one Trinidadian remarked, "If you were in the winning Panorama band, you didn't dare show your face in town for weeks." Nevertheless, by that time the bands had become an integral part of Carnival and had been taken up avidly in other West Indian islands as well.

Since then, steel bands have outgrown their underworld associations and have developed into a unique form of amateur, collective music making. Many Trinidadian youths play in school bands, while other bands, including top ones like the Amoco Renegades, are sponsored by businesses. Scattered around the country's towns are dozens of pan yards where instruments are stored and played. Only a few bands manage to get year-round professional gigs at dances and on cruise ships; the rest are purely amateur groups that unite only to compete in Panorama, the national competition climaxing on the Saturday before Dimanche Gras. In the two months before Carnival, the pan yards come alive as musicians rehearse nightly for up to eight hours. Spectators and supporters also turn out at the best yards to listen as the arrangements evolve and to refresh themselves with beer and aloo (potato) pies sold by vendors.

Generally, the bands do not play original material but perform arrangements of calypso hits and familiar classical pieces. For panmen raised in slums and lacking any formal musical training, it is a matter of pride to play pieces by Schubert and Saint-Saëns as well as Sparrow and Swallow. Even some of the leading pan arrangers cannot read music, but they nevertheless devise brilliantly intricate and driving arrangements. Nowadays, a few of the top bands compose their own elaborate tunes, but most restrict themselves to learning two or three calypsoes of the current season, in order to compete in the various levels of Panorama.

In Port of Spain's Carnival, the steel bands proceed along Queen's Park with the other mobile mayhem, stopping to perform in front of the judges' bandstand in the hope of making it to the Savannah semifinals. The pans themselves are mounted on frames with wheels, so that the ensemble, which can number up to the decreed limit of 120 musicians, becomes like a huge ship, complete with various floats, racks, and a roof. Its prow is formed by the bass drums, some of which point outward like cannons. Mounted above the surrounding tenor, cello, and melody pans is the "engine room," a

Bass steel-drum set (Ethnic Folk Arts Center)

rhythm section consisting of drum kit, congas, and men beating brake drums and wheel hubs.

In the 1980s, with the predominance of these elaborate, unwieldy, corporate-funded mega-bands, pan seemed to be losing its grass-roots earthiness, and public interest waned somewhat. Some Trinidadians worried that foreigners like American jazz pan virtuoso Andy Narell were stealing the limelight, while the Japanese were factory-producing standardized steel drums. By the early nineties, however, the genre was making a strong comeback, partly with the advent of smaller, more mobile "pan-around-the-neck" ensembles. These, as well as top bands like Exodus and the Tropical Angel Harps, generate tremendous enthusiasm among Trinidadians of all races, who love their national instrument and share the excitement generated by the music and by the intense rivalry between bands. With the Trinidad and Tobago government actively promoting steel bands and busying itself with such matters as standardizing tuning, pan music should be able to hold its own against the din of disc jockeys and disco.

CALYPSO AND CARNIVAL
OUTSIDE TRINIDAD

West Indians living in countries other than Trinidad and Tobago often take justified umbrage at outsiders' tendency to identify calypso and Carnival exclusively with Trinidad. It is true that Trinidad is the primary crucible of calypso and that its Carnival is by far the biggest and most extravagant in the West Indies. But other Caribbean islands have played their own roles in calypso's evolution. First of all, such calypso as existed in the eighteenth and nineteenth centuries appears to have been part of an Afro-French creole culture spread thoughout the French Caribbean; indeed, the first extant appearance of the word *cariso* refers to a singer from Martinique. Martinique was later the source of the tune of "Rum and Coca Cola," just as the Haitian folk song "Choucounne" provided the melody for "Yellow Bird." West Indian immigrants to the more affluent Trinidad have long enriched that island's music with their own traditions. More recently, several major figures have emerged in the calypso world who hail from other countries, including Arrow, from Montserrat, and Guyanese producer Eddy Grant.

Most West Indian countries also have their own versions of Carnival, of which some are recent gimmicks to attract tourists while others enjoy authentic grass-roots popularity. The festivities on the island of Carriacou, as documented by Donald Hill, are typical. Old-style Carnival there commenced with informal calypso singing, family *canbouley* feasts, and stick fighting with *calinda* songs on Sunday night. Early Monday morning, a rowdy *juvay* (*j'ouvert*) would take place to the accompaniment of steel bands. The rest of Monday and Shrove Tuesday would be devoted to traditional masquerade-band processions and "speech mas'," in which two opposing orators (called *paywoes, shortnees,* or kings), supported by local sidekicks, would hurl insults at each other and recite flowery speeches from Shakespeare (usually *Julius Caesar*) in a sort of Afro-Saxon call-and-response fashion. In recent decades, under Trinidadian influence, the calypso singing and *mas* processions have been organized into formal tent competitions held at schools.[5] With most of the various islands now holding their own festivals, Carnival and calypso now thrive year-round, albeit in different locales. Naturally, other West Indian countries have their own musical traditions, including various creole counterparts to calypso as well as distinctive Afro-Caribbean genres, such as Carriacou's "big drum" dance.

Last, but by no means least, there is New York City, which, as home to over half a million West Indians, is the largest West Indian city outside Jamaica. The city's West Indian community has long been dynamic and distinguished, its members renowned (or by some, begrudged) for their industriousness and economic progress. The community has generated such notables as Shirley Chisolm, Sidney Poitier, Kool Herc, and, among second-generation members, rappers like Africa Bambaataa, LL Cool J, and Heavy D. Accordingly, the city has also become a center for calypso, just as it did with French Caribbean and Latin music. New York is the hub of the West Indian recording industry, and due to the concentrated population, most records sell about five times the number there as in the islands themselves. Several calypsonians, from Calypso Rose to Mighty Sparrow himself, live in New York, performing regularly at venues like S.O.B.'s for mixed Caribbean and Anglo audiences. West Indians dominate entire areas of Brooklyn and Queens, and transplanted traditions from *parang* to pan thrive there.

But needless to say, New York is not exactly a Caribbean city, and its West Indian culture has naturally taken on a flavor distinct from its island counterparts. For one thing, there is much more social mixing among the diverse West Indian communities than would occur in the Caribbean itself. Barbadians ("Bajans"), Guyanese, Trinidadians, and others do maintain their own social clubs, but, living in such close proximity, it is inevitable that they intermingle, intermarry, and develop a more unified sense of identity. At the same time, many young West Indians increasingly identify with Afro-Americans, adopting hip-hop fashions, mannerisms, and music as their own, often to the dismay of their parents. As a result, the typical New York

West Indian may have various overlapping ethnic self-identities, for example, as Trinidadian, as West Indian, as black, and even as American. Musical tastes reflect these intersections, as young West Indians grow up enjoying rap and R & B as well as the Sparrow in their parents' record collections.

The U.S. West Indian community's main occasion to celebrate its identity is the Labor Day Carnival, in which *mas* groups, steel bands, and trucks with sound systems and accompanying dancers work their way down Brooklyn's Eastern Parkway. This event may have started as a miniature version of Trinidad Carnival but has long since acquired its own character. For one thing, it is hardly miniature, as it draws nearly a million people to the avenue, although most come to watch rather than to actively participate. More significant, it has much more of a pan–West Indian character than does its Trinidad counterpart, as it features processions and bands from all the various West Indian islands, some of which have no particular Carnival traditions of their own. It thus celebrates both the diversity and the unity of the West Indian community. As the ever-quotable Sparrow put it in his 1969 "Mas in Brooklyn":

> You can be from St. Clair or from John John,
> in New York, all that done.
> They haven't to know who is who;
> New York equalize you.
> Bajan, Grenadian, Jamaican, *tout moun* [everybody],
> drinking dey rum, beating dey bottle and spoon,
> and no one who see me can honestly say,
> they don't like to be in Brooklyn on Labor Day.

The growth and increasing self-consciousness of the community has led, among other things, to a movement to rename Eastern Parkway "Caribbean Parkway." This request has evoked little enthusiasm from the several thousand Hasidic Jews also living in Brooklyn, whose men can be seen on Labor Day wearing their black suits and derby hats in the sweltering heat, watching the raucous Carnival parade wanly from their front porches. ("You can just feel the love," as one reveler quipped.) In 1994, the Hasidic community made its own conflicting request for use of the parkway in connection with Jewish holidays. In a multicultural society, such are the issues that must continually be negotiated, in a spirit, one hopes, of compromise and mutual respect.

BIBLIOGRAPHY

Trinidadian scholars have produced several excellent books on calypso and carnival, notably Gordon Rohlehr's *Calypso and Society in Pre-Independence Trinidad* (Port of

Spain: G. Rohlehr, 1990); Errol Hill's *The Trinidad Carnival: Mandate for a National Theatre* (Austin: University of Texas Press, 1972); and Keith Warner's *Kaiso, the Trinidad Calypso* (Washington, D.C.: Three Continents, 1985); see also Donald Hill, *Calypso Calaloo: Early Carnival Music in Trinidad* (Gainesville: University Press of Florida, 1993).

RECORDS AND FILMS

Aside from recordings by the calypso and *soca* artists mentioned in this chapter, see "Calypso Carnival 1936–1941" (Rounder) and "An Island Carnival: Music of the West Indies" (Nonesuch 72091).

Films include *Mas Fever: Inside Trinidad Carnival,* by Glenn Micallef and Larry Johnson (Filmsound, Portland, Oregon, 1989), and *Pan in "A" Minor: Steelbands de Trinidad,* by Daniel Verba and Jean-Jacques Mrejen (Iskra Films).

9

The Other Caribbean

EAST INDIANS IN THE WEST INDIES

It is Sunday morning at the Newtown Sai Baba temple. As the neighborhood begins to awaken, the sounds of roosters crowing, songbirds chirping, and a distant Indian film song drift into the temple, where Jeevan Chowtie is preparing the room for the morning session. By 8:00 A.M., around two dozen Indian schoolchildren have trickled in and are seated on the floor, boys on one side and girls on the other. A ten-year-old boy tunes up a *tabla* drum pair, used in North Indian classical and light-classical music, while the other children flip through their songbooks. With Jeevan leading them on the harmonium, they start singing a *bhajan,* or Hindu devotional song, in the Hindi language: "Ishvar Allah tero nam, sab ko sammati de bhagwan" (Whether your name is God or Allah, let everyone give respect).

The scene could be anywhere in North India, except that the temple architecture is a bit different and the children's Hindi accents are slightly off. But they are close enough; for this is not India but Guyana, home to some four hundred thousand East Indians. These are not Amerindians but Indians from India—the ones Christopher Columbus thought he had found in the Caribbean. Columbus was clearly confused in calling the Arawaks "Indians," but the British partially rectified the misnomer by importing to the Caribbean some 425,000 peasants from India as indentured laborers between 1838 and 1917; the Dutch brought another 35,000 to Dutch Guiana, now Suriname. While life was hard for the immigrants, most of them stayed, re-creating aspects of traditional life from the Bhojpuri region of North India whence most had come. The descendants of these immigrants now constitute the largest ethnic groups in Trinidad and Guyana, and they make up over a third of Suriname's population.

With Trinidad known as the land of steel band and calypso and with

212

Hindu temple in rural Guyana, with *jhandi* flags in front (photo by Peter Manuel)

Guyana and Suriname little known at all, the Indo-Caribbeans have had a rather low international visibility. For that matter, even in the Caribbean they tended to remain somewhat insular and isolated on sugar plantations until recent decades. Such isolation, along with other factors, helped the Indians to retain much more of their ancestral homeland's culture than could West Indian blacks. The Indians came more recently to the Caribbean than the Africans and were not subjected to the same sorts of cultural repression. They could also look back to a mainstream North Indian, Hindi-language high culture with which they could maintain some ongoing contact through books, visits, and, from the 1940s, Indian films. In recent decades, the East Indians have entered their countries' economic, political, and cultural mainstreams, and their lively musical traditions have come into the open.

Jeevan Chowtie explains to me, "Here in Guyana, it's been an uphill battle all the way. For twenty-eight years we suffered under the last government, and tens of thousands of us Indians simply left, for Queens, Toronto, wherever." Chowtie is referring to the dictatorship of Forbes Burnham and the PNC (Peoples National Congress), who came into power in 1964 after the U.S. Central Intelligence Agency and the British destabilized the elected government of Cheddi Jagan, a fervently anti-imperialist East Indian leader. After Burnham's death in 1981, the PNC clung to power until 1992 when, holding free elections for the first time in thirty years, it lost to the indefatigable Jagan, then seventy-six years old.

Chowtie continues, "The country is bankrupt, but things may get better now, for us Indians and for everyone. Come to the TV station, where I work, and I'll show you."

We then ride on Chowtie's motorbike through the pot-holed streets of Georgetown to the studio of CNS, the country's only private television station, which opened in 1992. The studio consists of a single room cluttered with a few video machines, a camcorder, and a transmitter about the size of a refrigerator door. A rickety looking broadcast antenna reaches fifty feet or so above the house, the upper floor of which is inhabited by the owner, an Indian entrepreneur. CNS is oriented mostly toward the country's Indian community, which, Indians feel, has been otherwise neglected by the PNC-dominated state media. At the moment, they are broadcasting a Hindi film, and the three women working there are merrily singing along with one of the film songs.

Knowing that few Indo-Caribbeans speak Hindi, I ask one of the women how she knows the words to the song; she replies, "I love these songs; we listen to them all the time, so I know all the words, even if I don't really understand them." As another fan, in Trinidad, put it, "I cyan understan' dis t'ing, but I mus' hear it!"[1] And indeed, Indo-Caribbean people are crazy about Hindi films and film songs; many fans are amateur or even professional crooners, who will be praised by concert emcees as "The Voice of Mukesh" (an Indian singer) or "A True Imitator" (not one of your cheap imitators). But, as I learn, Indo-Caribbeans also make their own music. In Suriname, where Indians still speak Hindi, Indian folk music thrives, and even in English-speaking Trinidad and Guyana, young and old sing Hindi-language *bhajans* at temples and lively songs called *chowtal* at the springtime *phagwa* festival. In Guyana and Trinidad, as English gradually replaced Hindi, East Indians cultivated their own tradition of calypso-like, so-called "local" songs; in accordance with both calypso and North Indian folk customs, some of these songs could be quite ribald, as titles such as "Fowl Cock" and "Squash Long and Fine" might suggest.

But Chowtie laments, "We had a vibrant music tradition here in Guyana, but everything stagnated under Burnham. The older musicians are dying off, and the best of the younger ones all left, whether Indians like Devindra Pooran or blacks like Eddy Grant. Trinidad is the better place for Indo-Caribbean music."

Back at my hotel, I find the Afro-Guyanese staff sitting in the lobby, glumly watching the unsubtitled Hindi film on the TV. I can't help but ask, "Do you all like this film?"

"Frankly, no," says the clerk, "but there's nothing else on until the evening." Then they can tune in to the drab and underfunded government station or watch a pirated New York station, complete with local city news and ads for Brooklyn car dealers.

Trinidad, my next stop, does indeed turn out to have a more active musical scene, for both Indians and blacks. The country as a whole is much more affluent, and although some Indians feel they have been discriminated against, Trinidad's democratic government and openly multicultural ambience have allowed the Indians to develop quite a lively and varied musical culture. One venue for this is *Mastana Bahar*, an ongoing amateur competition series in which singers and dancers compete in weekly contests that are held around the island and broadcast on radio. Indians also celebrate various annual festivals with music. In springtime, Caribbean Hindus celebrate *phagwa* (or *holi*) much as in India, playfully dousing one another with colored powder and forming competing teams in singing raucous *chowtal* songs. Shia Muslims commemorate Muharram—or *Hosay*, as they call it—by constructing elaborate *taziya* floats, which are paraded through the streets to the accompaniment of *tassa* barrel drums. The *tassa* playing, based on Indian models, is fast, exciting, and deafeningly loud, and is also performed at weddings and other occasions.

Indo-Trinidadian weddings are particularly festive and elaborate. After a few days of preliminary rituals, the wedding culminates in a grand feast, called "tent night" or "cooking night," to which everyone in the neighborhood, regardless of race or creed, is invited. Around ten o'clock in the evening, an ensemble of hired musicians—a lead singer accompanied by harmonium, *dholak* barrel drum, and two metal rods struck against each other (*dantal*)—commences performing what Indo-Caribbeans call "*tan* singing" or local classical singing. *Tan* singing is a mixture of old folk songs from the Bhojpuri-speaking area of North India, somewhat garbled elements of North Indian classical music, and some features unique to Indo-Caribbean culture, all reinterpreted by local musicians who stress original composition and creation. As Trinidadian musician Mangal Patasar described it to me, "You take a capsule from India, leave it here for 150 years, and this is what you get." Although the singers don't really know Hindi, they know the words to the Hindi songs and are generally steeped in Hindu lore. For their part, audiences don't understand Hindi either, but they like the sound of it and prize its use as an emblem of Indianness. Basdeo "Lappo" Dindial, a Trinidadian singer, explained to me:

> I don't speak Hindi, but my mother knew it pretty well, since her parents were born in India. She taught me dozens of songs that I still sing. But we make up new songs too, gettin' the elders to help us with the Hindi; or else

Above, and on opposite page, *tassa* drummers, with *taziya*, at *Hosay* commemoration in Port of Spain, Trinidad (photos by Peter Manuel)

we take lyrics from old poetry books and set them to melodies as we please. I studied and practiced a lot when I was young. My friends used to laugh at me, they were always drinkin' rum and knockin' bench and table all over the place, but now they see the stage I reach. I'm singin' every weekend at weddings, tryin' to keep up the tradition. Here, no matter how poor a person is, they still want to have some singin' at a wedding, even if just for a few hours. And sometimes you see a poor person, he just loves music, and you cannot charge him for it.

Usually at a wedding, two singers will trade off singing all night, occasionally doing *picong*-style Hindi-language duels. By 4:00 A.M. or so, people are in a dancing mood, and the singers switch to what is now called "chutney," meaning up-tempo songs in folk style with simple, catchy tunes. At that point, men and women commence the most uninhibited and animated dancing, continuing until mid-morning.

Since the late 1980s, chutney has become something of a craze in Trinidad as Indians have taken it out of the closet and into big public dances,

held every weekend at open-air clubs throughout the island. These generally commence as film-music concerts (more "Voice of Rafi," etc.), but after a few hours, the beer takes effect, the chutney begins, and listeners—young and old, male and female—push aside the folding chairs, and a joyous pandemonium takes over. The dance style is quite unique, combining vigorous pelvic "wining" with graceful hand-and-arm gestures deriving from Indian folk dance. The result is a delight to behold, especially in its pervading sense of fun and its good, clean, wholesome, outrageous sexiness.

In studios and concerts, the rather sparse chutney instrumentation is sometimes jazzed up with soca rhythms and instruments (synthesizers, pressure drums, and whatnot). The soca beat mixes quite easily with the funky, heartbeat chutney rhythm (what Indians would call *kaherva*), and the result is called "chutney-soca." While generally lacking calypso's textual interest, chutney-soca has a flavor quite distinct from mainstream soca because of its Hindi lyrics, ornamented vocal style, often minor-sounding modal melodies, and the thumping and pumping *dholak*. As with calypso, some of the vocalists sing in tune and some don't. Those who do, like Trinidad's Anand Yankaran and Suriname's Kries Ramkhelawan, are mini-stars in constant demand. In a class by themselves are the duo Babla and Kanchan—vocalist Kanchan and her husband-producer, Babla—who hail directly from India but have their biggest following among Indo-Caribbeans. Their repertoire includes new and old chutney-soca tunes, a Hindi cover version of Arrow's song "Hot Hot Hot," and soca-style renditions of Guyanese "local" songs.

Babla and Kanchan's recordings are slick and professional products of fancy Bombay studios, unlike most of the chutney and *tan*-singing records, which are produced by little outfits in Trinidad or Queens, New York City. Many of these records are sponsored by local West Indian stores; some of the record jackets are plastered with ads (one advertises "beef in pail, toilet paper, mosquitoe coil"). Even some of the tunes sing the praises of products like Stag Beer and Balroop the Tire King. But the Indo-Caribbean recording industry is basically in its infancy and, furthermore, is merely an appendage to the live-performance scene—especially the wedding and chutney-show circuit.

The flowering of the chutney scene has paralleled the increased movement of East Indians away from rural sugar plantations and into the urban mainstream of Trinidadian and Guyanese society. Economic recession in Trinidad and the enmities engendered by the racist Burnham regime in Guyana have to some extent strained relations between the Indian and black

"Local classical" musicians (Ruplal Girdharrie and party) in Trinidad, playing *dholak*, two *dantals*, and harmonium (photo by Peter Manuel)

communities. But in both countries, the greater prominence and demographic growth of Indians have obligated everyone, including the traditionally more dominant Afro-Caribbeans, to acknowledge the multiracial nature of their societies. For their part, while Indians take pride in having left behind such ancestral evils as dowry, caste discrimination, and Hindu–Muslim enmity, they are proud of their ethnic ancestry. On the whole, they cherish their ties to India and, in some cases, look down on Afro-Caribbeans for having adopted the slave-masters' religion and lost touch with their traditional culture. Meanwhile, some Afro-Caribbeans regard Indians as unpatriotic foreigners—especially, for example, when they cheer for the visiting cricket teams from India or Pakistan!

In its own way, music has mirrored the complex relations between the two groups. Until recently, calypsoes generally tended either to portray East Indians as bizarre and exotic or, more typically, to ignore them. A prominent case of the latter tendency was Trinidad calypsonian Black Stalin's 1979 "Caribbean Unity," an oft-quoted appeal to Afro-Caribbean solidarity:

> Dem is one race, from de same place,
> that made the same trip, on the same ship,
> de Caribbean man.

For obvious reasons, aside from its perceived sexism, this message did not go over well with Indians, Chinese, and other Caribbeans, who are no longer content with being written out of their nations' history. Trinidad's modern East Indian calypsonian Rikki Jai made a more inclusive and judicious manifesto in his 1993 "Cry for Unity" (written for Jai by Afro-Trinidadian Ras Shorty I, formerly Lord Shorty):

> We both come down here by boat under the hands of the master,
> I from India, you from Africa . . .
> Between the two races since the days of slavery
> we was always enemies, is time we try unity.

Shorty's song goes on to urge Indians and blacks to "mix up cultures," and indeed, the cultures have been mixing up. East Indian singers like Jai and Drupatee Ramgoonai have made a splash in the soca scene, introducing *tassa* drums and other Indianisms. Drupatee's 1989 "Indian Soca" put the case plainly:

> The music of the steel drums from Laventille
> cannot help but mix with the rhythm from Caroni [an Indian area],
> for it's a symbol of how much we've come of age,

is a brand new stage.
Indian soca, sounding sweeter,
hotter than a chulha [stove];
rhythm from Africa and India,
blend together is a perfect mixture.

Similarly, the leader of the Amoco Renegades, a top steel band, is an Indian, Jit Samaroo; and Shorty himself has stated that the soca beat he invented was inspired partially by Indian *tassa* drumming (as heard in his late-1970s hits like "Endless Vibrations"). Meanwhile, calypsoes like Sparrow's "Maharajin" and Crazy's "Nani Wine" have highlighted East Indian themes, and Indian radio and TV programs are proliferating. While some non-Indians in Trinidad, Guyana, and Suriname continue to regard such shows as ethnically divisive, most are coming to accept the fundamentally multicultural nature of their societies and the increased role that Indians will play therein. For its part, Trinidad—the proverbial land of steel band and calypso—may eventually become known more inclusively as the land of steel band, calypso, and chutney.

Chowtal: An East Indian Folk Song

Afro-Caribbean rhythms are rightly celebrated for their richness and complexity, but they are not the only source of rhythmic vitality in Caribbean music. The traditional music of India, both folk and classical, displays other sorts of rhythmic complexity and drive, relying more on linear intricacies than on African-style simultaneous layerings of interlocking patterns. One common feature of Indian music is the use of "additive" meters, often involving measures of odd-numbered beats. *Chowtal,* a North Indian folk-song genre transplanted to the Caribbean, uses such a rhythm, which is also common in other North Indian styles and in Indo-Caribbean *tan* singing.

The *chowtal* meter can be regarded as in seven beats, divided into three plus four (hence the term *additive*). You can get the feel of it by counting "<u>one</u>–two–three–<u>one</u>–two–<u>three</u>–four" repeatedly, clapping on the underlined beats. A typical *chowtal* refrain is given in Musical Example 19.

MUSICAL EXAMPLE 19

e - go - ku - la   ke ja - ja-n men kan - ha - ye su - ra-na su - k   ja - e

Chowtal is sung during *phagwa*, when groups of enthusiasts (especially teenagers) form ensembles, ardently performing old and even newly composed songs. In Trinidad, where there are competition networks for just about every kind of music, *chowtal* groups also compete for prizes during springtime festivals.

INTRODUCING THE
POPULAR MUSIC OF SURINAME

Mention the name Suriname and most people, including world-music enthusiasts, draw a blank. Located on the northeastern coast of South America, this former Dutch colony, which gained independence in 1975, remains one of the least known nations on earth.

There are plenty of good reasons for lovers of Caribbean and African music to want to find out more about Suriname and its music. For one thing, this small country has the distinction of being home to the most strongly African societies and cultures in the Americas—those of the Maroon peoples who live in the interior rain forest. While many ethnologists interested in studying African culture in the Western Hemisphere have ended up in Suriname, few others are aware of this most African of African-American cultural legacies. Furthermore, aside from people of African descent, Suriname is an unusually diverse mix of different ethnic groups and their musics. As we have mentioned, the country is host to a thriving Indo-Caribbean population, whose fluency in Hindi and Dutch in some ways links them more closely to India and Holland than to the West Indies. And then, there are handfuls of Chinese, whites, and around forty thousand Indonesians, some of whom still speak Javanese and maintain their own musical traditions.

But it is the Afro-Surinamese culture that is perhaps the most unique and has come the closest to providing a national music. The African cultural legacy is the product of a history of colonization, plantation slavery, and African resistance—a past that is shared with much of the rest of the Caribbean. Like Jamaica and Haiti, Suriname was one of the world's major sugar-producing colonies during the eighteenth century and gave birth to a robust creole culture that owes a great deal to Africa. That the foundations of Afro-Surinamese culture were laid in the earliest years of settlement, while Suriname was still a fledgling English colony (before the Dutch took over in 1667), helps to explain why it has more in common today with Jamaican culture than with the creole cultures of the Netherlands Antilles and other parts of the Dutch-speaking Caribbean. The unofficial national language of

---

All material on Suriname was written by Kenneth Bilby.

Suriname, an English-related creole known as Sranan, is very close to Jamaican creole (though it shows heavier African influence).

In the last few decades, a host of vibrant new musics has sprung up from the Afro-Surinamese roots. The three most popular current styles—*kawina, kaseko,* and *aleke*—all remain virtually unknown outside of Suriname and the Netherlands. This isolation results primarily from the fact that Suriname's colonial language (Dutch) is not widely spoken elsewhere, and the country's indigenous creole languages, heard on its recordings, are not spoken or heard anywhere else in the world.

Kawina is the foremost drum-based dance music of coastal Suriname's Creole people—that is, Afro-Surinamese descendants of slaves who remained on coastal plantations, as opposed to Maroons, or *Bosnegers,* who fled and set up independent communities in the interior rain forest. Although its roots go back to religious and secular African-derived slave-plantation styles, the *kawina* style heard today is thought to have developed during the late nineteenth century. It was during this period that the Creoles, Maroons, and migrant gold prospectors from neighboring countries found themselves working alongside one another and making music together during evening festivities. In the early years, the resulting musical blends incorporated European instruments like accordions and clarinets, but over time, these either receded or were dropped as the drums were brought to the fore. Today, most *kawina* bands feature only drums and other percussion, with an occasional ukulele-like *kwatro* (*cuatro*).

By the turn of the century, the rural area around the Commewijne River in northeastern Suriname had become the stronghold of this new music, which flourished in two similar forms: *prisiri kawina* (good-time *kawina*) for social dances and other secular occasions and *winti kawina,* which is attached to the ceremonial music of the Afro-Surinamese religion called *Winti* (which also has its own repertoire of sacred drumming and dance styles).

The instruments of a typical *kawina* band include a small wooden bench beaten with sticks, a number of rattles, one or more large standing drums (*timbal*), and two double-headed drums (*koti kawina* and *hari kawina*) held sideways on the lap. While the rest of the ensemble lays down a solid groove, the *koti kawina* drummer, playing with a stick and the palm of one hand, takes the lead, conversing with the other drummers and contributing punctuations to the subtle cross-play and shifting accents of the deeper drums. *Kawina* songs are always done in call-and-response style. Many of the secular songs comment on local current events and people, while others are traditional, having been passed down over the generations. While the melodies and harmonies usually betray a clear European influence, the rhythmic foundation—the interlocking play of skins and percussion—is deeply African.

Although *kawina*'s reliance on drums and percussion might make it seem old-fashioned to some listeners, it has continued to keep pace with changing times. Popular recordings of *kawina* began to emerge in the late 1950s, when artists such as Big Jones and Oscar Nieuwendam started making records for urban audiences. Subsequent bands added new instruments, such as congas and the *skratji* bass drum used in *kaseko*. During the 1970s, Surinamese emigrating to the Netherlands brought *kawina* with them. Today, now that roughly half of the Surinamese population lives in Dutch cities, developments and trends in Holland play as important a role in the continuing life of the *kawina* tradition as those taking place in Suriname itself. For Surinamese youths living in the cold, high-rise housing projects of Amsterdam's Bijlmermeer section, *kawina* has provided a positive, living cultural tie to the homeland. Today, some of the most popular *kawina* bands are based in the Netherlands, and many of the best recordings are made there.

By the late 1980s, the rising costs of purchasing instruments and hiring electric dance bands in Paramaribo, Suriname's capital, and a growing pride in local culture combined to produce a new upsurge in popularity for *kawina* music in Suriname. Innovations continue as bands experiment with new instrumentation, different Afro-Caribbean rhythms, and Congolese *soukous* dance-music influences. But these outside influences remain subtle, and *kawina* today retains its uniquely Surinamese feeling. The latest trend is a fusion of *kawina* with *kaseko* music, called *kaskawi*, which blends the roots sound of *kawina* drums and vocals with electric instrumentation and high-tech studio wizardry.

KASEKO: ENTER THE STRINGS AND HORNS

The origins of *kaseko*, Suriname's homegrown counterpart to calypso, are not entirely clear. The name is most likely derived from French creole, *cassé-co* (meaning, literally, "break the body"). In turn-of-the-century Suriname, the French Guianese Creole drumming style called *cassé-co*, known for the physically grueling dance that went with it, was among the ingredients tossed into the musical brew at the same Creole get-togethers where *kawina* was born. But it was not until after World War II that the modern style called *kaseko* surfaced, absorbing influences from all sides and gradually emerging as the all-embracing national popular music of Suriname.

First came *bigi poku*, an offshoot of *kawina* that added the large *skratji* bass drum and, subsequently, horns, especially the tuba. Other formative influences in the 1940s and 1950s included Trinidad calypso; Afro-Cuban dance music; a British Guianese style of topical song called *badji*, backed by string band with horns; and a banjo- and snare-drum style called *boengoe-boengoe*. But it was the 1970s that saw the flowering of *kaseko*, as the new style came into its own as the local dance beat with the widest appeal. *Kaseko* was, by now, electrically amplified, its bands typically featuring electric guitars, bass, keyboards, traps, *skratji* drum, cowbells, and other percussion, and various horns. Perhaps the most distinctive thing about *kaseko*, other than the language of the songs, was the unique rhythm, notable for its busy snare work and the heavy accents pounded out on the newly refurbished *skratji*-and-cymbal combination.

It was during this period that Hugo "Iko" Uiterloo—otherwise known as Lieve Hugo—reigned as the "King of *Kaseko*," releasing, along with other singers, a chain of hits focusing on local themes and capturing the mood of the country during the preindependence period. Hugo's sometime backing band, Orchestra Washboard, was particularly influential in popularizing a horn-based sound and what came to be called *winti kaseko*, which melds traditional Afro-Surinamese drum rhythms with electric *kaseko*. Suddenly, dancers in urban nightclubs found themselves moving to amplified African-based *Winti* rhythms, which had been grafted onto guitars, keyboard, and bass. The results in many cases came to bear remarkable resemblance to some styles of West African popular music, such as early Nigerian Afrobeat and other styles using 12/8 polyrhythms like those discussed in Chapter 1 of this book.

Throughout the 1970s, influences from Trinidadian, Cuban, French Antillean, and black American music continued to crop up in *kaseko*, but the local roots of the music remained strong. Increasing emigration to Holland led to a new crop of overseas *kaseko* bands, along with a greater sense of professionalism and "sophistication," as in the slick, brassy sound of producer-arranger Stan Lokhin's various bands.

Toward the end of the 1970s, a particularly interesting new phase commenced as Maroon musicians entered the *kaseko* scene in full force. During the preceding decade, unprecedented numbers of young people from the interior, especially Saramaka and Ndjuka Maroons, had migrated to the coastal towns. They became attracted to the new urban sounds, and within a few years, their contributions came to dominate developments in *kaseko*, which was now often sung in the Maroon languages Saramaccan and Ndjuka as well as Creole Sranan.

The new Maroon presence in *kaseko* had profound repercussions. Ever since the seventeenth and eighteenth centuries, when their ancestors escaped from coastal plantations and established their independence, Maroons had remained relatively isolated in their forest villages. Their rich musical culture, which combined elements from several different parts of the African continent, had remained almost entirely free of European influence. The many musical traditions that formed part of the rhythm of daily life in Maroon communities—ranging from social dance styles to religious music of the *kumanti, vodu,* and *ampuku* possession rites (called *obia pee,* "obeah plays")—constituted what was probably the most thoroughly African musical corpus in the entire Western Hemisphere. This wealth of Maroon musical traditions called for a variety of complex drumming styles and special songs, many of them in esoteric African-derived languages such as *papa* and *kumanti.*

Specific, direct carryovers from these traditional Maroon styles into urban popular music were more the exception than the rule, but the musical sensibility embodied in Maroon music gradually began to permeate *kaseko* recordings. One could hear the Maroon influence, for instance, in the Saramaka and Ndjuka texts of many songs, in the constant references to Maroon culture and to traditional life in the interior, in vocal and guitar stylings, in the occasional *kaseko* recordings containing sections based on rhythms of one or another kind of *obia pee,* in the transfer of specific Maroon rhythmic patterns to *kaseko* instruments like the *skratji,* and in the occasional appearance of actual Maroon drums. Even Creole and Holland-based bands began to incorporate these influences.

Over the last few years, the local record industry has suffered greatly as a result of worsening economic conditions in Suriname. A further blow was dealt by the advent of the compact disc, a format that remains prohibitively expensive for producers tapping a relatively small market such as Suriname's. *Kaseko* CD production is limited almost entirely to the Netherlands, where most of the technically better recordings are now made. But the studios of Paramaribo keep busy anyway, and record stores still abound with cassettes of current local releases.

Kaseko today presents a kaleidoscopic panorama of stylistic influences from diverse sources. The sound may jump from calypso- or reggae-inflected rhythms one moment to strong hints of *zouk,* dancehall, or *soukous* the next. While some artists consistently favor one or two particular styles, others range over a whole rainbow of musical influences in a single song (as might also be said of eclectic Indo-Surinamese pop musician Kries Ramkhelawan). But as varied as the music has become, certain generalizations about *kaseko* still hold true. Contemporary pieces are almost always divided into two or more contrasting sections, often in very different tempos. The snare drum,

Surinamese *kaseko* band Ghabiang (Iwan Esseboom)

with its rolls and fills, plays a particularly prominent part, as does its companion, the *skratji*, with its rapid, off-center punches. Other hallmarks of contemporary *kaseko* are the bright, snappy brass arrangements; long stretches of instrumental vamping, with lots of jazzy horn solos; and especially, the characteristic transitional sections marked by dizzying stop-and-go breaks—staccato bursts of counterrhythm that temporarily play havoc with the otherwise rock-solid beat. Finally, most *kaseko* bands today mix in what they call "bubbling," meaning a blend of reggae, dancehall, and *kaseko*.

All of this adds up to a distinctive contemporary Caribbean dance music that has so far remained hidden from the rest of the world, even as it reaches out and creatively soaks up influences from far and wide. *Kaseko*, no matter how danceable, remains for the time being a well-kept secret, a cherished example of what the Surinamese proudly call *wi egi sani*—"our own thing."

ALEKE: THE DRUM RULES AGAIN

Disco Amigo in downtown Paramaribo is Suriname's main record store. Alongside the stacks of cassettes filled with recent *kaseko* and *kawina* releases, a visitor who manages to elbow his or her way through the crowd of customers will notice a selection of tapes labeled "*aleke* band," followed by what appears to be the name of a group. *Aleke*, a rootsy, drum-based music created by and for young Maroons, is a newcomer to the local music industry. Although the style has flourished in Maroon communities since the 1970s, the first studio recordings of *aleke* did not come on the market until around 1990.

Aleke's origins can be traced back to an earlier drumming style known as *lonsei*—itself a relatively recent innovation, developed by Ndjuka Maroons in the interior of Suriname. Said to have been introduced by a spirit that possessed a Ndjuka medium, *lonsei* music quickly grew in popularity, reaching its height in the 1960s. With its distinctive drumming and dance and its emphasis on topical songs, it became an important vehicle of expression for the younger generation of Ndjukas during that period.

As increasing numbers of Ndjuka men migrated to coastal Suriname, the *lonsei* they brought with them soon mutated, under the influence of Creole drumming traditions, into *aleke*, which clearly bore the marks of its mixed Maroon-Creole parentage. As a hybrid, modern style associated with the young, *aleke* proved particularly adaptable and was soon seized upon by Maroon youths living in the coastal towns, who made it their own by introducing a series of innovations. Originally played on traditional Ndjuka drums, by the late 1970s *aleke* came to be played on an ensemble of three

Ghabiang, with leader Iwan Esseboom holding cowbell (I. Esseboom)

Maroon *aleke* band Sapatia, 1987 (Ken Bilby)

conga-like "*aleke* drums," a bass drum and high-hat set called *djas* (jazz), and other percussion instruments.

In the shared spaces of coastal Suriname and French Guiana, *aleke* brought together young Maroons from different clans and ethnic groups. By the early 1980s, it had come to reflect the wide range of influences around them, both in lyrics and in sound. Singers experimented with Pentecostal church melodies and French Antillean Carnival tunes; they stripped down reggae rhythms, transferring them to drums and percussion to come up with something like a Rastafarian *nyabinghi* beat. New songs were constantly composed, reflecting contemporary life on the margins of the coastal towns. Many songs were concerned with relations between the sexes, but political commentary became common, especially after the outbreak of civil war in 1986. Many *aleke* songs obliquely denounced the atrocities perpetrated against Maroon civilians by the military government, while other songs called for a healing of wounds and the restoration of democracy, peace, and harmony—a goal that, as of 1995, has yet to be fully accomplished, although fighting has stopped for the time being.

It was not until the late 1980s that Disco Amigo and other record stores began bringing out studio recordings of *aleke* on cassette. While the drum-

Sapatia band (photo by Ken Bilby)

Aleke drum of band Sapatia (photo by Ken Bilby)

Maroon *aleke* drummer playing *djas* bass drum and high-hat set (photo by Ken Bilby)

ming style of *aleke* remains firmly anchored in tradition, many modern *aleke* songs sold on cassette today deal with decidedly modern themes, from AIDS and poverty to the pros and cons of condoms. Yet traditional Maroon concerns remain as much in the foreground as ever, and it is this mixture of new and old that makes *aleke* special: it speaks to the experience of both those living in the traditional Maroon villages and those who have settled in coastal towns. Indeed, on some occasions *aleke* is still played in the old way, on traditional Ndjuka drums, and is danced in ring formation; at other times, the same musical style appears in its newer incarnation, featuring the long drums and *djas,* electrically amplified vocals, and dance floors filled with couples in close embrace. One of the latest developments is the emergence of a new blend called *aleke-kaseko,* played by electric dance bands on modern instruments. This new type of *kaseko* is among the most popular Surinamese styles today, both in Paramaribo and in the Netherlands.

Amid the extraordinary diversity of Surinamese music styles, the African-rooted music has had the greatest popular impact, successfully crossing ethnic boundaries and becoming a national music. While doing so, it has borrowed freely from other traditions. Yet even in the Netherlands, where Sur-

inamese music strays farthest from its roots, musicians have spurred a revival of the neo-African drum-and-percussion styles associated with the
Winti religion and other fundamental Afro-Surinamese cultural expressions.
Amid so much creative blending and eclecticism, there is no sign that the
deeper roots are losing ground—which just goes to show that despite all
the changes in Surinamese music, the drum still rules.

INDO-CARIBBEAN BIBLIOGRAPHY

For a thorough ethnography of Indo-Trinidadian society with reference to music,
see Steven Vertovec's *Hindu Trinidad: Religion, Ethnicity, and Socio-economic Change*
(London: Warwick University Press, 1992).

INDO-CARIBBEAN RECORDS

Commercial recordings of Indo-Caribbean genres (aside from Rounder's CD *Caribbean Currents*, a companion to this text) are mostly inaccessible outside the Caribbean and diaspora neighborhoods.

SURINAME BIBLIOGRAPHY

Melville and Frances Herskovits, *Suriname Folk-Lore* (New York: Columbia University Press, 1936); Jan Voorhoeve and Ursy Lichtveld, *Creole Drum* (New Haven:
Yale University Press, 1975); and Marcel Weltak, ed., *Surinaamse Muziek in Neder-
land en Suriname* (Utrecht: Cosmos, 1990), which includes an excellent companion
cassette.

SURINAME RECORDS

TRADITIONAL GENRES: *The Creole Music of Suriname* (Folkways 4233); *Music from
Saramaka* (Folkways 4255); *From Slavery to Freedom: Music of the Saramaka Maroons
of Suriname* (LLST 7354); *The Spirit Cries: Rainforest Music from South America and
the Caribbean* (Rykodisc RCD 10250).

MODERN DANCE MUSIC: *Sranan Pokoe Wowojo* (Imperial 5N 126-26123/24); *Kaseko: Surinaamse Roots Muziek* (Kaseko SUCD 35040); *Switi: Hot! Kaseko Music*
(SPN 010); *Caribbean Beat*, vol. 1 (Intuition INT 31122).

10

Five Themes in the Study of Caribbean Music

UNITY AND DIVERSITY
IN A CONTINENT OF ISLANDS

In the opening chapter of this book, we briefly looked at some aspects of unity and diversity in Caribbean culture and music. Having surveyed the region's individual music styles, we may now be better poised to tackle some fundamental questions: To what extent does the Caribbean constitute a unified musical area? Is Caribbean music just a colorful collage of diverse genres, without any pan-regional continuity? Aside from curiosities like the Haitian/Cuban/calypso *cinquillo*, has music in any significant way transcended linguistic boundaries?

As we have noted, the region has always been culturally and politically divided by geography, language, and ethnicity. The linguistic and colonial boundaries are the most obvious, and one can to some extent divide the area into three major cultural zones, that is, Spanish, English, and French. However, even these subregions are internally fragmented in terms of rivalries and factionalisms, as well as musical traditions. Residents of the nearby French islands of Martinique and Guadeloupe manage to look down on each other, and the calypso line "small island, go back where you came from" long expressed the Trinidadian attitude toward its neighbors. The end of colonialism has only exacerbated such fragmentation. The pan–West Indian federation fell apart in 1962, and a few years later, tiny Anguilla saw fit to secede from St. Kitts-Nevis, even though it had no telephones, power, or paved roads. In what ways, then, have musical tastes and traditions reflected such divisions, and in what ways has music transcended them?

The parallels between musical and linguistic boundaries are obvious. A Martinican feels closer to France than to nearby Barbados. Similarly, despite Cuba's proximity to Jamaica, its similar history, and its overwhelming musi-

232

cal influence on the Spanish Caribbean, Cuban music does not seem to have much impact on Jamaican popular music. The Linguistic fragmentation reaches an extreme in the southern Caribbean Basin, where the national languages of the adjacent Venezuela, Guyana, Suriname, French Guiana, and Brazil, are, respectively, Spanish, English, Dutch, French, and Portuguese.

However, such disparities represent only part of the picture. For one thing, as we noted in Chapter 1, the entire region shares a set of basic sociomusical attributes, including the presence of an Afro-Caribbean cultural common denominator; a history of musical syncretization; the strength of oral traditions; and the emergence of lower-class, African-influenced work songs, religious musics, Carnival traditions, and creole, duple-metered dance-music genres. Further, even the boundaries between the Spanish, French, and English zones have often been fluid and permeable. The French creole zone formerly extended to Trinidad and elsewhere in the present Anglophone realm (including New Orleans), and in terms of language and musical tastes, Dominica and St. Lucia still straddle the two.

Internal migrations have also left musical traces. Franco-Haitian culture and music pervade eastern Cuba, just as Cuban dance music heavily influenced the 1950s Haitian *konpa*. West Indian migrants to southern Puerto Rico appear to have contributed to the emergence of *bomba*, and the Trinidad calypso was enriched by melodies brought from throughout the region. Afro-American migrants from the southern United States preserve their own traditions in the Dominican peninsula of Samaná, and laborers from just about everywhere migrated to Panama to work on the canal. Internal migrations have continued in recent decades as Haitians seek work in the Dominican Republic, Dominicans flock to Puerto Rico, and people throughout the Lesser Antilles migrate to prosperous Trinidad. Similarly, despite strained relations between Haitians and Dominicans (including disputes about the origin of the *méringue*/merengue), the two nations' musical histories are inseparable. As we saw in Chapter 6, the mid-twentieth century Haitian *konpa* emerged as a local variant of the Dominican merengue, while modern Dominican bandleaders like Wilfrido Vargas have mercilessly plagiarized Haitian hits.

Since the 1950s, the conflicting trends toward unity and diversity have acquired a new dimension with the advent of the mass media. It may seem contradictory to speak of simultaneous homogenization and diversification, but that is in many ways what has happened. The new common denominator is popular music from the United States, which now pervades the entire region. Rap, rock, and R & B have their own undeniable appeal and vitality, and when backed by powerful multinational record companies, they tend to put local musics on the defensive throughout the Caribbean. In many countries, local broadcast media are so poorly funded that they can barely compete with the United States. In several smaller countries, there is no local TV at all; instead, everyone watches pirated satellite transmissions from the United States, complete with New York City news and ads for products that are unavailable as well as unaffordable. So it is not surprising that disco and R & B tend to dominate much of the West Indian airwaves, constituting a new sort of musical lingua franca. In the process, the foreign media onslaught displaces and devalues local musics, reinforcing Caribbean inferiority complexes and alienating people from their own cultures.

But as was noted in Chapter 1, the mass media, together with interaction of migrant communities in New York and elsewhere, also facilitate all sorts of musical cross-fertilization and fusions. Some of these products, like Latin rap and Garifuna *punta* rock, mix local languages and styles with Yankee influences. Others are purely Caribbean fusions, like the Trinidadian and Puerto Rican adaptations of Jamaican dancehall style. Many of these hybrids are just ephemeral gimmicks and fads, but others may be more than that. Indeed, in an age of multiple identities and crisscrossing media networks, some of the most vital and dynamic artistic creation may be coming from the borders and interstices rather than the stylistic hinterlands. As the media and musical trends transcend geographical distances and borders, a new sort of Caribbean unity may yet emerge, based not on homogeneity but on a cosmopolitan multiculturalism.

RACE AND ETHNICITY

The history, styles, and meanings of Caribbean music are intimately linked to issues of race in several ways. Musical genres are often associated with or claimed (plausibly or not) by specific ethnic groups; alternately, they may be celebrated as national patrimonies whose appeal transcends such boundaries. Throughout the region, song texts chronicle and articulate popular attitudes regarding race. Perhaps most significant are the ways in which music not only passively reflects race relations but actively influences them; in some cases, it serves as a powerful symbol of racial syncretism and harmony, often situating local versions of Afro-Caribbean music in the mainstream of national culture.

It is quite impossible to generalize about race relations and attitudes in the Caribbean, except to say that they are complex, diverse, and often different from those in the United States. Thus, for example, throughout the West Indies black people may have historically internalized colonial prejudices, but because they generally constitute demographic majorities, unlike many North American blacks, they do not regard themselves as members of an alienated and marginalized minority. Racism in the Spanish-speaking Caribbean is generally somewhat milder than in the English-speaking world; for many Puerto Ricans, this tradition of tolerance and mixing has been a source of nationalistic pride vis-à-vis the United States. Certainly, North American and English racial ideology, which recognizes only black and white, is relatively unusual in the Spanish and French Caribbean, especially since so many people are of mixed ancestry. Instead, people tend to be highly conscious of shades of coloring; even within Afro-Caribbean communities, social preferences for lighter skin, thin noses, and straight ("good") hair remain widespread. For North Americans, understanding such attitudes is complicated by the entirely different norms of discourse about race; especially in the Hispanic Caribbean, people simply do not talk about race in the same ways that Yankees do.

Song lyrics do articulate racial attitudes and situations in various ways. Many colonial-era calypsoes mocked people with negroid features, reflecting the hegemony of British imperial ideology even among Afro-Trinidadians. Since the 1970s, however, in the wake of the Black Power movement, such calypsoes have seldom been encountered. In the 1980s and 1990s, reggae songs have voiced attitudes with particular frankness; after singer Buju Banton was criticized for his "Love me Browning," which eulogized fair-skinned girls, he released his own rejoinder, "Love Black Woman." Latin music song texts also confront these issues in their own fashion. An old Puerto Rican folk song "¿Tu abuela, dónde está?" (Where's your grandmother?) reminded listeners of the island's African heritage, while in a popular *chachachá* of the 1950s, an Afro-Cuban mocked a *mulata* (mulatto woman) for her pretensions:

> You passed by me yesterday, *mulata*,
> and glared at me contemptuously
> with your self-consuming conceit,
> you put me down for my color. . . .
> Because you've ironed your kinky hair
> and you've got a bit less color,
> you think you're the queen of the house.
> But the truth is more glaring,
> that you don't know what you are,
> you're a thick-lipped black, just like me.[1]

Such songs often express racial attitudes more openly than other forms of discourse. At the same time, one must be careful in trying to draw conclusions from song texts. For example, in Latin music, the woman beloved by the song's narrator, if racially identifed at all, is typically described as *morena* (dark, mulatto) or *negra*—seldom as white or blond. But aside from the ambiguity of *negra* (a common term of endearment meaning either "negress" or "dark-eyed one"), one might ask whether such references indicate a profound racial attitude, a purely aesthetic preference for dark women, or merely a conventional and superficial stereotype of such women as being exotic and sexy.

In broader terms, the styles, associations, and breadth of individual music genres tell us much about the racial and cultural composition of Caribbean societies as a whole. Most Caribbean musical cultures exhibit a continuum of genres, ranging from the African-derived to the European-derived. The proportions vary considerably from island to island, however. An obvious contrast is between some smaller West Indian countries, where neo-African cult musics are relatively weak and marginal, and Cuba and Haiti, where they are extremely widespread. Even in Trinidad, for example, *Shango* worship has remained a private subculture to such an extent that calypsonians have generally portrayed it as an exotic and bizarre cult, to be feared or ridiculed. By contrast, innumerable Cuban popular songs refer with easy familiarity to the *orishas* (spirits) whose religion pervades lower-class Afro-Cuban life. Similarly, one can trace a direct evolution from Congolese secular dances through the traditional rumba and on to modern Cuban dance music and salsa—as reflected, for example, in modern salsa versions of old rumbas like "Díle como yo acere ko, ahí na' má'," with its (essentially untranslatable) combination of African words and colloquial Spanish. The weakness of such threads of continuity in the West Indies led Trinidad's prime minister Eric Williams to speak, however exaggeratedly, of Afro-Trinidadians as a "deracinated" people with "nothing indigenous."

Throughout much of the Caribbean, the emergence of creole popular musics has involved a process of accepting and legitimizing local forms of Afro-Caribbean music. While some Dominicans have tried to deny the African-derived elements of merengue, in most countries, the Afro-Caribbean elements of modern popular musics are now recognized and celebrated. Reggae, the Cuban *son,* and the *plenas* and *bombas* of Puerto Rican bandleader Rafael Cortijo are all so overtly Afro-Caribbean that their popularity at once reflected and helped create a wholesale mainstreaming of black identity. After the emergence and fame of Bob Marley, Jamaicans have felt proud to be black as never before.

However, the tendency to celebrate Afro-Caribbean culture as national culture is complicated by the presence of other ethnic groups. Even leaving aside Cuba and Puerto Rico, with their substantial white populations, many West Indian islands have significant East Indian, Chinese, Syrian, and European communities. As we saw in Chapter 9, the identity question is particularly marked in Trinidad and Guyana, where East Indians are coming to outnumber blacks. The prevailing ideal, however, is a multiculturalism of the kind expressed in the oft-heard saying "All o' we is one." Although ethnic stereotypes still abound and communities are often polarized by politics, the norm remains one of interracial courtesy and tolerance, not Balkan-style fratricide. And typically, the contradictions raised by Afrocentricism are expressed not in violence but in whimsical songs, like the calypso "Split me in two," of Mighty Dougla. Dougla, whose sobriquet denotes an Indian-African mulatto, contemplates his fate under an imaginary law repatriating all Trinidadians to their ancestral homeland:

> Can somebody just tell me
> where they sending poor me?
> I am neither one nor the other,
> six of one, half dozen of the other.
> If they serious about sending back people for true,
> they got to split me in two.

Such complexities and contradictions are reflected in the ethnic associations of musical styles in general. Many music genres remain identified with particular communities, with tastes and affiliations serving as boundary markers. For example, one Indo-Guyanese youth told me, "I like all kinds of Indian music, and nothing else." However, what is perhaps more marked is the tendency for Afro-Caribbean popular musics—*son,* reggae, soca, and *konpa*—to become integrating symbols, uniting audiences of all communities. In such cases, music serves less as a flame beneath a melting pot than as a dressing poured over a mixed salad, integrating its diverse elements into a coherent whole.

MUSIC, SEX, AND SEXISM

In the Caribbean as throughout the world, love and male–female relationships have always been favorite song topics. Throughout the region, music relates the perennial themes of love, betrayal, and loss. Caribbean men, especially in the Spanish-speaking areas, often use songs to convey their feelings, singing softly in a lover's ear, playing a romantic record over and over for a beloved woman, or even giving a sweetheart a chosen recording. In a lighter vein, songs throughout the region display an uninhibited delight in sexuality, typically expressed in whimsical, thinly disguised puns and double entendres. Beyond this level, however, the particular sentiments expressed in Caribbean music reflect the attitudes and values in the region, many of which, rather than being universal, are products of specific sociohistorical conditions.

It is difficult to generalize about gender relations in the Caribbean, as in most complex societies. Throughout the region, for example, one finds nuclear families as well as strong extended family structures. Kinship networks help provide stability and cohesion to families in situations where the men are absent or peripheral, for whatever reason. In the twentieth century, it has become quite common for men to have only loose ties to their children and partners. To a considerable extent, this condition is a legacy of slavery, which undermined the role of the male provider and, more significant, destroyed traditional African kinship structures, which had to be rebuilt afresh after emancipation.

With modernization, familial ties have been further strained by urbanization and greater mobility, which disrupted village kinship networks, and above all, by poverty and unemployment. As traditional male occupations like cutting sugarcane have been mechanized, the role of the male breadwinner has been increasingly weakened; in some cases, women stand better chances than men do of finding jobs, whether as domestics or as workers in factories whose managers prefer women because they are less likely to organize. Such conditions can put a tremendous strain on family cohesion. The devoted but unemployed father unable to feed his children can suffer unbearable grief and guilt, as chronicled in Zeigfield's 1938 calypso "Depression":

> Five children and a wife and myself to mind,
> but to me the world is so unkind.
> No work, no food, no clothes to wear.
> If things go on, I'll die in despair.

Such a father, however well-meaning, may even be ejected by a wife who, out of duress, finds a better provider or who is herself employed but unable to feed a dependent man. Alternately, the man may simply avoid responsibility, going from one mate to another, ignoring whatever children he sires, and hoping ideally to shack up with some woman whom he can charm into supporting him. Thus throughout the Caribbean, as elsewhere, many lower-class men and even women have tended to avoid marital or even emotional ties that may become burdensome and frustrating. When relationships become mediated primarily by money, some employed women shun male hangers-on, and unemployed women accept men's advances only if they get something tangible in return. As Growling Tiger's calypso "Money is King" (1935) relates:

> If you have money and things going nice,
> any woman will call you honey and spice.
> If you can't give her a dress or a new pair of shoe,
> she'll say she have no uses for you.

At worst, the women struggle to support the children, and the under-employed and demoralized men hang out in bars, listening to songs that pump up their egos and soothe their frustrations.

Music is part of this condition, but on the whole, it reflects not universal feelings but predominantly male viewpoints, in accordance with male domination of most aspects of the music world and of public culture in general. Hence some Caribbean music, especially of the twentieth century, articulates the most self-indulgent forms of male boasting and its flip side, self-pity. Such songs may be extremely influential in presenting a certain male ideal, that of the swaggering macho stud or calypso "saga boy," attracting women by his charm alone and promising nothing more than a good time. Some songs offer specific advice to other men, like the several calypsoes warning against marriage (e.g., Atilla's "I'll Never Burden Myself with a Wife"). As we have seen, the double standard is often explicit, as women are expected to be sexually available to the singer while still being denounced for their promiscuity.

Portrayals of women in Caribbean music vary according to individual genres and their respective social backgrounds. Overtly sexist songs are relatively unusual in Cuba and Puerto Rico, perhaps due to the persistence of Hispanic ideals of family honor—ideals which many West Indian women might find repressive in their own way. The norm in most Latin music, whether weepy boleros or upbeat salsa songs, is a genteel sentimentality, often idealizing women, however unrealistically. Sexism was more overt in 1970s–1980s Dominican *bachata* and in West Indian genres like colonial-era calypso. "Roots reggae" songs generally portrayed women respectfully, although not necessarily as equals. For its part, Rastafarianism certainly had a streak of misogyny (quoth Peter Tosh, "Women are instruments of the devil"). But for sheer crudity, however whimsical, there is little to compete with Jamaican dancehall hits like Admiral Bailey's 1987 "Punanny." Dancehall has also been faulted for its homophobia, as in Buju Banton's controversial "Boom Bye Bye," which appears to advocate murdering gays.

Attitudes toward such songs vary within the Caribbean. Many people find them offensive, but even educated, enlightened women may enjoy them while shrugging off the problematic aspects. One West Indian college coed told me, "I like dancehall, and I don't mind the sexist songs; I just don't take the words seriously." Another told me, "'Boom Bye Bye' is one of my favorite songs; I don't agree with the message, but I like the way he expresses it, and it's got a good beat." Such attitudes, which are quite widespread, certainly have their own legitimacy, especially because in dancehall, as in rap, the driving rhythms and rhetorical cleverness may be more important to listeners than the actual message of the text. The danger, however, is that among some listeners, sexism and homophobia may be so rampant and ingrained that they are taken for granted.

What would change the situation would be for women (and gays) to be able to make their own viewpoints heard in popular music. Women have always played important roles in performing certain kinds of Caribbean music, from domestic lullabies to church hymns; but in the Caribbean, as elsewhere, the worlds of professional folk music and commercial popular music have always been dominated by men. Women have entered these genres, but often have to contend with predominantly male performance norms and personnel structures. And in patriarchal societies, any woman who expresses her sensuality in public runs the risk of being perceived as a sex object by men, especially in a genre so oriented toward "slackness" as Jamaican dancehall. Thus, for example, the flamboyantly sexy dancehall performer Patra may be seen by some women as an embarrassment, and by others as a liberated woman fully in control of her situation.

Ultimately, transcending sexism in popular music may depend on transforming social norms as a whole. To some extent, this change is slowly taking place, as women throughout the Caribbean enter the socioeconomic mainstream and challenge chauvinist traditions. (In doing so, of course, they may provoke more sexist backlash, articulated in music.) Women have made particularly marked progress under the Cuban Revolution. Since coming to power in 1959, the Cuban socialist government has vigorously promoted the equality of the sexes, encouraging the participation of women in all levels of work and society, providing unrivaled and unprecedented socioeconomic stability, and launching a sustained media barrage against still-persistent machismo. Music played its own part in this movement, not only in the form of progressive *nueva trova* songs but in the self-conscious general avoidance of sexism. As of the mid-1990s, however, the likelihood of such state-supported reforms occurring elsewhere in the region appears slimmer than ever.

CARIBBEAN MUSIC INTERNATIONAL

Liberty Avenue in Queens and Brooklyn's Nostrand Avenue typify the new kind of polyglot Caribbean migrant neighborhoods that have emerged in New York City and elsewhere. West Indian snack bars offering calaloo and roti adjoin Chinese-Cuban eateries, while groceries hawk coconuts, curry powder, fresh fish from Guyana, cassava, and day-old Caribbean newspapers. On the sidewalk, one hears a Babel-like chatter of Spanish, Jamaican patwa, Haitian creole, Afro-American jive, and even standard English (though usually with a Caribbean lilt). Meanwhile, ghetto-blasters, car stereos and storefront cassette players boom out the throbbing rhythms of merengue, salsa, soca, and reggae, which intertwine like some perpetually changing postmodern polyrhythm.

New York has become a Caribbean city, especially since the 1980s, when its Caribbean population reached a sort of critical mass of over two million. It is now the biggest Caribbean city and the second biggest Jamaican, Haitian, and Guyanese city. There are more people from Nevis in New York than there are in Nevis itself. Dominicans have become the dominant community in Washington Heights ("Quisqueya Heights"), as have Puerto Ricans in Spanish Harlem and the Lower East Side ("Loisaida") and English-speaking West Indians in Brooklyn and Queens. While other North American cities like Detroit have degenerated into depopulated rotting shells, New York's economy has been revitalized by Caribbeans who bring their traditions of initiative and self-reliance. As the saying goes, when a West Indian gets ten cents above a beggar, he opens a business. More often, he or she joins the service sector, while adding color and vitality to the city's street life and culture.

Many Caribbean migrants keep closely in touch with their homelands by way of the telephone, satellite TV, and frequent visits. For others, "home" is a distant island that they may have never seen, barely remember, or remember in a way that hasn't existed for decades. For all of them, music and food assume new significance as symbols of identity; meat patties and reggae music *are* Jamaica, just as roti and calypso signify Trinidad. Caribbean migrants and their descendants develop complex and multiple senses of identity, so that a second-generation Jamaican may see him- or herself in various contexts as Jamaican, West Indian, Afro-Caribbean, Afro-American, Brooklynite, or just plain American. Most Caribbeans, rather than wishing to assimilate totally, want to retain some sense of their origins, and their musical tastes generally reflect these cosmopolitan and overlapping senses of identity.

Emigration has mixed effects on musical culture in the homelands. Emigrants can enrich island culture by sending money home and by serving as conduits for new trends and ideas. At the same time, the tendency for the best and brightest to emigrate can deplete the ranks of talented musicians on the islands; lesser folk music genres that fail to thrive in emigrant communities can decline altogether. For example, folk-song traditions formerly maintained in lively "tea meetings" on islands like Nevis and St. Vincent have declined markedly because most of the creative performers have left.[2] Islanders left behind express their demoralization in songs like the early 1990s calypso from Dominica, "Dominicans Come Home."

Such instances of cultural impoverishment are to some extent counterbalanced by the thriving of Caribbean culture abroad. As we have seen, New York, with its media infrastructure and concentrated Caribbean enclaves, has been a center for Caribbean music for many decades. From the 1920s, most of the leading Puerto Rican composers and performers, from Manuel "Canario" Jiménez to Rafael Hernández, came to live in the city, and much of the evolution of Latin dance music took place here. The mambo evolved mostly in clubs like the Palladium, and salsa emerged as a barrio reinterpretation and resignification of Cuban music in the late 1960s. New York continues to be the center of the recording industries for Haitian and West Indian music. Other cities, like Toronto, Birmingham, and Paris, have played similar roles in the development of modern Caribbean music, hosting more clubs, record producers, and top groups than the islands themselves.

Of course, the international presence of Caribbean music has never been limited to immigrant communities. Ever since the habanera charmed European dancers in the 1800s, Caribbean music has found its own international audiences. 1940s calypsoes like "Rum and Coca Cola" were hits in the United States, while the mambo and *chachachá* enjoyed their own crazes among North American whites and blacks. The mass media allowed Caribbean musics to spread way beyond the reach of Caribbean musicians themselves, so that Cuban dance music became the dominant urban popular music in Africa during the mid-twentieth century. Since the 1970s, the most remarkable case has been that of roots reggae, which is perhaps the single most popular form of music in Africa. Whether in the form of old Bob Marley records or of new songs by local groups, reggae dominates such countries as Gambia, and performers like Alpha Blondy sing reggae in various African languages. With the added input of dynamic groups like Steel Pulse in Great Britain, roots reggae now flourishes outside the Caribbean much more than in its homeland, Jamaica.

In general, musics like salsa, reggae, and *zouk* have taken on lives of their own outside the Caribbean, becoming truly international. This process, however, does not signify a global co-optation of Caribbean music, for the region itself and its émigré musicians continue to be sources for the most dynamic innovations. For the most creative artists, Caribbean music now involves combining international sounds and Caribbean cross-fertilizations, while often reaching deep into local traditions for inspiration.

MUSIC AND POLITICS

There is a widespread myth that most Caribbean people pass their lives dancing, partying, and lolling about on the beach. The fact that most outsiders know of the region only through its music may reinforce this misconception. In fact, most Caribbean people, now as always, have passed their lives in toil and relative poverty. In many cases, from the slave period to the present, Caribbeans have had to endure brutal political repression on top of hunger and deprivation.

One function of music in the Caribbean, as elsewhere, has always been to provide some sort of escape from such adversity. In dancing and singing, people can temporarily forget their woes, reaffirm community ties and values, and enjoy their own artistic creativity. But it has also been the nature of music and verse to express the full range of human emotions, including those related to sociopolitical conditions. Through music, men and women can voice aspirations and ideals, strengthen group solidarity, and transcend adversity by confronting it and transmuting it into song. Accordingly, music in the Caribbean has often been explicitly linked to sociopolitical struggles.

Local music genres, whether overtly political or not, can be important symbols of nationalistic pride and identity. In the nineteenth century, both Cuban habaneras and Puerto Rican *danzas* were celebrated as symbols of bourgeois and petit bourgeois opposition to Spanish rule. The unofficial Puerto Rican anthem, "La Borinqueña," is a gentle *danza* rather than a military march. Many other songs and *décimas* of this period also explicitly celebrated the independence struggle and, later, nationalistic opposition to Yankee domination.

Some musicians themselves have entered the realm of politics. Harry Belafonte, however criticized for his commercialization of calypso, has long been a champion of progressive causes and a critic of racism and American imperialism. Merengue innovator Johnny Ventura was an outspoken opponent of the Balaguer dictatorship in the Dominican Republic, while salsa artists Ruben Blades and Willie Colon both have run energetically for political office. While Colon has composed songs dealing with everything from military despots to AIDS, he said during his 1994 campaign for U.S. Congress, "Sometimes writing a song is not enough."

In the twentieth century, one of the greatest challenges for Caribbean countries has been to ameliorate poverty by gaining control over their own natural resources and by creating social justice. For independent countries, North American imperialism has been a significant obstacle to such progress. Virtually whenever a Caribbean state has attempted significant reform—redistribution of wealth, land reform, or nationalization of resources—the United States has intervened, often by overthrowing governments in the name of "safeguarding American interests" and "fighting communism." Aside from the numerous regional military occupations in the early twentieth century,[3] the CIA destabilized elected governments in Guatemala (1954) and Guyana (1962–1964), effectively replacing them with corrupt and brutal military regimes. In 1964, the Marines invaded the Dominican Republic to restore the Trujillo elite to power. In the 1970s, U.S. hostility helped undermine the reformist PNP (Peoples National Party) government in Jamaica, leading to its defeat in 1980 by the more pliant Jamaican Labour Party. The 1983 invasion of Grenada did away with the progressive New Jewel Movement, and since 1959, the Cuban people have endured all manner of Yankee hostility, including armed invasion in 1962, ongoing CIA-backed sabotage and terrorism,[4] and a crippling embargo. And such interventions have not ended with the Cold War; while the embargo on Cuba was tightened in the 1990s, in 1991, U.S.-trained Haitian generals on the CIA payroll ousted elected Prime Minister Jean-Bertrand Aristide and instituted a reign of terror. While American intervention in 1994 nominally restored Aristide to office, it has served to sustain the infrastructure of military and para-military repression.

During this period, much of the Caribbean music industry has been dominated by North American–owned multinationals with a vested interest in maintaining the status quo. There has been a marked tendency—and often explicit pressure from producers—for musicians in the industry to avoid controversial song lyrics and stick to stock romantic themes. Nevertheless, different forms of Caribbean music have, in their own way, confronted social reality and reflected, however idiosyncratically, the demand for social justice. Such uses of music were particularly prominent in the 1960s and '70s, which were a period of sociopolitical ferment, mobilization, and optimism throughout the region as in much of the world. The Cuban Revolution was thriving, Dominican dictator Rafael Trujillo was dead at last, and the newly independent West Indian states thought that they could for the first time control their own national destinies. In the United States, this was the era of the '60s youth counterculture and the Black Power movement, whose influence spilled over into the Caribbean. And last, even if the Soviet bloc itself did not constitute an attractive model, at least its existence and the aid it could provide implied the possibility of an alternative to Yankee domination and cultural "Coca-Colonization."

The *nueva canción* of Cuba and, to a lesser extent, of Puerto Rico and the Dominican Republic has been the form of music most explicitly linked to the optimism and idealism of the era. Other genres have mirrored the spirit of the age in their own ways. Early salsa emerged as the youthful voice of the barrio, militant and optimistic, chronicling the vicissitudes of lower-class urban life with a dynamic exuberance. In Jamaica, the sociopolitical ferment of urban youth found expression in roots reggae, which was linked not only to Rastafarianism but also to the activism and idealism of the 1970s PNP government. Calypsoes by Black Stalin, Chalkdust, and others also reflected the influence of the Black Power movement and the broader political consciousness of the period.

In subsequent years, however, political developments frustrated most of the aspirations of the 1960s and '70s, leading to the decline of the idealism expressed in that period's music. By the 1980s, hippies had grown into yuppies, and rock had become co-opted by the corporate music industry. With the triumph of Reaganomics (still dominant in the mid-1990s), the urban underclass became accepted as a permanent feature of North American society, and salsa turned from barrio militancy to commercial complacency and soap-opera sentimentality. The late 1980s found the Cuban Revolution in crisis, the Trujillo/Balaguer elite back in power, and the Puerto Rican independence movement marginalized for good; the *nueva trova* movement seemed to sputter out accordingly. In Jamaica, the PNP experiment collapsed under hostility from the United States and the International Monetary Fund, leading to a return to the status quo of multinational exploitation, laissez-faire capitalism, and worsening poverty. With the Jamaican poor despairing of changing their collective situation, roots reggae's militancy has largely given way to the boasting and slackness of dancehall. Meanwhile, Trinidad's post-oil-boom recession seems to have accompanied the increasing preference for light "jam-and-wine" soca over trenchant calypso.

Throughout the region, the fervor and optimism of the 1960s and '70s seem to have subsided as the various challenges to the status quo have been defeated, and youthful idealists of all stripes seem to have lost hope in change. In the "new world order," singing of revolution and redemption has become like spitting into the wind, and popular music seems to have retreated into sensuality, sentimentality, and lumpen nihilism. But if the old revolutionary models failed, new ones may yet arise to challenge the Pax Americana, and the musical scene, like the political one, is too volatile and unpredictable for us to declare the end of history. Music itself may yet play a role in forging a new multicultural sense of Caribbean unity, which could help the weak and divided islands of the region collectively to challenge their multinational masters and take control of their own destinies.

Glossary

abakuá. A secretive urban Afro-Cuban brotherhood, derived from the Efik people of Calabar.

abeng. A cow's horn, blown as a trumpet in Haiti, Jamaica, and elsewhere.

afranchi. Creole mulatto class in Haiti.

aguinaldo. A kind of Puerto Rican *jíbaro* (peasant) music, performed especially during Christmas season.

aleke. A modern Surinamese syncretic music genre associated with Maroons.

arará. A Dahomeyan-derived Afro-Cuban sect.

areito. An Arawak socioreligious ritual with music and dance.

bachata. A romantic, guitar-based bolero style of the urban Dominican Republic.

balada. A sentimental Spanish-language song (ballad) in mainstream, commercial pop style.

bandu. The deeper voiced of the two drums normally played in traditional Jamaican *Kumina* music, on which an unvarying supporting rhythm is played.

bandurria. A Spanish-derived, mandolin-like instrument used in Cuban peasant music (especially *punto*).

bann rara. A Haitian *rara* band.

batá. A double-headed, hourglass-shaped drum played in a trio, used in Afro-Cuban *santería/lucumí* music.

bembé. (1) In Cuba, a type of *santería* party, using eponymous drums and rhythms, wherein possession may occur, despite the prevailing festive air. (2) The staved barrel drums used in the *bembé* party. (3) In New York City, a term used loosely to describe any *santería* ceremony with music and dance.

biguine. A creole early and mid-twentieth-century dance-music genre of Martinique and Guadeloupe.

247

bogle. A Jamaican popular dance style of the 1990s.

bolero. A sentimental, danceable song in slow quadratic meter, popular throughout the Spanish Caribbean, with a characteristic bass pattern (when bass is present) of a half note followed by two quarter notes.

bomba. An Afro–Puerto Rican dance and music genre using drums of the same name.

bombo. A Spanish drum used in military bands and in Cuban *conga/comparsa* processions.

bongó. Bongo; (1) a pair of small, joined hand drums. (2) An archaic Afro-Trinidadian social dance genre, traditionally performed at wakes.

botánica. A store selling articles pertaining to Afro-Caribbean religions, especially *santería*.

boula. An accompanying drum in Haitian *vodou* music.

bubbling. A Jamaican generic term for dancing.

buru. A specific style of neo-African Jamaican music, played primarily in the parishes of Clarendon and St. Catherine, that uses three drums and a variety of percussion instruments; the term is also used more broadly in Jamaican to refer to any music of obviously African origin.

buttafly. A Jamaican popular dance of the 1990s.

cabildo. Town Council; in Cuba, an Afro-Cuban mutual-aid society.

cadens. See *kadans*.

cajones. Spanish: literally, "boxes." The wooden boxes sometimes used as drums in Cuban *rumba columbia*.

camboulay (canboulay). A nineteenth-century Afro-Trinidadian festival with drumming and dancing.

campesino. A peasant.

canción. Literally, "song," especially a through-composed, sentimental, slow song, not associated with dance.

canto. Spanish: literally, "chant." The first section of a *rumba* (synonym, *largo*).

catá. A log played with sticks, especially in *santería* and *tumba francesa* music.

chacha. Uncovered baskets shaken like rattles in Santiago de Cuba *comparsa*.

chachachá. A Cuban popular dance and music genre in medium tempo, which originated in the early 1950s.

cha madigra. In Haitian Carnival, mobile floats carrying bands.

charanga. A Cuban dance ensemble consisting of flute, two violins, piano, bass, and percussion (originally called *charanga francesa*).

chowtal. An Indo-Caribbean folk-song genre, performed at the vernal *phagwa* (*holi*) festival, derived from North India.

chutney. (1) An East Indian spiced condiment. (2) A light, fast Indo-Caribbean song and dance in modernized Indian folk style.

Cibao. Densely populated valley of central-northern Dominican Republic.

cinquillo. A Cuban term for the rhythmic ostinato pervading *danzón* and related genres (in note values, long–short–long–short–long).

clave. (1) Literally, "key" (especially used metaphorically). (2) One of a pair of hard wooden sticks, struck together. (3) The characteristic ostinato played on *clave* sticks. (4) A nineteenth- and early twentieth-century urban genre of Cuba, in 6/8 meter, sung by strolling choruses. (5) Spanish, masculine: "clavichord."

cocolo. Puerto Rican slang for fans of Afro-Latin dance music and, recently, hip-hop; loosely, "coconut-head."

colmado. Dominican Republic: a neighborhood store.

columbia. One of the three main types of Cuban rumba, danced by a solo man, in what could be regarded as 12/8 meter.

comparsa. A street procession associated with Cuban Carnival, incorporating music and ambulatory dance (especially *conga*).

compas. See *konpa dirèk.*

conga. (1) A single-headed drum used in Cuban dance music. (2) A song and dance genre, characteristically used in *comparsa* processions.

conjunto. In Afro-Latin music, a standard dance ensemble consisting of a rhythm section, two to four horns, and vocals.

contradanza. (1) A nineteenth-century Cuban salon and popular dance and music genre, known more commonly abroad as habanera. (2) A Spanish salon dance and music genre of the eighteenth and early nineteenth centuries.

contredanse. A French and Franco-Haitian salon and popular dance and music genre, dating from the late eighteenth century.

controversia. (1) Spanish: literally, "debate, argument." (2) A Cuban and Puerto Rican campesino music genre in the form of a duel between two singers.

cuatro. (1) Spanish: literally, "four." (2) A Puerto Rican guitar-like instrument with five doubled strings, used in *jíbaro* (peasant) music. (3) A ukulele-like instrument used in Venezuela and Suriname and in Trinidadian *parang.*

cuchifrito. A kind of fried snack.

cumbia. A popular music genre of Colombia and, subsequently, Central America and elsewhere.

dancehall. A style of Jamaican popular music that arose out of reggae in the 1980s and currently remains the dominant popular style.

dantal (dand-tal, dhantal). In Indo-Caribbean and Bhojpuri Indian music, two steel rods (one long and straight, the other short and U-shaped) struck together rhythmically.

danza. (1) A popular and salon dance and music genre of Puerto Rico. (2) An alternative term for Cuban *contradanza*.

danzón. A Cuban salon music genre popular from the late nineteenth to early twentieth centuries.

décima. A Spanish-derived text form of ten-line stanzas, usually with the *espinela* rhyme scheme *abbaaccddc*.

deejay music. A substyle of Jamaican music, centering on stylized "toasting," or rapping, in Jamaican creole over prerecorded tracks.

deshoukaj. Haitian creole: literally, "uprooting," referring to the popular attempts to destroy vestiges of the Jean-Claude Duvalier dictatorship in Haiti in the late 1980s.

dholak. An East Indian barrel drum used in folk and popular music.

dub. A substyle of reggae that arose during the 1970s, characterized by special studio effects such as fades, echo, reverb, and shifting of recorded tracks.

dub poetry. A Jamaican genre of poetry, usually performed with reggae or dub music, using Jamaican creole language and uncompromising political lyrics.

estribillo. Spanish: "chorus, refrain."

etu. A Yoruba-influenced genre of neo-African music played in Western Jamaica.

fiesta patronal. In Puerto Rico and elsewhere, the festival in which a town honors its patron saint.

funde. (1) The "time-keeping" drum in traditional Rastafarian *nyabinghi* music. (2) The name of one of the three drums used in traditional *buru* music.

fusilamiento. Spanish: literally, "firing." In Dominican music, the adaptation of a preexisting song to merengue format.

galleta. A military-style bass drum used in Cuban *conga* processions.

guaguancó. The most popular kind of Cuban traditional *rumba*.

guajeo. In Cuban dance music, a melodic ostinato.

guajira. (1) A female peasant of Cuba. (2) A kind of folk and popular music associated with Cuban peasants (from *música guajira*).

guajiro. A Cuban peasant.

guaracha. An up-tempo dance genre of Cuba and, subsequently, Puerto Rico, originally with a light, often satirical or bawdy text and verse–chorus form (rather than the *son's largo–montuno* form).

güiro (güira). A gourd or metal scraper.

gumbe. (1) An African-derived Jamaican religion and the neo-African music associated with it. (2) The square-frame drum used in this music, which is also used by Maroons in some communities.

habanera. Alternate term for Cuba *contradanza* (from *contradanza habanera,* or Havana-style *contradanza*).

harmonium. A hand-pumped keyboard instrument popular in India and in Indo-Caribbean music.

iyesá. An Afro-Cuban, Yoruba-derived religious sect.

Jab-Jab. A ghoulishly costumed stock character in Trinidad Carnival.

jíbaro. A Puerto Rican peasant, implicitly white or mulatto.

joropo. A Venezuelan Hispanic-derived folk-song genre.

kadans ranpa. Haitian creole: literally, "rampart rhythm." A Haitian dance rhythm popularized by Weber Sicot in the 1950s.

kaseko. An Afro-Surinamese popular urban dance-music style.

kawina. A percussion-based music genre of Creole blacks of coastal Suriname.

kete. The ensemble of three drums used in traditional Rastafarian music, consisting of repeater, *funde,* and bass; also sometimes used to refer to the repeater drum alone.

konpa dirèk (compas direct). A Haitian dance rhythm popularized by Nemours Jean-Baptiste in the 1950s.

Kromanti Play. Traditional religion of the Maroons living in the Blue Mountains of eastern Jamaica.

Kumina. (1) An African-derived religion in eastern Jamaica and the neo-African music associated with it. (2) (Lowercase) The name of a new, secular, urban style of drumming that developed in Kingston and contributed to the development of *nyabinghi* drumming.

*kyas (*also, *playing kyas).* The higher-pitched of the two drums normally used in *Kumina* music, which plays the more complex rhythmic patterns.

largo. The initial section of a Cuban rumba (following the short introductory *diana*), where the lead vocalist sings an extended text.

Latin jazz. A predominantly instrumental, latter twentieth-century genre featuring jazz-oriented solos over Afro-Cuban rhythms, intended primarily for listening rather than for dance.

lonsei. An Afro-Surinamese drum music, out of which developed *aleke.*

lucumí. An Afro-Cuban of Yoruba descent.

lwa (loa). A spirit in Haitian *vodou.*

malimba. Haitian term for *marimbula.*

mambo. (1) An up-tempo, predominantly instrumental dance-music genre, featuring antiphonal sectional arrangements for contrasting brass instruments. (2) An instrumental interlude in the *montuno* section of a salsa or Cuban-style dance-music song. (3) A vamp-like, harmonically static coda of a *danzón*.

manman. The largest drum in the Haitian *vodou* ensemble.

marimba. (1) In the Dominican Republic, the term for the Cuban marimbula. (2) Elsewhere, a xylophone with wooden keys.

marimbula. In Cuba, a bass instrument consisting of plucked metal keys mounted on a wooden box.

maroon. A runaway slave or a descendant thereof (Haitian creole: *mawon*).

mason. A dance genre in Cuban *tumba francesa*.

mbira. One African name for a family of hand-held melodic instruments, each featuring plucked metal keys mounted on a small wooden box, with or without a gourd amplifier.

mento. A Jamaican creole folk-song genre played on a variety of instruments, most typically featuring guitar, banjo, fife (or fiddle), and rhumba box.

mereng. A Haitian creole social-dance genre.

merengue. A popular creole music and dance genre of the Dominican Republic.

méringue. A popular creole music and dance genre of Haiti.

mini-djaz. A Haitian popular dance music of the 1960s.

Moko Jumbie. A stilted, costumed, stock character in Trinidad Carnival.

moña. Similar to definition # 2 of *mambo; moñas*, unlike mambos, occur over the same chordal ostinato used in the rest of the *montuno*.

montuno. The final and, usually, longest part of a rumba, *son*, or other Afro-Cuban-derived dance-music piece, employing call-and-response vocals over a rhythmic and harmonic ostinato.

ñañigo. A member of a Calabari-derived Afro-Cuban *abakuá* society.

negritud. A literary and cultural movement of the Spanish and French Caribbean, celebrating the Afro-Caribbean heritage.

ngoma. (1) In Cuba, a Congolese-derived cylindrical drum. (2) In Africa, the term for a variety of regional drums and music and dance genres.

nouvel jenerasyon. Haitian creole: literally, "new generation." Haitian pop music of the 1980s and 1990s.

nueva canción. Spanish: literally, "new song." The Latin American variety of singer-songwriter music, explicitly or implicitly identifed with progressive politics and cultural policies.

nueva trova. A Cuban efflorescence of *nueva canción*.

nyabinghi. (1) A traditional, drum-based Rastafarian musical style. (2) Formal Rastafarian gatherings or ceremonies.

obeah. A body of African-derived beliefs and practices relating to medicine, ritual, and, especially, magic.

orisha. A deity in Yoruba and Afro-Caribbean Yoruba-derived religion.

orquesta típica. In the latter half of the nineteenth century, a horn-dominated ensemble primarily playing *danzón* and *contradanza,* consisting of cornet, trombone, *figle, bombardino* (saxhorn), two clarinets, two or more violins, contrabass, *timbales,* and *güiro.*

oru del igbodú. The initial, semiprivate part of a *santería* ceremony.

palitos. Spanish: literally, "little sticks," such as are used to play rhythmic ostinatos on the side of a drum or a log in traditional rumba and other Afro-Cuban genres.

palo. Spanish: literally, "stick." A Congolese-derived Afro-Cuban religion.

pandereta (pandero). A jingle-less tambourine (frame drum) used in Puerto Rico and elsewhere.

parang. A Trinidadian Christmas-season song and dance genre, of Venezuelan derivation (from Spanish, *parranda*—"spree, party").

perico ripiao. Spanish: literally, "ripped parrot." The traditional style of Cibao merengue, played on a ensemble of accordion, marimba, *tambora, güira,* and optional saxophone.

picong. A musical verbal duel between two calypso singers (from French, *piquant*—"spicy").

playing kyas. See *kyas.*

plena. A creole song form of Puerto Rico, existing in both folk and danceband versions.

Poco. Shorter, more common term for *Pocomania.*

Pocomania (Pukkumina). A blanket term for the Afro-Protestant religions that developed in Jamaica during the nineteenth century, as well as the music associated with them; also sometimes used to refer to a specific, more African branch of the larger category of religions known as Revival.

polyrhythm (polymeter). A composite rhythmic structure combining two or more regular meters.

punta. A folk music and dance genre of the Garifuna ("Black Caribs") of coastal Honduras and Belize.

punto. In Cuba, the campesino-style musical rendering of a *décima.*

quinto. Spanish: literally, "fifth." The higher-pitched conga in Cuban rumba.

ragga. Shortened form of *raggamuffin.*

raggamuffin. (1) A substyle of Jamaican dancehall music that developed in the late 1980s. (2) Since at least the 1970s in Jamaica, a poor young resident of the ghetto.

ranchera. A popular sentimental song genre of northern Mexico and Tex-Mex music.

rara. Haitian street celebrations, with music provided by *bann rara* ("rara bands").

Rastafarianism. A politico-religious movement that developed in Jamaica in the 1930s and has since grown to become a world religion; its original prophets proclaimed the divinity of Emperor Haile Selassie (Ras Tefari) of Ethiopia and predicted the imminent repatriation of the faithful to Africa.

reggae. A specific genre of Jamaican popular music that developed around 1968 and remained the dominant form until the early or mid-1980s; the term is often used nowadays, however, to refer to all styles of Jamaican popular music since the late 1960s.

repeater. The highest-pitched of the Rastafarian drums used in traditional *nyabinghi* music, which plays the more complex rhythmic patterns.

Revival. A blanket term for the indigenous Afro-Protestant religions that developed in Jamaica during the nineteenth century, as well as the music associated with them (see also *Poco, Pocomania*).

rhumba box. A Jamaican bass instrument with plucked metal lamellae; equivalent to Cuban *marimbula*, Dominican marimba.

riddim. A Jamaican term (derived from "rhythm") used to refer to the underlying recorded rhythm tracks that are often recycled to create new songs or to back deejay lyrics in Jamaican popular music; a "riddim" is usually defined by a bass melody and the basic accompanying drum patterns.

rockero (roquero). In Puerto Rico and elsewhere, one who likes rock music (as opposed, for example, to *cocolos,* who prefer Latin music).

rock steady. A Jamaican popular music style that supplanted ska and was dominant around 1966–1968.

rumba. An Afro-Cuban secular dance and music genre.

salsa brava (also salsa caliente). "Strong," "hot," hard-driving salsa music, as opposed to *salsa romántica.*

salsa romántica (also salsa sensual). "Romantic," "sensual," sentimental salsa.

sans humanité. French: literally, "without mercy." A standard and essentially meaningless rhetorical phrase (corrupted to *santimanitey*) inserted at the end of early twentieth-century calypso verses (later replaced by "in this colony" and, after 1962, "in this country").

santería. A Yoruba-derived Afro-Cuban religion.

segon. A accompanying drum in Haitian *vodou* music.

seis. Spanish: literally, "six." The most important subgenre of Puerto Rican campesino (*jíbaro*) music; also a kind of dance done by altar boys in the cathedral of Seville, Spain.

ska. A Jamaican popular music that emerged in the early 1960s, derived in part from American rhythm and blues.

skratji. A large bass drum used in Surinamese *kaseko* and *kawina*.

son. The most popular Cuban music and dance genre of the twentieth century.

songo. A modern Afro-Cuban dance-music rhythm, popularized in the 1970s by Los Van Van.

soukous. A popular Congolese dance-music genre.

tabla. A North Indian drum pair used in classical and light-classical music.

tambora. Spanish: "drum." The double-headed drum used in Dominican merengue.

tambu. (1) A genre of neo-African music played in western Jamaica, rhythmically similar to *Kumina* music. (2) A Maroon genre of drumming and song within *Kromanti Play* that has been influenced by *Kumina* music.

tan. In North Indian classical music, a fast melodic run.

tan singing. Indo-Caribbean "local classical" music.

tcha-tcha. The Haitian term for maracas (small gourd rattles).

telenovela. Spanish: literally, "television soap opera."

tigueraje. Spanish: literally, "tigerness." Dominican slang for feistiness, vigor.

timbales. In Latin music, a pair of drums, usually mounted on a stand, with a cowbell.

típico. Spanish: "traditional, typical."

toasting. A type of indigenous Jamaican rapping by deejays, which came to dominate Jamaican popular music during the dancehall era of the 1980s.

toque de santo. A *santería* ceremony with music and dance.

tres. Spanish: literally, "three." A Cuban guitar-like instrument with three doubled courses, tuned D–G–B.

tumba francesa. A Franco-Haitian-derived mutual-aid and social-recreation society of eastern Cuba.

twoubadou. Haitian creole: "troubador." A Haitian singer of topical or popular songs, usually accompanied by guitar, maracas (*tcha-tcha*), *malimba,* and *tanbou* drum.

vaksin. A bamboo trumpet used in Haitian *rara* and Dominican *gaga* bands.

vallenato (música vallenata). An accordion- and vocal-dominated folk and popular music genre of northeastern Colombia.

vejigante. In the *fiesta de Santiago apóstol* of Loíza, Puerto Rico, a ghoulishly costumed stock character.

velación. In the Dominican Republic, a nightlong ceremony and social dance with Afro-Dominican music.

vodou (voodoo, vodun, voudoun). A Dahomeyan-derived Afro-Haitian religion.

yambú. One of the three extant forms of Afro-Cuban traditional rumba, with a rhythm and dance style similar to that of the *guaguancó* but somewhat slower.

yanvalou. A polyrhythmic Haitian *vodou* rhythm.

yeye. The 1960s Haitian term for rock music.

yuba. An archaic *tumba francesa* dance; also a term for other archaic, now-extinct Afro-Caribbean dances.

zapateo. A Spanish-derived, nearly extinct Cuban folk dance, featuring heel stomping (cf. Spanish *zapateado*).

zarzuela. Spanish and Spanish-Caribbean light opera.

zouk. A popular dance music of Martinique and Guadeloupe.

Notes

CHAPTER 1

1. We shall avoid the term *tribe*, with its pejorative connotations, until it becomes equally common to speak of the "Serbian tribe" or, for that matter, the "Anglo-Saxon tribe."

2. The Inquisition, although not exactly an indication of cultural tolerance, was a religious, not a racial, campaign and was aimed at Jews and Moors, not blacks.

3. In Trinidad and Guyana, a "creole" is a black person and "creolization" thus has a different meaning, referring, for example, to the phenomenon of an East Indian adopting Afro-Trinidadian manners.

CHAPTER 2

1. *Guaguancó* is pronounced "wa-wan-có"; and perhaps this is a good point for a word on Spanish pronunciation in general, with which all North Americans should be familiar. Briefly, *j* is an aspirated *h*, *ll* is like *y*, *h* is silent, *z* is like *s*, *gue* is like *gay*, *güe* is like *gway* (or *way*), and *qui* is like *key*. Hence *jolla* is pronounced like "hoya," *hija* like "ee-ha," *quinto* like "keen-toe," and *son* somewhere between "sun" and "sone."

2. Note that this *décima* uses the word "American" to refer to the United States. Today, many Cubans, Puerto Ricans, and other Caribbean peoples (who are also "Americans") would resent such a usage, preferring the term *North American*. In deference to this school of thought, I favor that usage in this book.

3. Alejo Carpentier, *La música en Cuba* (Mexico City: Fonda de Cultura Económica, 1946), pp. 104–5.

4. John Storm Roberts, *The Latin Tinge: The Impact of Latin American Music on the United States* (New York and Oxford: Oxford University Press, 1979), p. 133.

5. Pablo Menéndez, quoted in Mark Kurlansky, *A Continent of Islands* (New York: Addison-Wesley, 1992), p. 113.

6. Silvio Rodríguez, "Pequeña serenata diurna" (Little daytime serenade): "Vivo en un país libre / cual solamente puede ser libre / en esta tierra, en este instante / y soy feliz porque soy gigante. . . . Soy feliz, soy un hombre feliz / y quiero que me perdonen / por este día / los muertos / de mi felicidad."

7. A reference to the oft-quoted lines of nineteenth-century Puerto Rican poet

Lola Rodríguez de Tió. This song's final line invokes the *macheteros,* the militant wing of Puerto Rico's *independentistas.*

8. Congressman Robert Torricelli, sponsor of the early 1990s law tightening the embargo, has stated, "I want to wreak havoc on that island." Bombs away, Enola Gay!

CHAPTER 3

1. *Chuitín*: "Vamos conmigo mi pana / para la banda allá del Ejío / que hay prendío que dura / y que hasta la mañana. / Mi mujer como está tan sana / en la casa se quedó. / Compay no digas que no / vamonos a parrandear, / que te voy a demostrar / que en mi casa mando yo."
Chuito: "Contigo no voy pa'allá, / porque es bueno que se aprenda / que tu mujer es tremenda / y no se quiere pa'na'. / Ella no te dejará / bendito sea Díos / que te vayas a beber. / No te podras ni mover / a la esquina de la plaza, / porque yo sé que en tu casa / la que manda es tu mujer."
Chuitín: "Tú está bien equivocado, / tú sabes que voy en coche / y me amanezco esta noche / porque nunca me ha sentado. / Cuando estoy medio pica'o / yo bailo hasta un guaguancó. / Como el baile ya empezó / vamonos a vacillar."
Chuito: "Y aunque ya estés *very fool,* / no vayas que no conviene / porque esa mujer te tiene / sentadito en el baul. / Te dejará un ojo azul, / escucha Chuitín, porque te llega a ver. / Llegando al amanecer / más caliente que una braza / porque yo sé que en tu casa / la que manda es tu mujer." (Chuitín and Chuito, "Quién manda en la casa," on *Un jíbaro terminao,* vol. 2 [Ansonia SALP 1519]).

2. Baltazar Carrero, "El jíbaro de rincón," on *Tierra adentro* (Ansonia SALP 1537).

3. "Mi Borinquen está cambiado, / para mi es una sorpresa / y me sirve de tristeza / el ayer qué transformado. / Estás tan modernizado / yo mismo ni me lo cuento. / Hoy cantando comento, / noto en mi alma un vacío, / pues me cambiaron un bohío / por la casa de cemento.

"Ni a la yegua ni al caballo / hay quien ponga una heradura, / y para [llevar?] la verdura / no quieren usar el guayo. / Ya ni al cantillo del gallo / el jíbaro escucha atento, / y para buscar su elemento / no sale de madrugada / si está el río y la quebrada / en canala de cemento." (Ramito, "Puerto Rico cambiado," on *Parrandeando* [Ansonia SALP 1492]).

4. James McCoy, "The Bomba and Aguinaldo of Puerto Rico as They Have Evolved from Indigenous, African, and European Cultures" (Ph.D. diss., Florida State University, 1968), p. 167. A typical *bomba* text is: "The policeman's wife ran off with the fireman / to see if he could put out the fire" (La mujer del policía se fue con el bombero / porque ella quería saber cómo se apagaba el fuego). In *Nueva colección de bombas Puertorriqueñas,* by Mohammed Dua (San Juan, 1990).

5. Quoted in Juan Flores, "Cortijo's Revenge," *Centro de estudios puertorriqueños Bulletin* (Spring 1991): 18.

6. "Si yo vine a Nueva York / con el fin de progresar / si allá lo pasaba mal / aquí lo paso peor. / Unas veces el calor / y otras el maldito frío, / a veces parezco un lío / por la nieve patinando. / Eso no me está gustando / yo me vuelvo a mi bohío" (*décima*). Rafael Hernández, "Yo vuelvo a mi bohío."

7. "Un día por la mañana / salí en buscar un remedio / para sana un enfermo / muy grave que se encontraba. / Era un amigo que estaba / apuntado a pulmonía, / y como yo no sabía / caminar en Nueva York / cogí un subway y era error / y volví a los cinco días" (also in *décima* form). (El Gallito de Manatí, "Culpando el subway," on *Tierra adentro* [Ansonia SALP 1537]).

8. "Yo vine por Nueva York / porque yo me imaginaba / que aquí se hablaba / el inglés que el español / pero me dijo un señor, / 'No, tú estás muy equivocado, / cuando quiere bacalao / tiene que decir *co'fi*" . . . en qué apuros me veo / cuando llego al restaurant / al decirme '*Wha' you wan*'?' / les señalo con el dedo" (*décima*). Baltazar Carrero, "Un jíbaro en Nueva York," (on *Tierra adentro* [Ansonia SALP 1537]).

9. "No sufren por nada / aunque estén ausente / si brille en sus mentes / su tierra adorada / siempre recordara / una vida entera. / Si un día cualquiera / verás tu regreso, / vente con un beso; / tu patria te espera / en la Navidad, Borinquen" (*aguinaldo orocoveño, décima* text).

10. Jorge Javariz, quoted in Ruth Glasser, "The Backstage View: Musicians Piece Together a Living," *Centro de estudios puertorriqueños Bulletin* (Spring 1991)

11. "Yo tuve un sueño feliz, quise hacerlo una canción, y mi guitarra cogí, puse todo el corazón, concentré pensando en ti. . . . Era en una playa de mi tierra tan querida, a la orilla del mar, era que allí estaba celebrándose una jira, debajo de un palmar." BAJO UN PALMAR by Pedro Flores, copyright (c) 1942 by Peer International Corporation; copyright renewed; English lyric, copyright (C) 1995 by Peer International Corporation.

12. John Storm Roberts, *The Latin Tinge: The Impact of Latin American Music on the United States* (New York and Oxford: Oxford University Press, 1979), p. 87.

13. Ibid., p. 86, and Glasser, op. cit.

14. Flores, "Cortijo's Revenge," p. 18.

CHAPTER 4

1. In fact, several of Pacheco's early hits were simply well-executed covers of forgotten and by then unavailable recordings by Cuban bandleader Felix Chappotin.

2. Sergio George, interviewed by Vernon Boggs, in *Latin Beat* 3, 1 (February 1993).

3. A reference to Cuban nationalist José Martí, who wrote of the United States, "I know the monster, for I have lived in his entrails."

4. Willie Colon, "Calle lune calle sol," on *Lomato* (Fania SLP 00044). (Copyright by José Flores, Sonido Inc.).

5. From Willie Colon's 1967 "El malo": "El malo de aquí soy yo, porque tengo corazón."

6. The second line of "Juanito Alimaña" bitterly parodies Rafael Hernández's 1930s "Lamento Borincano," with its romanticization of traditional island life ("Sale loco de contento con su cargamento por la ciudad."—"He leaves, full of joy, for work in the city . . ."). "Juanito Alimaña" is on *Vigilante* (Fania JM 610).

7. Salsa's rise in Venezuela is documented by Lise Waxer (manuscript) and Juan Carlos Baéz, *El vínculo es la salsa* (Caracas, 1989).

8. Ruben Blades, quoted in Jeremy Marre and Hannah Charleton, *Beats of the Heart: Popular Music of the World* (New York: Pantheon, 1985), p. 80.

9. Ruben Blades, quoted in "Singer, Actor, Politico," *Time* (January 29, 1990): 50.

10. Ibid., p. 52.

11. Eddie Palmieri, "Ven ven," on *Cheo y Quintana* (Barbera LP B205 SENI 0798).

12. The cover bands, which are thus generally unable to get original scores for the hits they play, have to have someone transcribe the songs, including the complex horn parts, from records. Chris Washburne, who plays for both original and cover bands, relates, "Sometimes I'll be playing in a cover band, doing a song that I also play in its original version. It can really throw me off when I'll be playing my part, more or less on automatic pilot, and then all of a sudden there's a change, because the guy who transcribed it from the record got the part wrong."

13. As one record-company executive put it, "Salsa divides the market, and the ballad unites it."

14. Jorge Manuel López, interviewed in *El Diario*, 24 September 1993, p. 32.

15. Enrique Fernández, "Is Salsa Sinking?" *Village Voice*, 2 September 1986, p. 21.

16. Pablo Guzmán "¡Siempre Salsa!" *Village Voice*, 25 June 1979, p. 92.

17. Gerardo, "It's a Latin Thang," on *Gerardo Dos* (Interscope 7 92184-4).

18. "Puerto Rico tiene bomba para brincar, Venezuela tiene bomba para pegar, Colombia tiene bomba para gozar. . . . Y a me que me gusta vestir, tengo mi ropa rasta para lucir, mi chino quiero incluir y su sangre con la nuestra poder unir, pero un poco de salsa mezcla con calypso que suena en este cuero se haciendo un hechizo." (Vico C, "Bomba pará afincar," on *Hispanic Soul* [Prime CD 1014]).

19. Mangú (Freddy Garcia), "La playa," (on Polygram 162-440 578-4).

20. Latin Empire, interview with Juan Flores, "Latin Empire: Puerto Rap," *Centro de estudios puertorriqueños Bulletin* (Spring 1991): 81. A number of black English-language rappers (including Dres of Black Sheep and ex–Fat Boy Prince Markie Dee) are Latino.

21. See her *Bachata* (Temple University Press, 1995).

22. Edgardo Díaz, "Pablo Milanés: Un canto sin dirección," *El Mundo* (San Juan), 2 February 1985, p. 52.

CHAPTER 5

1. Paul Austerlitz's *Dominican Merengue in Regional, National, and International Perspectives* (Philadelphia: Temple University Press, forthcoming) is the primary source for information on merengue in this chapter.

2. "Tropicó, mira tu chivo, después de muerto, cantando" (Manuel del Cabral).

3. After all, the Nobel prize was given to Vietnam War architect Henry Kissinger.

4. "Puerto Rico queda cerca, pero móntate en avión, y si consigues la visa, no hay problemas en inmigración; pero no te vayas en yola, no te llenes de ilusiones, porque en el Canal de la Mona, te comen los tiburones" (Wilfrido Vargas).

5. "Aquí la vida no vale una guayaba podrida; si un tigre no te mata, te mata la factoría" (Sandy Reyes).

6. Willie Rodríguez, cited in Deborah Pacini, *Bachata: A Social History of a Dominican Popular Music* (Philadelphia: Temple University Press, 1995).

7. E.g., journalist Alex Soto, *Listin,* 6 October 1993.

8. Daisane McLane, "Uptown and Downhome," *Village Voice's* Rock 'n' Roll Quarterly (Winter 1991): 15.

9. Pacini, *Bachata,* Sponsorship of cultural events by liquor companies is common throughout the Caribbean (except in Cuba).

10. All *bachata* texts cited in this section are from Pacini, *Bachata.*

11. This song is adapted from a Congolese *soukous* tune by Lea Lignanzi, "Dede Priscilla," (Island ISSP 4008).

12. Hector Guttierez, *Latin Beat* 3, 2 (March 1993): 37.

CHAPTER 6

1. Gage Averill, "Haitian Dance Bands, 1915–1970: Class, Race and Authenticity," *Latin American Music Review* 10, 2 (1989), is the principal source of information on Haitian popular music for this chapter.

2. The *contredanse,* which was among the most popular dances of the colonial elite, was eventually adopted by the rural Haitian population and is still performed today at outdoor festivals known as *fèt champèt.*

3. "Kompam ce pam," by Tabou Combo. *Aux Antilles* (Zafem Records TC 8056CD).

4. "Tout moun ale nan kanaval," Mancuso Productions. Video shown on Telenationale Haiti, 1988.

5. Jocelyne Guilbault, Gage Averill, Édouard Benoit, and Gregory Rabiss, *Zouk: World Music in the West Indies* (Chicago: University of Chicago Press, 1993), is the prinicipal source of information on *zouk* for this chapter.

6. "An-ba-chenin la," by Kassav'. *Kassav'* (GD Productions MRS 1182-I GD 027).

CHAPTER 7

1. For a recent examination of the spread of reggae and Rastafarianism around the world—including other parts of the Caribbean, North America, Europe, Africa, and the Pacific—see Neil Savishinsky, "Transnational Popular Culture and the Global Spread of the Jamaican Rastafarian Movement," *New West Indian Guide* 68, 3 & 4 (1994): 259–281.

2. Maureen Sheridan, "Jamaican Studios Jumping with Success of Dancehall," *Billboard* 101 (July 18, 1992): 1.

3. Chris Wilson liner notes to the Starlights' 1993 CD *Soldering: Reggae's Greatest Hits* (Cambridge, Mass., Heartbeat HB 102).

4. Partly because *Kumina* is one of Jamaica's most African musics, popular books and films on Jamaican music continue to make the error of equating it with Maroon music. For instance, a recent film, *Before Reggae Hit the Town* (written and directed by Mark Gorney, University of California Extension Center for Media and Independent Learning, 1990), includes a scene of *Kumina* drumming and dancing and represents it as "Maroon music." In fact, the main music-and-dance tradition of the

Maroons, called *Kromanti Play,* is entirely separate from *Kumina,* going back to the eighteenth century and featuring entirely different kinds of drums and musical genres. *Kumina,* in contrast, is derived largely from traditions introduced to Jamaica during the nineteenth century by African contract laborers, primarily from the Congo region. Unlike *Kumina,* Maroon *Kromanti Play* has had almost no influence on Jamaican popular music, since it has traditionally been considered secret and, until recently, was never played outside of Maroon communities. The only way in which Maroon music has been able to exert a slight influence on outside styles is by way of the *Kumina* tradition, to which it has lent a number of songs, learned by *Kumina* musicians from Maroons visiting their ceremonies.

5. Robert Witmer, "'Local and Foreign': The Popular Music Culture of Kingston, Jamaica, before Ska, Rock Steady, and Reggae," *Latin American Music Review* 8, 1 (1987): 18–19.

6. Cited in Balford Henry, *A Short History of Jamaican Music* (Kingston: Buckley Communications, 1992), pp. 2–4.

7. Cited in Howard Johnson and Jim Pines, *Reggae: Deep Roots Music* (London: Proteus Books, 1982), 53–54.

8. For more on the influence of the *Kumina* religion and its music on the Howellite Rastafarians, see Kenneth Bilby and Elliott Leib, "Kumina, the Howellite Church and the Emergence of Rastafarian Traditional Music in Jamaica," *Jamaica Journal* 19, 3 (1985): 22–28.

9. Bob Marley and the Wailers, "Trench Town," on the 1983 LP *Confrontation* (Tuff Gong/Island 90085-1).

10. I am grateful to Professor Simpson for making available the materials he recorded in 1953, on which this reconstruction is based.

11. "Uptown Babies," on the 1976 LP *War ina Babylon* (Island ILPS 9392).

12. "Them Belly Full (But We Hungry)," on the 1974 LP *Natty Dread* (Island 90037-1).

13. Oku Onuora, quoted in Brian Jahn and Tom Weber, *Reggae Island: Jamaican Music in the Digital Age* (Kingston: Kingston Publishers Limited, 1992), p. 91.

14. Dub music is characterized by the artful fading in and out of various tracks and a number of other studio techniques used to create new sound textures.

15. Dub poetry, known for its socially conscious, politically uncompromising lyrics, is a rich genre that deserves an entire book to itself. It stems in part from the earlier deejaying tradition, which had been given a new boost by the advent of dub music during the 1970s. Unlike deejay lyrics, however, those of dub poetry exist in both written and oral form (in the latter case, performed with reggae music). Among its major practitioners are Oku Onuora, Mutabaruka, the late Michael Smith, Jean Binta Breeze, and the London-based Jamaican poet and music historian Linton Kwesi Johnson.

16. Half Pint, quoted in Jahn and Weber, *Reggae Island,* p. 108.

17. Wayne Armond, quoted in Jahn and Weber, *Reggae Island,* p. 129.

18. "Pocomania Jump," a 1984 12″ 45rpm record (Ashantites 010).

19. Linton Kwesi Johnson, "Introduction," in *Tougher than Tough: Thirty-five Years of Jamaican Hits* (booklet accompanying four-CD boxed set (1993) *Tougher than Tough: The Story of Jamaican Music* [Mango CD 1–4, 518 400-3]).

20. Bob Andy, "Jamaican Music is not Reggae," in *Jamaica Beat* (Kingston), no. 3 (February–March 1989): 5.

21. Sheridan, "Jamaican Studios Jumping," p. 1.

22. Transcribed from a video recording made by John Homiak, Clarendon, Jamaica, May 1989. The videotape is in the collections of the Human Studies Film Archives at the Smithsonian Institution.

CHAPTER 8

1. "Jean and Dinah" (words and music by Don Raye and Mighty Sparrow), © 1957 MCA Music Publishing, a Division of MCA, Inc. Copyright Renewed. International Copyright Secured. All Rights Reserved. Used by Permission.

2. Mighty Sparrow and Lord Melody "Picong," on *Calypso Kings and Pink Gin* (Cook 1185).

3. Chalkdust, "Kaiso in the Hospital," on *Chalkdust—Visions* (Straker GS2365).

4. See Gordon Rohlehr, *Calypso and Society in Pre-Independence Trinidad* (Tunapuna, Trinidad, 1990), chapter 5; and Keith Warner, *Kaiso! The Trinidad Calypso* (Washington, D.C.: Three Continents, 1985), chapter 4.

5. See Donald Hill's *The Big Drum and Other Ritual and Social Music of Carriacou* (Folkways FE 34002).

CHAPTER 9

1. In Steven Vertovec, *Hindu Trinidad: Religion, Ethnicity, and Socio-Economic Change* (London: MacMillan Education, 1992), p. 224.

2. Rikki Jai, "Cry for Unity" (lyrics by Ras Shorty I), on *More Bacchanal* (Spice Island).

CHAPTER 10

1. Arcaño, "Negra bembón," on *Al Santiago's "The Best of Cuba"* (Funny CD-507).

2. Roger Abrahams, *The Man-of-Words in the West Indies* (Baltimore: Johns Hopkins University Press, 1983), pp. 12, 16.

3. These include occupations of the following countries: Nicaragua (1910; 1912–1933), Honduras (1903; 1907; 1911–1912; 1919; 1924–1925), Cuba (1906–1909; 1912; 1917–1920; 1933–1934), Mexico (1913–1917; 1918–1919), Panama (1921; 1925; 1989), the Dominican Republic (1916–1924), and Haiti (1915–1934).

4. In 1976, for example, CIA-trained terrorist Orlando Bosch blew up a Cuban civilian airliner, killing all seventy-three people aboard. Bosch now lives free in Miami.

Index

264